AF244206

WHAT
FRESH
HELL?

WHAT FRESH HELL?

The Best of

Blogging on Post-Katrina New Orleans
and America, 2005–2015

TENTH ANNIVERSARY EDITION

Mid-City Books

NEW YORK • NEW ORLEANS

What Fresh Hell? The Best of Levees Not War:
Blogging on Post-Katrina New Orleans and America, 2005–2015

Copyright © 2015 by Mark LaFlaur
Tenth Anniversary Edition copyright © 2025 by Mark LaFlaur

Published in the United States by Mid-City Books

Mid-City Books
Kew Gardens, New York

ISBN: 978-0-9887-9093-3 (pbk)
ISBN: 978-0-9887-9094-0 (ebook)

Library of Congress Control Number (LCCN): 2015908665

The contents of this book originally appeared online at *LeveesNotWar.org*.

Interior design and composition by Beverly Butterfield, Girl of the West Productions, Petaluma, California. Cover design by Richard Sheppard, Cloverdale, California. New Orleans street tile designs by Evelyn Menge, New Orleans. For the Tenth Anniversary Edition, additional typesetting by Kyle Kabel, New York, and cover design work by Richard Sheppard, Chicago. Cover photograph credit: NASA: Hurricane Katrina, 2005.

marklaflaur.com
leveesnotwar.org
Facebook.com/LeveesNotWar

To those who lost their lives in Hurricane Katrina,
those who came back to rebuild home and find new lives,
with courage and good cheer, and those of the diaspora who long for home;

To the many volunteers from all over who have helped
in rebuilding New Orleans and the Gulf Coast;

To the community of bloggers in and about New Orleans, my friends;

. . . and, as always, to Janet, steadfast partner in heart and mind

Every gun that is made, every warship launched, every rocket fired signifies, in the final sense, a theft from those who hunger and are not fed, those who are cold and are not clothed.
Dwight D. Eisenhower

The responsibility of ministers for the public safety is absolute, and requires no mandate. It is in fact the prime object for which governments come into existence.
Winston Churchill

I know of no safe depository of the ultimate powers of the society but the people themselves; and if we think them not enlightened enough to exercise their control with a wholesome discretion, the remedy is not to take it from them, but to inform their discretion by education.
Thomas Jefferson

Contents

CONTENTS

CONTENTS

Preface to the Tenth Anniversary Edition

Ten years after . . .

This book was first published a year before a New York City real estate developer and reality TV personality rose to prominence in American politics and then, to widespread surprise, was elected president, perhaps with a little outside help. That time feels not only like a more innocent age (see the Afterword for a sense of contrast) but like the era before a comet struck the earth. His name, which now seems inescapable, does not appear in this book, though ten years ago the name and the face were familiar. Indeed, I had actually met him and his wife once at a publication party given for one of my company's authors, the late congressman Charles Rangel of Harlem, by Mayor Michael Bloomberg at Gracie Mansion in Manhattan. It was in the spring of 2007, and they were standing alone in a roomful of Democrats, so I introduced myself and we talked agreeably for a few minutes about what a great guy Charlie Rangel was (I was his editor so it was my job to schmooze). At the time, Senator Barack Obama was not yet a leading contender for the White House, so it was well before this man began to poison the national consciousness with his pernicious "birther" campaign. Again, it was a long time ago, when *Levees Not War* was but a young blog.

To paraphrase the late Queen Elizabeth II, the ten years since this book was published are not a decade on which we look back with undiluted pleasure. (That was from her famous "Annus Horribilis" speech of 1992 after a year when Windsor Castle burned and her son the Prince of Wales and his glamorous wife were publicly splitting apart.) Our recent troubles have been of a more long-lasting and chronic nature. It is true that we haven't suffered yearly crises of the magnitude of the 2010 Deepwater Horizon oil spill in the Gulf of Mexico off the coast of Louisiana from which lawsuits drag on and victims continue to suffer, but time and the Republican death grip on state and national politics have yielded other catastrophes aplenty.

There have been bright spots of comparative good fortune for Louisiana, as with the leadership of Governor John Bel Edwards and Mayors Sharon Weston Broome in Baton Rouge and LaToya Cantrell in New Orleans, all Democrats, during the Covid-19 pandemic that began in early 2020. The pandemic could have been even worse for Louisiana. Fortunately, these leaders took the public health emergency (and science) seriously, which made Louisiana "something of an outlier in the South," as described by Mark Moseley, a blogger and former columnist at *The* [New Orleans] *Lens*.

There was a time when Louisiana politicians in the United States Congress were among the most powerful and influential in Washington (Huey Long, Russell Long, Hale Boggs, and F. Edward Hébert), and they brought home the pork so that Louisiana benefited from their high positions. Now a Louisiana congressman is the Speaker of the House, which theoretically could benefit the state, except that this one is the sanctimonious Mike Johnson of Shreveport who like the rest of his party is ambitiously subservient to the bullying and social media directives from the Oval Office.

The entire ten-year span since this book was published has passed under the shadow of one man and his many, many helpers. (Where did they all come from?) We once wrote, about former governor Bobby Jindal, that with today's increasingly extreme G.O.P., to have a Republican governor with presidential ambitions is a curse that we would not wish upon any state (see page 43). This remains our view of radical, partisan governors such as Jeff Landry of Louisiana, Greg Abbott of Texas, and Ron DeSantis of Florida, who strive to outdo each other in serving as "willing executioners" in carrying out the White House's scheme for mass deportations of dark-skinned immigrants. We thought Bobby Jindal was bad (and he was), but we had no idea to what depths an already antidemocratic party would sink, turbocharged by ambition, greed, and fearful submission to a malignant authoritarian's cult of personality.

The Republicans, as usual (for most of this century), have *no ideas*, no constructive plans for building or improving anything, but only schemes to cut taxes on the wealthy and corporations and to undo, repeal, roll back the twentieth century's people-helping New Deal and Great Society programs, environmental protections, and the Affordable Care Act of 2010 ("Obamacare"), and eviscerate the Voting Rights Act, all enabled by the Supreme Court's radical majority. In the past ten years and especially since January 2025 the demolition crew has been working overtime. This is widely known, painfully felt, and does not need belaboring.

How's the Weather?

Over the past ten years the Gulf Coast has been relatively safe from massively destructive storms—there's always next year—but the temperatures and sea levels are rising inexorably, summer and the hurricane season seem to last longer, and the weather has occasionally been extreme. The most powerful storm to threaten New Orleans since Hurricane Katrina in 2005 was named Ida (2021), whose arrival on Sunday, August 29, the exact date of Katrina, added extra spookiness to the sense of threat. One wit on Twitter, with a sense of humor worthy of the satirical Krewe du Vieux, asked, "Who invited Ida to Katrina's sweet sixteenth?" Particularly alarming about Ida—a *ferocious* f'ing storm—was how rapidly it intensified in the warm Gulf waters from Category 1 to 3 and then 4, bordering on 5: only a day or two. There was no time to order a contraflow evacuation of the city (all lanes outbound), because that takes about 72 hours' advance notice. "Ida astonished meteorologists with its rapid intensification in the days before it made landfall on Sunday near Port Fourchon as a Category 4 storm," *The New York Times* reported. "And it maintained its intensity for longer after coming ashore than is typical for hurricanes, a result of the swampy terrain and the fact it was still growing in strength as it reached the coast."

Ida didn't stop there, but swept up the eastern part of the United States and on September 1–2 brought fresh destruction to Pennsylvania, New Jersey, and New York City and environs: unexpected flash flooding inundated streets in Newark, Hoboken, Staten Island, Brooklyn, and Queens; and spawned tornadoes across Pennsylvania and New Jersey, the first tornado emergency ever issued for a tropical cyclone and the first ever issued for the northeastern United States. Flash flood waters drowned eleven people living in basements in Brooklyn and Queens; burst into subway entrances in Manhattan, pouring down to the tracks; and filled streets in Brooklyn, where passengers were filmed standing on the (already high) seats of city buses and looking like *What is going on?*

The good news was that the post-Katrina reinforced flood protection system around New Orleans held up and the pumps worked well enough to keep the water from rising too high. "This was a victory under extreme duress," says Mark Moseley. "We largely passed the stress test in not having catastrophic damage or levee breaks that caused flooding." But the failure of Entergy to keep its power flowing, its long delay in restoring service, and the unconscionable nonfunctioning of (privatized) garbage pickup for weeks into months for some neighborhoods—all this gave a dispiriting sense of municipal services and infrastructure breaking down. After Ida, some families left town for good.

Among the most extreme seasons in the annals of climate change was the summer of 2023. Over that year, temperatures in New Orleans and Baton Rouge were on average four degrees warmer than usual. New Orleans had the second-longest streak of days with extreme heat across the world, tied with Jakarta, Indonesia. *The Times-Picayune* reported that, starting in July, extreme temperatures lasted in New Orleans for 17 days, with 10 of those days reaching triple-digit temperatures—which for New Orleans used to not be normal. (I recall the highs in the 1970s, '80s, and '90s being more like 85 to 87 degrees, which, with the humidity, were quite warm enough.) Ben Schott, the director of the National Weather Service in New Orleans, said of 2023, "No person alive in the city has ever experienced a summer like this." To be sure, during that summer the entire midsection of North America was suffering from extreme heat, but southern Louisiana's natural humidity compounded the extraordinary temperatures. As they say, it's not the heat, it's the humidity. (There's a local variant on this folk wisdom, "it's not the heat, it's the stupidity," which now applies as well to national as to Louisiana politics.)

A Government Dismantling Itself

The current administration, guided by the radical (not at all "conservative") blueprint for restructuring the federal government known as Project 2025, brought to us by the folks at the Heritage Foundation, has been breaking apart the National Weather Service (including its Weather Prediction Center) and the Environmental Protection Agency. It proposes to slash funding for the National Oceanic and Atmospheric Administration (founded in 1970 under President Richard Nixon), which monitors tropical storms and inland weather and provides forecasting data to meteorologists and news organizations. The regime wants to shut down the National Severe Storms Laboratory and other research centers funded by NOAA. Project 2025 complains that the National Oceanic and Atmospheric Administration is a "colossal operation that has become one of the main drivers of the climate change alarm industry." In the past half year NOAA has lost nearly six hundred employees, many of them highly skilled, either through firings or encouraged early retirements.

The Federal Emergency Management Administration (FEMA) was established in 1979 by an executive order of President Jimmy Carter to unify the federal civil defense functions of disaster preparedness and relief into one agency when it became clear that states alone did not have the resources to manage responses to natural disasters. After the attacks of September 11, 2001, FEMA was placed under the newly created Department of Homeland Security. Republican administrations tended not to take its functions seriously, appointing directors in name only who lacked emergency management experience ("Heck of a job, Brownie"), while Democratic presidents such as Carter, Bill Clinton, and Barack Obama nominated authentic disaster management professionals. The two best FEMA directors ever were James Lee Witt of Arkansas under Clinton and Craig Fugate of Florida under Obama: both served full, eight-year terms with distinction. (See *Levees Not War*'s interview [online] with Christopher Cooper and Robert Block, authors of *Disaster: Hurricane Katrina and the Failure of Homeland Security* [2007].) The new regime appointed as administrator a former Marine Corps officer with no emergency management experience who admitted in June 2025 that he was unaware that there is such a thing as a *hurricane season*. When, amid howls of outrage, he was asked if he was serious, he claimed he was only joking (that's what they always say).

This administration aims to shut down FEMA and to return all responsibility to the individual states—the same basic plan they have for the Department of Education—as Republicans have long aimed to do. You're on your own, as people in western North Carolina learned after Hurricane Helene's catastrophic flooding in September 2024. Republicans train their voters to expect nothing and to hate the government. FEMA's threatened demise was slowed in July 2025 when a terrible flash-flooding rainstorm along the Guadalupe River in central Texas swept away the lives of about two dozen children at a summer camp and killed some 135 people. The deaths were a public relations inconvenience for the Republican-controlled state of Texas and the new administration, which had already forced the downsizing of the National Weather Service and its forecasting functions. As is becoming more common amid global warming, storms can escalate rapidly in severity, as Hurricane Ida did in 2021. The warmer atmosphere causes excessive rainfall, as with Hurricane Harvey of August 2017, which parked over Houston for days and dumped more than fifty inches of rain. "The hotter the air, the more moisture it can hold," as *The New Yorker*'s Elizabeth Kolbert explains. "According to the Fifth National Climate Assessment, published in 2023, the amount of rain falling on so-called 'extreme precipitation days' has, during the past several decades, increased by twenty per cent in the region that includes Texas, by almost half in the Midwest, and by a staggering sixty per cent in the Northeast." (Elizabeth Kolbert, "Flash Floods and Climate Policy," *The New Yorker*, July 12, 2025) The new regime, however, denies the reality of global warming, of climate change, or any human (or corporate) responsibility for extreme weather. Meanwhile the director of DHS, FEMA's nominal overseer, enjoys dressing up in military garb, toting a gun and posing toughly in front of cages of captive brown-skinned immigrants in prison photo-ops in El Salvador and Florida.

Leave No Social Safety Net Behind

The mendaciously titled, doubleplus ungood budget legislation known as the One Big Beautiful Bill Act, whose passage was forced through by the afore-mentioned Speaker of the House, a "more Christian than thou" kind of man, was signed on the Fourth of July 2025. There is so much evil and avarice in OBBBA that the irony of its false name will smolder like toxic waste for many years to come. This might be wishful thinking, but the bill's passage may well be viewed in retrospect as the high point of political success for this adminis-tration, after which everything will be downhill. For at least half the country, everything already feels downhill, like we're on a ski slope of ashes and charred bones. Even many Republicans denounced the bill before voting for it. It could only be "beautiful" to someone who takes pleasure in human suffering. "The cruelty is the point," as they say. The damage to be inflicted by this roughly $5.5 trillion, deficit-maximizing OBBBA goes in many directions, mostly kicking downward at levels beneath the ultrarich. Some 10 million people will lose access to Medicaid—these are *individual human lives*, not mere statistics—and 2.5 million will be cut off of food stamps in order to pay for massive tax cuts for corporations and the rich, including an extension of the 2017 tax cut, totaling $4.6 trillion over ten years, that primarily benefited the ultrarich. As *The New Yorker*'s John Cassidy observes,

> By stripping almost a trillion dollars in funding for Medicaid,
> the public health-care system that covers more than seventy
> million low-income American adults and their children, and also
> slashing subsidies to health-care insurance policies purchased
> on the Obamacare exchanges, [Republicans on Capitol Hill and
> in the White House] found more than $1.2 trillion in savings.
> They also hacked about a hundred and forty billion dollars
> from nutritional-assistance programs, once known as food
> stamps, and three hundred and thirty billion from student-loan
> programs and other commitments to education. To save another
> five hundred and forty billion dollars or so, they repealed Joe
> Biden's tax credits for purchases of electric vehicles and business
> investments in clean-energy systems and green manufacturing,
> climate action be damned. ("The Economic Consequences of the
> Big Odious Bill," *The New Yorker*, July 7, 2025)

With its slashing of Medicaid and $230 billion from the Supplemental Nutritional Assistance Program (SNAP, formerly known as food stamps) over the next ten years—a 20 percent reduction—OBBBA will inflict additional suffering upon a city (indeed a nation) that already has a large population of low-income people, most of whom work but struggle to make ends meet. The Center for Budget and Policy Priorities estimates that in Louisiana nearly a quarter million will lose their health coverage. Because the bill eliminates federal tax credits and funding for clean energy initiatives put in place by Joe Biden's Inflation Reduction Act (2022), the Center for American Progress projects that households could see an average increase of $110 per year in electricity costs; other estimates are as high as an extra $280 per year by 2035.

The Times-Picayune reports that federal budget cuts will also stop the U.S. Army Corps of Engineers from conducting regular inspections of the city's and surrounding area's levees in 2025 and 2026, inspections that had been stepped up and more generously funded after Hurricane Katrina. According to FEMA there are more than 3,100 miles of levees in Louisiana, about one-fifth of the state's total area. Budget cuts have also forced the pause (or end?) of a major Corps study on the future of the lower Mississippi River—on shipping, flooding concerns, salt water intrusion, the quality of drinking water, and the operations of the Old River Control Structure—("previous president budget funds received during FY25 must be returned to the United States Treasury"), and the New Orleans district of the Corps is losing about eighty of its 1,160 employees.

But, even as OBBBA taketh away, it giveth: the oil and gas industry received some $18 billion in new or expanded tax incentives, and will have less competition from the solar- and wind-energy industries that were weakened by the bill. What's more, the increasingly Gestapo-like Immigration and Customs Enforcement agency (ICE) was awarded a massive increase in funding for detention and deportation. According to the American Immigration Council, "With approximately $28 billion given to [ICE] annually, the agency now has a budget larger than the Federal Bureau of Investigation (FBI), Drug Enforcement Administration (DEA), Bureau of Alcohol, Tobacco, Firearms and Explosives (ATF), U.S. Marshals Service, and Bureau of Prisons combined."

"It Is Tossed by the Waves, but Does Not Sink"

The Latin motto of the city of Paris, *Fluctuat nec mergitur*, could apply as well to New Orleans—but for how long? With a combination of determination, good cheer, and dark humor, the city struggles with the perennial challenges of sustaining the electricity, providing a safe supply of water, worries about the strength of the levees and the municipal system of pumps that are needed to push excess rainwater out to Lake Pontchartrain, and efforts to limit the damage to the city's affordability and sense of identity amid the pressures of short-term rental services. There are more issues than this Preface's brief summary can mention—I know, it can feel overwhelming, and *there is simply too much to worry about*—but here's a start.

Over the past two decades Charity Hospital might have been a source of succor to the poor when they're ill, as it was devotedly for centuries, but the nearly three-hundred-year-old institution (est. 1736) was never reopened—rather, its closure was forced by the state, including LSU, in a coup of disaster capitalism—after it was only glancingly damaged by minimal floodwaters in Hurricane Katrina in 2005. (Charity's emergency room once helped this writer, at the time a freelancer without health insurance, when a certain medication had side effects that *felt* like a heart attack. The nurse and doctor couldn't have been kinder.) The massive, twenty-story, million-square-foot hospital building on Tulane Avenue that Huey Long built and micromanaged (completed in 1938) has been shuttered, surrounded by razor-wire fencing, while the LSU Medical Center and the Veterans Administration built a large medical complex in the adjacent neighborhood—demolishing several blocks' worth of vintage middle-class homes and displacing hundreds of people to make room for shiny new buildings in what is now called the BioDistrict. Tulane University plans to redevelop the Charity Hospital building and will occupy part of it; other parts of the building will be set aside for retail and residential apartment units.

Infrastructure issues have bedeviled the city for many years, but a decade and a half after repairs from the widespread damage of Hurricane Katrina, benefiting from serious increases in funding from Congress, for a change, after the Bush administration's shameful federal response—even after all those repairs, after Hurricane Ida the reliability of electricity, garbage pickup, and the robustness of the city's pumping system were again in question. Frequent power outages have led to pump failures that result in "boil water" advisories, in which the water flowing through the city's pipes cannot be trusted for cleanliness or potability. Climate change has brought longer, more drenching rains, and the pumping stations can only work so fast. Pumps at several stations around the city broke down in 2024. The stations can handle an inch per hour for the first hour of rain and then a half inch per hour thereafter, but sometimes the rain just keeps on falling and the pumps cannot keep up. It is also common to see major intersections' traffic lights not working for weeks at a time, replaced by stop signs until lights are fixed. On a more positive and charming note, a clever initiative called Green Light has partnered with Entergy to provide large, 55-gallon rain barrels that can be attached to your downspout to siphon off excess rainwater and collect it for gardening or other practical uses, reducing (by at least 55 gallons) the rainwater in your yard and saving on the water bill. It has become a very popular program citywide, and there's a waiting list for rain barrels. Students paint the barrels in vivid colors, each one an individual creation. It's little things like this that keep the civilization going.

Entergy New Orleans, which is regulated by the New Orleans City Council, succeeds in delivering profits for its shareholders but often fails in providing reliable energy in tropical storms—and sometimes even when there isn't a storm, as in the "outage event" over Memorial Day weekend in 2025. More than 100,000 customers lost electricity during a series of rolling blackouts, about half of them in the city of New Orleans. To explain Entergy's history and way of doing business would take a whole 'nother book, but suffice it to say that New Orleans is not well served overall by this utility firm. Entergy is a living disproof, a corporate refutation of zombie Reagan rhetoric like "magic of the marketplace" and "government is the problem." Entergy, like most cities' utilities, is in business to make a profit and holds a monopoly over the power lines. It belongs to a regional grid operator called the Mid-Continent Independent System Operator (MISO), but Entergy is not interested in participating fully in a cooperative grid that transmits power on a regional basis because then it would have to rely on other regional utilities' power supplies and would be obligated to charge less to its New Orleans area customers. The structure and terms of the arrangement are too complicated to explain here, but, as John Norris, a former Federal Energy Regulatory Commission (FERC) commissioner who voted for approval of Entergy's joining MISO, writes in *The Lens*:

> Entergy continues to block long-range transmission planning, a necessary part of electric reliability. . . . Entergy has a history of using its transmission system to prevent competition and maximize profits from its fleet of gas plants. That strategy prioritizes Entergy's bottom line but sacrifices reliability for its customers. . . .
>
> Throughout Entergy's membership in MISO, I have witnessed and heard of numerous efforts by Entergy and its staff or consultants to the Public Service Commissioners and NOLA City Council to stall, block, interfere—or throw up barriers of any type, all to stop efforts to conduct [a Long Range Transmission Plan (LRTP)] in MISO South. . . .
>
> The state public service commissions and New Orleans City Council, who regulate Entergy, must require Entergy to fully participate in MISO's LRTP process. This is the key to planning and building a transmission system that will bring greater reliability for New Orleans and all of Entergy's service territory, along with more competitively priced electricity and more diverse electric generation. ("Entergy wants to use power it creates. That led to the May [2025] blackout," John Norris, *The Lens*, July 31, 2025)

The short-term rentals of apartments have been driven by Airbnb, VRBO (Vacation Rentals by Owner), and similar app services. The city has sought since 2016 to regulate and limit the industry to balance residents' concerns about the rising cost of living and complaints of noise with other residents' right to earn money by renting out their units to visitors—the usual capitalist economic tension between the profit motive and the need for shelter made worse by post-storm housing shortages and escalating tourism. A short-term rental is defined as a space offered for rentals of thirty days or less. The city has passed a series of ordinances designed to limit the number of rental units to one per square block, which Airbnb has fought with lawsuits, often joined by property owners who wish to rent their units. Post-Katrina tourism has been enabled by the smartphone apps that were initially unregulated. Local and out-of-town investors, including real estate investment firms, bought properties, renovated them, and then rented one or two halves of a shotgun double (what other cities call a duplex) for profitable short-term rents—particularly during the Sugar Bowl, Mardi Gras, and the two weekends of Jazz Fest. This drove up real estate prices and rents and property taxes for New Orleanians trying to hold on to or find an affordable place to live. The monthly rent for half a double rose to between $1,500 and $2,000 per month. (In the mid '90s to 2001 my rent for a spacious half of a double in Mid-City was about a quarter of my monthly freelance income; nowadays the rent could eat up three-quarters of my budget.) Many have been driven out of the central city to New Orleans East or out of Orleans Parish to neighboring Jefferson Parish (Metairie or Kenner) or across the Mississippi to Algiers, Gretna, or farther from town. The short-term rentals are a vexing issue, as they make tourism attractive and affordable, which can stimulate shops and restaurants, but residents find the increase of tourism has a bad effect on the neighborhoods' sense of community cohesiveness. Some observe that you don't hear so many New Orleans accents anymore, and you hear more people who don't know how to pronounce Calliope, Melpomene, or Telemachus—though, to be sure, any New Orleanian will tell you that there are usually at least two local pronunciations for any street, and even the name of the city itself.

The year 2025 began ominously with a terrible, shocking terrorist attack by truck on Bourbon Street at 3:15 a.m. on January 1, when, after planting two IEDs in the Quarter, one Shamsud-Din Jabbar, a U.S. Army veteran from Texas who had pledged his allegiance to ISIS, drove his pickup around bollards at Canal Street and plowed into pedestrians on Bourbon, killing fourteen and injuring fifty-seven others. Jabbar was killed when he opened fire on police, wounding two officers. This attack caused a one-day postponement of the Sugar Bowl—that shows how seriously the authorities took the attack—and occurred a month before the city's first hosting of the Super Bowl (LIX) since 2013 and just days before the start of the Carnival season that begins with king cake parties on Twelfth Night, a traditional and more peaceful way of celebrating January 6. Later in January a polar vortex brought a rare snow-fall of eight to ten inches on New Orleans and southern Louisiana, drawing people out for snowball fights, snowmen, and general merriment amid the unfamiliar white crystals. Although doubtless it was difficult getting to work, and New Orleanians don't get much practice driving in the snow, there were beautiful views of snow in the Quarter and on St. Charles Avenue and a viral video of three white-robed nuns at St. Catherine of Siena Church in Metairie getting the better of a black-clad priest in an impromptu snowball fight out in the churchyard.

How many wars are we involved in now? Since U.S. troops were pulled rather hastily from Afghanistan in August 2021—after a twenty-year stay—American forces have not been engaged in active conflicts in large numbers, though peacekeeping or stabilization forces are in place in Syria, Iraq, and elsewhere. For the first year after Russia's invasion of Ukraine in March 2022, the U.S. provided arms and financial and logistical support, but the new administration prioritizes Putin over Zelensky (why might that be?). Peacemaking and settling of that conflict has not been as easy as promised because the aggressor does not want peace. Then, in another intractable conflict, between Israel and Iran (and virtually all of Israel's neighbors), in June 2025, with no declaration of war from Congress, no advance notice to Democratic congressional leaders, and no preparation of the American public for involvement in what could be a long and messy war—possibly World War III—the world leader pretend made his decision in his own little mind and 30,000-pound "bunker-buster" bombs were dropped on three Iranian nuclear facilities, at Fordo, Isfahan, and Natanz, inserting the United States into a war with Iran that Israel started on a Friday the 13th. Thus far the repercussions from Iran have been restrained, but American support of Israel's punitive leveling of Gaza and deliberate starvation campaign—all this has sickened the conscience of the world, and retribution cannot be far away.

The unsmiling strongman, embittered that he was talked out of using the U.S. military against civilians in the George Floyd / Black Lives Matter protests in 2020 ("Can't you just shoot them in the legs or something?" he asked General Mark Milley), actually seems more likely to use armed force against the people in Democratic-controlled cities and states—L.A., Washington, D.C., maybe Chicago and New York—than against foreign foes. "The homegrowns are next," he said in one of his humorless jokes during a visit to the White House by Salvadoran president Nayib Bukele in April. He was referring to extralegal shipments to foreign jails, such as to Bukele's notorious CECOT mega prison. Claiming in all seriousness that its actions are backed by the 1798 Alien Enemies Act, asserting that the nation is under attack by a hostile invader (a Venezuelan gang), and directed by White House anti-immigration adviser Stephen "Final Solution" Miller, the administration has so far deported nearly 60,000 migrants, sending them to El Salvador, Honduras, and Guatemala, among other destinations. (Miller reportedly wants the dreaded ICE to nab three thousand a day, a million a year.) Courts are being ignored, lied to, circumvented, and defunded. Other captives, most of them with no police record, are being held in inhumane conditions in Louisiana and Florida's new and legally challenged Alcatraz in the Everglades; the latter is reportedly to receive funds repurposed from FEMA's Shelter and Services Program. The strongman has already called out the National Guard on "scare" pretexts about "bloodthirsty criminals" to occupy parts of Los Angeles and Washington, D.C., and has at least temporarily federalized the D.C. police department (making a strong case for D.C. statehood).

He is not an authentic president of the United States—he just plays one on TV and social media.

I recognize that this Preface is a lot to digest, and I'm sorry if you feel overwhelmed after reading this far. A lot has happened in the past ten years, and this survey is just scratching the surface. It's understandable that many of us have tuned out and stopped reading the news altogether. As I mention in the Introduction, "what fresh hell?" was the attitude with which we used to open the daily paper during the Bush-Cheney years, and it's even worse now.

What the next ten years will bring is unimaginable—just like the past six months have been—but, as ever, I believe in the goodness and common sense

of the people, without whose consent no government can long stand. And I
have faith that, as the Rev. Martin Luther King Jr. famously said, "the arc of
the moral universe is long, but it bends toward justice." Fight the good fight.
Never give up.

diligentibus deum omnia convertuntur in bonum . . .

And we know that in everything God works for good
with those who love him, who are called according to his purpose.

Romans 8:28

August 29, 2005   Hurricane Katrina

August 29, 2015   *What Fresh Hell?* published

August 29, 2025   Tenth Anniversary Edition

WHAT
FRESH
HELL?

Introduction

What fresh hell can this be?
Dorothy Parker

Isn't it a bit backward to take a blog and make it into a book? Well, maybe, but at the same time, what's the point of writing a blog if you can't make a book out of it? As for backward, it's always struck us as worse than reverse for an advanced nation like the United States to practically ignore its schools and public health and roads and levees while spending ever more billions on wars and overseas military bases. And isn't it also retrograde to pretend our industries and our consuming ways of living don't have some connection to the increasingly extreme weather and rising sea levels?

Levees Not War is a New Orleans–dedicated, New York–based blog that focuses on the environment, infrastructure, war and peace, and progressive politics—sexy things like that. We see these subjects as interrelated, inseparable, so it's important to stay focused on multiple fronts at once, particularly as they affect New Orleans, Louisiana, the Gulf Coast, and America. The blog includes well-stocked sections on political action and how to help, with names and contact info of elected officials and relief and recovery organizations; a literature page with links to resources, reports, and videos; and interviews with authors and experts.

I started *Levees Not War* in the months following Hurricane Katrina (August 29, 2005). What would soon take shape as a website and then a blog began as a determined, persistent series of letters faxed and snail-mailed to members of Congress and to the news media, imploring them to keep the financial and humanitarian assistance coming to New Orleans and the Gulf Coast, and keep sending reporters and camera crews, *please*.

The name of the blog comes from a sign I made for an anti–Iraq War march in Washington, D.C., on September 24, 2005, the weekend of Hurricane Rita, a month after Katrina. I'd thought I was being clever when

Mark and Janet (with signs) with Louisiana friends Chris and Molly near the Washington Monument, September 24, 2005.

I wrote "MAKE LEVEES, NOT WAR" on a big poster board. When we got to Washington (after our Amtrak train from Penn Station was delayed by a mysterious signal outage somewhere in New Jersey—more evidence of needed repairs to national infrastructure!), I found I was not as original as I'd thought: at least two dozen other protesters, all apparently independent of one another, had the same bright idea. The peace activism group Code Pink, too, carried a huge banner with the legend MAKE LEVEES NOT WAR.

The title of this book may sound familiar. "WHAT FRESH HELL?" was the header that appeared at the top of an early version of *Levees Not War*, when it was more a crude website than a WordPress-style blog. During those years, so much bad news came in such a relentless barrage, on all fronts and with such intense velocity, that "What fresh hell do we have today?" was the attitude with which one unfolded the newspaper each morning. (There's still as much bad news as ever, but in the George W. Bush years much of the hell was generated *by the administration in power* as it systematically dismantled or privatized key functions of government, reversed environmental protections, and went after the social safety net with chainsaws.) The phrase comes from Dorothy Parker, who is said to have grumbled "What fresh hell can this be?" each time the telephone or doorbell rang.

For someone who came of age around the time personal computers were being developed, before the Internet or the iPhone, there is something wonderful about the Web's expanding universe of blogs and social media. Depending on where you click, it can be a nearly infinite storehouse of knowledge (e.g., Project Gutenberg) and a superb venue for good writing and investigative reporting—as long as the servers are up and the domain name is kept current, anyway. But there is also something reassuring, in a way that the Internet cannot quite duplicate, about a printed book as an enduring, time-tested preserver of an author's writings. The book form (including the eBook) *in addition to the blog* is that extra bit of assurance that one's words will not perish too quickly—and might reach new readers. And, besides, I've worked my whole adult life in publishing, so making a book feels like a natural thing to do. In a blog, of course, unless you keep listing previous writings in newer, related posts, the earlier pieces may easily be buried, like old newspapers piled in a corner: out of sight, out of mind. So, even though it may seem to be going against nature to publish a dead-tree edition of originally digital content, this Best Of collection is an attempt to keep readily accessible some writings from the past ten years that I hope will still be of interest even as more waves of fresh hell wash over us in the news cycles and Facebook and Twitter feeds.

Levees Not War was prompted by a wish to help my beloved home state and former residence—I had moved from New Orleans to New York City in 2001, just months before September 11. The letters and then the blog, launched in December 2005, were a way for a homesick transplant to try to help after the most destructive and traumatizing catastrophe in New Orleans's three-hundred-year history.

In the aftermath of the storm, many electrical and phone lines were not working and cell phone towers were out, but text messages could be sent. *The Times-Picayune* hosted online message boards for community information, and New Orleans area bloggers posted updates about where essential services could (or could not) be found; which neighborhoods had regained electricity; where hot meals and cold drinks were being served; where you could recharge your laptop and mobile phone; which intersections' traffic lights were still not working, and so on. There formed a community of bloggers in New Orleans, in some ways tight-knit and yet loose and informal. To name just a few: *Your*

Right Hand Thief, People Get Ready, Hurricane Radio, Fix the Pumps, Library Chronicles, Humid City, Maitri's VatulBlog, Tim's Nameless Blog, and many more—see *Levees Not War*'s blogroll under In the Sunken City. One long-enduring event that grew out of this community is the annual Rising Tide conference on the future of New Orleans (see Part VI). Many of these bloggers are still active today, and a good sampling of their work appears in the excellent anthologies *A Howling in the Wires* (2010), edited by Sam Jasper and Mark Folse, and in *Please Forward: How Blogging Reconnected New Orleans After Katrina* (2015), edited by Cynthia Joyce. I am indebted to them all for ideas, inspiration, and friendship.

Now, part of the emotional energy behind *Levees Not War*—the indignant sense of injustice and determination to make things right—was unleashed when I read that a local Army Corps of Engineers project manager, Alfred Naomi, said that for $2.5 billion (modest on the scale of federal expenditures), the New Orleans area's flood protection defenses could have been brought up to Category 5 strength—and yes, there were such plans ready for funding—which probably would have prevented what has become known as the federal flood. The U.S. at that time was (deficit) spending about *$12 billion per week* in Iraq, so $2.5 billion would have been about two and a half days' worth.

Because of George W. Bush's $1.35 trillion tax cut in 2001, unanticipated expenditures for homeland security after 9/11, and the costs of two wars, funding for Southeast Louisiana flood control projects in place since the mid 1990s was cut drastically. Nearly a dozen articles in the *Times-Picayune* in 2004 and 2005 cited the Iraq War as the reason for the huge cutbacks in funding for projects that had been approved by Congress and were under way when Bush took office. After the 2004 hurricane season, one of the worst in decades, the Bush administration and the Republican-led Congress slashed the Corps of Engineers New Orleans district's FY2006 budget by $71.2 million, even as they were pushing a repeal of the estate tax on the wealthiest 2 percent. Predictably, after Katrina they claimed that a storm of this magnitude and destructiveness could not have been anticipated.

*He shall judge the poor of the people, he shall save the children
of the needy, and shall break in pieces the oppressor . . . he shall
deliver the needy when he crieth; the poor also, and him that hath
no helper.*

Psalm 72

In an interview in 2014 with Bruce R. Magee and Stephen Payne of the *Louisiana Anthology* podcast series, I was asked if there is a philosophy or moral vision behind *Levees Not War*. At the time Hurricane Katrina came knocking, I was already about a year and several hundred pages into a sprawling rough draft of what could charitably be described as political philosophy: an argument on behalf of the idea of the social contract. I wasn't quite sure whether "social contract" was the exact term—it's an age-old concept, as explained below—but what I was trying to get at was the idea that for moral reasons as well as for social stability there should be some kind of Golden Rule–like equilibrium of fairness in the society, in the conditions of life. (See "Does Believing in Social Contract Make Us Socialists?" in Part IV.) During the George W. Bush years, described by former labor secretary Robert B. Reich as a time of "corporate power in overdrive," unfairness, greed, and indifference were all around, and coming in blows—as they are still. Especially amid widening wealth and income disparity—with the rich getting ever richer, corporate profits reaching new heights as corporate taxes drop to new lows, with jobs ever harder to find (or keep), and the nation's social safety net for the poor and the middle class disintegrating (and not by accident) in a death by a thousand cuts—those who are very well-to-do ought to help the less fortunate without begrudging or insulting.

The idea of the social contract (or compact), an ancient concept that has taken various forms over the years (Rousseau, Locke, medieval coronation oaths, etc.) and dates at least as far back as King David's covenant with the elders of Israel, holds that political authority derives from the consent of the governed (as it says in the Declaration of Independence). "The people themselves are the originating source of all the powers of government," as Justice Ruth Bader Ginsburg wrote in a Supreme Court ruling in June 2015. (Some of these ideas are enshrined in Magna Carta, whose eight-hundredth anniversary was being celebrated as this book was being assembled.) There is or should be a reciprocal agreement by which the people can rely upon the leader's protection and benevolence in exchange for their allegiance. A balanced social contract would also rightly expect that all able-bodied citizens shall contribute to the common good through some kind of labor. Similarly, as the people agree to work and produce the goods of society, the wealthy and powerful share some of their abundance for the protection of the less affluent. Everyone should have *some* kind of work, and all who labor should not be without food and shelter. Everyone unable to work—the very young, the infirm, and disabled—should be assisted by the community. And the state, for the people's labor and payments of taxes, shall in turn help educate and house the populace. The poor will always be with us, so programs and policies should be in place to assist them, with no grumbling from the blessed.

Conservative politicians are always paying homage to Ronald Reagan, so why not restore the upper-income tax rates to the 50 percent that the wealthy paid during the Reagan years of 1982–86? They can afford it. After all, in the past thirty years, more than four-fifths of the total increase in American incomes has gone to the richest 1 percent. Meanwhile, according to data from the 2010 U.S. Census, more than half the American population lives in poverty or is low-income.

A social contract would also involve taking better care of the earth, as good stewards of nature, God's creation—not plundering and laying waste our only planet.

These, anyway, are some of the ideas I was working on at the time Hurricane Katrina struck, when all the shortcomings of American society—particularly of the downsized, privatized, and underfunded functions of its federal and state governments—became so starkly, painfully obvious to all who had eyes to see. After August 29, 2005, the leisurely work of composing a treatise of political philosophy had to give way to more urgent advocacy and action.

. . . It is here, under this oak where Evangeline waited for her lover, Gabriel, who never came. This oak is an immortal spot, made so by Longfellow's poem, but Evangeline is not the only one who has waited here in disappointment.

> *Where are the schools that you have waited for your children to have, that have never come?*
> *Where are the roads and the highways that you send your money to build, that are no nearer now than ever before?*
> *Where are the institutions to care for the sick and disabled? . . .*
>
> **Huey P. Long, 1928, St. Martinville, Louisiana**

One of the reasons why I care so strongly about the social safety net and public works is that I came of age in a state where there was a proud and still-breathing tradition of progressive, liberal spending on behalf of public schools, hospitals for the poor, roads and bridges, and a good, low-priced state university on a beautiful campus. Louisiana, though a largely traditional and conservative state, once was a place where populist and agrarian-socialist ideas were not uncommon. When Huey P. Long took office as governor in 1928, the state had 30 miles of paved roads, no bridges across major rivers, and half the state's children were unschooled. In three years 2,500 miles of paved roads, 6,000 miles of gravel roads, and 12 bridges were built, and by the end of the Great Depression about two-thirds of black children were attending public schools. Long provided new schools, hospitals—including a grand and massive new state-of-the-art facility for the centuries-old Charity Hospital in New Orleans—courthouses, free bridges across bayous, and a beautiful, well-funded and affordable state university at a time when other schools were contracting or closing. Importantly—and today's elected officials might take note—he shifted most of the tax burden from individuals to industry, and slashed personal property taxes and fees. In order to fund the free textbooks for public schools, taxes were raised on the oil companies doing business in the state. (Standard Oil led an attempt to have him impeached.) It is well known that Huey Long grew corrupt and dictatorial, but when he was good he was very good for the state, in a way that no Louisiana governor had ever been before. It should be mentioned, too, that while he was generous to the public, Long was also fiscally conservative: in his term as governor (1928–32), taxes rose 2.2 percent compared to the 4.7 percent national average.

In this ten years' collection you will find pieces on hurricanes, Louisiana's environmental predicament, the BP disaster, and climate change; on infrastructure and public works in a time of job-killing scrooges (with a definite nostalgia for Franklin Roosevelt's WPA and CCC programs); on the wars in Iraq and Afghanistan and beyond; plenty about politics, including a mad tea party and half-mute Democrats; blogging and merrymaking with friends in New Orleans, with a dash of burlesquery; on-the-scene reporting from Occupy Wall Street; remembrances of Katrina and 9/11, and tributes to activist leaders such as Medgar Evers, Tom Hayden, John F. Kennedy, and an early founder of Greenpeace. After the interviews with Harry Shearer and experts on the environment and infrastructure, there's a bibliography to point readers to further sources of information, organizing, and activism. This and much more. Jump in at any point. I hope you enjoy the book—and the blog.

Hurricane Katrina and the Environment

Remember August 29, 2005

AUG. 29, 2014—If you don't live in or around New Orleans you may have forgotten, but August 29 is the day when, in 2005, Hurricane Katrina assaulted the Gulf Coast with Category 3 winds (up to 175 mph) and storm surges of 25 to 28 feet, killing 1,833 and costing some $108 billion in damages, the costliest tropical storm in U.S. history. It was not until the following day that we began to realize that although the eye of the storm had curved eastward and the city was spared the worst—"we dodged a bullet"—*the city was flooding!* In addition to coastal St. Bernard, Plaquemines, and other parishes, 80 percent of New Orleans flooded when Katrina's massive storm surge burst through the city's outflow canals to Lake Pontchartrain, the Mississippi River–Gulf Outlet (MR-GO), the Inner Harbor Navigation Canal, etc.—53 different levee breaches in all. (The surge was about 10 to 20 feet around New Orleans, and nearly 28 feet at nearby Pass Christian, Miss., exceeding the previous record set by Camille in 1969 by about 4 feet.)

The most dramatic and infamous of the flooded areas was the already poor Lower Ninth Ward. An animated graphic produced by *The Times-Picayune* called "Flash Flood" shows the sequence of events, still horrifying to watch. It was a catastrophic failure of the mostly federally built storm protection system, and in the years since the scorned and humiliated Army Corps of Engineers has worked overtime to rebuild and reinforce the area's defenses against flooding. (The Corps' funding and directives come—or don't come—from Congress, one of the reasons why this blog does not hold the Corps alone responsible for the failures.) For more about the flooding, and recommendations on reinforcement of the area's flood defense system, see our interviews with Mark Schleifstein and Ivor Van Heerden in Part VII

New Orleans: Proud to Rebuild Home

Much of the city has been rebuilt, and in some ways life in New Orleans is better than ever (see Magazine Street, for example). Other parts of town are still damaged, depressed. There are neighborhoods that will never be the same. Many people had to leave and will never return—they left to avoid the storm and could not have imagined they would not be able to return, or would not want to—but those who remain are bravely, determinedly rebuilding, and there are also thousands and thousands of new residents, many of them young, talented, imaginative and energetic. There is a relatively new and improved mayor, Mitch Landrieu, and the New Orleans Saints won the Super Bowl in 2010 the same weekend Landrieu was elected—a good warm-up for Mardi Gras a week later. And then, lest anyone get too optimistic, a few months later, on Earth Day (April 22) 2010, BP's Deepwater Horizon oil drilling platform exploded nearby in the Gulf of Mexico and became the most destructive marine oil spill in history, devastating the state's coastline, seafood industry, wiping out livelihoods beyond measure. The lawsuits go on . . .

Much has improved since the storm, and much remains the same, or worse. The United States remains embroiled in Middle East and Central Asian wars, some of our own making (or making worse). The nation continues to spend far more on its military than on its crumbling infrastructure, and the Pentagon receives hundreds of billions per year that could instead go to a national healthcare system that covers everyone, to an improved educational system in which teachers are compensated as though their work is valuable, and so on. Scroll through this blog's posts and you'll see that the issues are plenty, and the work goes on. Congress remains dysfunctional or, worse, actively hostile amid widespread unemployment, persistent and seemingly deliberate shredding of the middle class and its safety net (rolling back the New Deal and the Great Society), and ever-increasing corporate profits and tax evasion, and diminishing taxation of the super-wealthy. The earth's environment is under increasing stress from carbon emissions (again, one party in Congress stubbornly denies that global warming / climate change even exist, or that humanity is responsible), so the warming and rising seas threaten not only coastal Louisiana but the entire globe, as New York and New Jersey learned from Superstorm Sandy in October 2012.

Well, on the bright side, there is plenty of work to be done: we shall not lack for causes to advocate for, write about, and urge elected officials and community and business leaders to assist with. Readers' ideas are always welcome. E-mail us at leveesnotwar@mac.com.

As we have said many times, *National Security Begins at Home*. And, as we wrote on our ABOUT US page years ago:

> If New Orleans is not safe, no place in this country is safe. . . .
> Where will the federal government be when you're down and
> out? Earthquakes, wildfires, tornadoes, collapsing bridges,
> hijacked planes . . . If the federal government neglects one
> city's disaster, it can neglect them all. Without funding,
> without investment, things fall apart. The collapse of the
> physical infrastructure and the hospitals and schools and the
> justice system after the storm—what's happening to New
> Orleans is happening to the entire country—except perhaps
> in luxury high-rises and gated communities. The Lower Ninth
> Ward is the national predicament carried to an extreme.

TAGS: BP Oil Flood, Hurricane Katrina, New Orleans, Superstorm Sandy,
U.S. Army Corps of Engineers

http://www.leveesnotwar.org/remember-august-29-2005/

Understanding Louisiana's Environmental Crisis

After Hurricanes Katrina and Rita, people outside southern Louisiana asked why on earth (and why in hell) people would live below sea level in a place where there is a perennial risk of hurricanes and flooding.

First of all, New Orleans's historic, originally settled areas, along the Mississippi River, are *not below sea level*—some parts of the French Quarter are about 10 feet *above* sea level—but it is true that most of the 20th-century developments are.

It is also true that the sea is encroaching almost inevitably, almost irrevocably.

Louisiana was not always so vulnerable. Choctaw and other tribes lived here for millennia before the arrival of European and African settlers about three hundred years ago. It is only since about the late 1920s that man-made, industrial factors—principally oil exploration and the channelizing of the Mississippi River—have caused the land to erode at a rapid and alarming pace. (It could be viewed as the Gulf Coast equivalent of melting ice caps.)

About 1,900 square miles have disappeared in the past century, and the erosion is accelerating. Katrina tore away four years' worth of land loss—about 100 square miles—in only a few hours. No other state in the Union has ever lost so much land. The two main causes of land loss are erosion and subsidence, or sinking—and both ultimately are caused by human actions. Erosion is caused largely by man-made canals (see below), which allow the inflow of salt water from the Gulf of Mexico. Salt water kills freshwater plant life. As the swamp grass dies, the roots decompose, lose their grip on the soil, and the marshy ground crumbles and sinks into seawater.

A Sinking Feeling

The ground is sinking because the Mississippi River has been channelized by the Army Corps of Engineers ever since the great flood of 1927. In a truly monumental achievement, the Corps built massive earthen levees a hundred feet across at the top and three hundred feet wide at the base. (These levees stood strong during Katrina.) Human settlements have been mainly safe from flooding since the river was "tamed," but the ecological cost is that in spring the swollen waters from melted winter snows are no longer allowed to flood out across the land and deposit sediment and replenish the soil and plant life as they always did before. Over the past 7,000 years, as the Mississippi changed course every millennium or so, it built up the land of southern Louisiana through its spring floods. The Mississippi used to deposit about 85 million tons of sediment across its delta in coastal Louisiana; now all those potential minerals and nutrients are funneled straight off the continental shelf into the Gulf of Mexico where they serve no ecological benefit. And the wetlands wither, the cypress trees die, and the unreplenished lowlands sink still lower.

Since oil exploration began in southern Louisiana in the late 1920s, coastal erosion has been accelerated by oil industry pipeline canals and navigation channels. Lower Louisiana is crisscrossed by about 10,000 miles of oil and natural gas pipelines—the source of 18 percent of oil and 24 percent of natural gas supplies for the U.S. The canals trigger erosion: salt water rushes in, burns the delicate marsh grass, and wave-action erosion beats the dying grass and roots to pieces. Because of the incursion of salt water, the canals tend to double their width every 14 years. Scientists at LSU estimate that at least one-third of coastal erosion is directly attributable to these industrial canals.

Why does it matter if the wetlands are lost—aside from the deaths of cypresses, alligators, turtles, egrets, and other swamp life? Wetlands are critical because they help absorb hurricanes' storm surge and form a natural buffer against flooding. Scientists say about every 2.5 square miles of wetlands absorbs a foot of storm surge. Therefore, to protect against the awesome 25- to 30-foot storm surges brought by massive cyclones like Katrina and the Category 5 Hurricane Camille in 1969, for safety southern Louisiana would want (in addition to the barrier islands that have all but washed away) about 50 to 75 miles of wetlands between the Gulf of Mexico and the city of New Orleans. Environmental writer Mike Tidwell (*Bayou Farewell*) says that around 1900 the Gulf shore was about 50 miles from New Orleans. That distance has shrunk to only about 20 miles today, and it is closing fast. Some experts fear that if serious coastal restoration is not begun immediately, in another ten years the Gulf may be lapping at New Orleans's suburbs.

At the same time, global warming has caused the level of the Gulf of Mexico to rise, and warmer waters intensify the ferocity of hurricanes. There is some question whether global warming causes an increase in the *number* of hurricanes per season, but it is known that the hurricanes spawned are strengthened by warm water—this was certainly the case with Katrina and Rita. Further, the erosion of barrier islands (the first line of defense that helps break the tidal surge) and behind them the marshlands that help absorb the tidal surge reduce the buffer zone that once helped diminish the effects of hurricanes on cities along the Gulf Coast. (Ship and Horn Islands that formerly served as a buffer for Gulfport and Biloxi have been shredded in recent decades.)

But All Is Not Lost—Yet

The defense of New Orleans could be envisioned as a castle or fortress ringed by three concentric walls: (1) restored wetlands to help fend off the tidal surge; (2) storm gates at the Rigolets Pass and the drainage canals between the city and Lake Pontchartrain; (3) Category 5-strength levees all around New Orleans (before Katrina the Corps of Engineers said Category 3 would be strong enough; nothing has changed). In his straight-talking book *The Storm*, Ivor van Heerden of the LSU Hurricane Center proposes a robust, Dutch-style flood and hurricane protection system that could be built for roughly $20 billion—about the amount the U.S. spends in three months on the wars in Iraq and Afghanistan. (See interview with van Heerden in Part VII.)

Another remedy that has been proposed to help reverse coastal erosion and restore the wetlands is a 95-mile-long controlled diversion of the Mississippi around Donaldsonville, Louisiana, between Baton Rouge and New Orleans. The idea is to divert about one-third of the Mississippi's volume westward and send its waters on either side of Bayou Lafourche (a remnant of the former path of the Mississippi) to spread the Big Muddy's rich sediment across the wetlands north of Barataria Bay and Terrebonne Bay.

Yet another line of defense that engineers recommend would be a series of storm gates at the Rigolets Pass, a strait connecting Lake Pontchartrain to the Gulf of Mexico, to block the hurricane's tidal surge from entering the lake, and at the mouths of the drainage and navigation canals around New Orleans. Storm gates have also been proposed near the juncture of the Intracoastal Waterway and the Mississippi River–Gulf Outlet ("MR-GO") and where the Industrial Canal flows into Lake Pontchartrain. "You don't want to let your enemy invade deeply into your territory," explains Jurjen Battjes, a professor of civil engineering in the Netherlands. "Close your fence at the outside." That is why Battjes and others have urged that the city's canal pumping stations be moved to the edge of Lake Pontchartrain—and protected by the storm gates described above.

There is also a well-developed plan called *Coast 2050: Toward a Sustainable Coastal Louisiana* that details specific policy recommendations. The cost of *Coast 2050* could reach about $14 billion (the U.S. spends that amount every 3 months in Iraq), but the plan could prevent the loss of about $100 billion in jobs, infrastructure, the profitable Louisiana seafood industry, and wildlife. The main practical and economic benefit, however, would be the rebuilding of the buffers against hurricanes that once existed naturally along southern Louisiana. This in turn would protect the oil and natural gas industry and the Port of New Orleans, the seafood industry, and the countless petrochemical plants in the industrial corridor between Baton Rouge and New Orleans. The Port of New Orleans is the nation's largest in tonnage, the fifth-largest in the world. It handles some two-thirds of America's grain and wheat—the Midwest would be crippled without New Orleans—and most of the nation's oil and steel imports, and the minerals and raw materials feeding the industrial heartland.

If an enemy wanted to cripple the United States, he would strike New Orleans. As Thomas Jefferson understood when he authorized the Louisiana Purchase in 1803 (signed in Jackson Square a hundred yards from where President Bush spoke), possessing and protecting New Orleans is a matter of national security, and essential to economic prosperity.

We believe national security begins at home. And we believe in doing something to reclaim our security. If you want to be secure, get involved.

http://www.leveesnotwar.org/environment-ecology/

Louisiana Flood Protection Agency
Sues Big Oil to Repair Wetlands

Historic case is compared to 1990s litigation against Big Tobacco

JULY 25, 2013—About 100 oil and gas companies must pay to repair the Louisiana wetlands damaged by a century of oil exploration and extraction, according to a lawsuit filed July 24 in civil district court in Orleans Parish by the Southeast Louisiana Flood Protection Authority–East. The Authority (SLFPA-E) was established by the Louisiana legislature in 2006 after Hurricane Katrina to ensure the integrity of the state's flood risk management systems.

John M. Barry, vice president of SLFPA-E (and the widely respected author of the award-winning *Rising Tide: The Great Mississippi Flood of 1927 and How It Changed America* [1998]), said:

> With this lawsuit, the Authority is carrying out its mandate to help protect southern Louisiana by strengthening our first line of defense against catastrophic flooding. That first defensive perimeter is of course the buffer of land and marsh that cuts down hurricane storm surge before it reaches the levees. . . . The industry recognizes that it is responsible for a significant part of the problem. We want energy companies to fix the part of the problem they caused—and which they promised to address. We want them to do what they said they'd do.

The suit has been denounced by Louisiana Governor Bobby Jindal, who said in a statement that the Authority has "overstepped its authority." The governor asserted, "We're not going to allow a single levee board that has been hijacked by a group of trial lawyers to determine flood protection, coastal restoration and economic repercussions for the entire state of Louisiana."

The state's attorney general, Buddy Caldwell, however, has authorized SLFPA-E to proceed in filing its suit.

An attorney for the Authority, Gladstone N. Jones III, has successfully brought suit against Big Oil firms in the past. He told Clancy Dubos of *Gambit* that the suit has the potential to be bigger than the ongoing BP litigation, and, according to *The New York Times*, Jones said the plaintiffs are seeking damages equal to "many billions of dollars. Many, many billions of dollars." Dubos writes, "The case ultimately could seek environmental recovery for all oil and gas activity along Louisiana's coast. If that happens, this case will be to Big Oil what the Tobacco Litigation was to that industry: a game-changer."

The lawsuit asserts that the Authority is obligated by law to restore Louisiana's coastal land areas, and charges that oil, gas, and pipeline companies that have cut at least 10,000 miles of oil and gas canals and pipelines have damaged the state's environmental buffer zones that formerly protected the state from storm surge and flooding. As experienced in recent hurricanes, Southeastern Louisiana has been rendered vulnerable to frequent and often catastrophic flooding.

Every year Louisiana loses 25 square miles of land— 50 acres every day.

Wetlands protect human settlements from hurricane storm surges, which can rise as high as 25 feet. Every 2.5 to 4 miles of wetlands reduce hurricane storm surges by about a foot; measured another way, each mile of marsh reduces storm surges by 3 to 9 inches. Metro New Orleans, home to about 1.5 million, is now protected by a buffer no more than about 20 miles of wetlands.

The suit summarizes the environmental significance of coastal wetlands and the consequences of oil exploration (quoting from *Gambit* and from SLFPA-E's press release):

- "Coastal lands are the natural protective buffer without which the levees that protect the cities and towns of southern Louisiana are left exposed to unabated destructive forces. This protective buffer took 6,000 years to form. Yet . . . it has been brought to the brink of destruction over the course of a single human lifetime. Hundreds of thousands of acres of the coastal lands that once offered protection to south Louisiana are now gone as a result of oil and gas industry activities. . . .

- "For nearly a century, the oil and gas industry has continuously and relentlessly traversed, dredged, drilled and extracted in coastal Louisiana. It reaps enormous financial gain by exploiting the resources found there, sharing some of that bounty with the many residents whom it employs. Yet it also ravages Louisiana's coastal landscape. An extensive network of oil and gas access and pipeline canals slashes the coastline at every angle, functioning as a mercilessly efficient, continuously expanding system of ecological destruction. This canal network injects corrosive salt water into interior coastal lands, killing vegetation and carrying away mountains of soil. What remains of these coastal lands is so seriously diseased that if nothing is done, it will slip into the Gulf of Mexico by the end of this century, if not sooner. . . .

- "Oil and gas activities continue to transform what was once a stable ecosystem of naturally occurring bayous, small canals, and ditches into an extensive—and expanding—network of large and deep canals that continues to widen due to Defendants' ongoing failure to maintain this network or restore the ecosystem to its natural state. That canal network continues to introduce increasingly larger volumes of damaging salt water, at increasingly greater velocity, ever deeper into Louisiana's coastal landscape and interior wetlands. The increasing intrusion of salt water stresses the vegetation that holds wetlands together, weakening—and ultimately killing—that vegetation. Thus weakened, the remaining soil is washed away even by minor storms. **The canal network thus comprises a highly effective system of coastal landscape degradation.** The product of this network is an ecosystem so seriously diseased that its complete demise is inevitable if no action is taken." [LNW's emphasis]

Mark Schleifstein of *The Times-Picayune* reports, "A study conducted by the late University of New Orleans geologist Shea Penland in 1996 for the U.S. Geological Survey and the Gas Research Institute concluded that about 36 percent of the wetland loss in southeastern Louisiana between 1932 and 1990 was the result of the direct and indirect effects of actions taken by the oil and gas industry." By a conservative estimate, since 1932 Louisiana has lost more than 1,900 square miles of coastal lands, equivalent to the state of Delaware, and if the present rate continues, some 700 more square miles of coastal Louisiana are expected to be lost in coming decades.

John Barry told *The Lens*'s environmental writer Bob Marshall, "No one denies—not even the oil industry—that the canals they dredged helped cause this problem. . . . Now, people will say there are other causes, and we're not denying that. The levees on the river, obviously, are a major cause. But the federal government built those levees, and they've been spending billions of dollars on better flood protection and coastal restoration projects in this area. What we're saying to the oil companies is, 'It's time for you to step up now for the damage you did.'"

The Flood Protection Authority's lawsuit is grounded in long-established legal principles and in state and federal law, such as the Rivers and Harbors Act of 1899, the federal Clean Water Act of 1972, and the state Coastal Zone Management Act of 1972.

Barry explained to *The Times-Picayune* that the suit is founded upon three principal legal arguments:

> Most of the damaging oil, gas and pipeline activities were conducted under federal and state permits that "explicitly require the operators to maintain and restore the canals they dredged," Barry said. He said the oil and gas industry dredged more than 10,000 miles of canals through the state's wetlands, which provided pathways for salt water from the Gulf of Mexico to kill fresh and brackish water marshes.
>
> The federal Rivers and Harbors Act of 1899 prohibits actions that impair the effectiveness of flood protection levees. "Clearly, increasing storm surge makes a levee less effective," Barry said.
>
> A tenet of civil law called "servitude of drainage" prohibits someone taking actions on property that they own or control that sends more water onto someone else's property. Again, Barry said, the oil and gas projects clearly focus increased storm surge onto the levee system.
>
> The Southeast Louisiana Flood Protection Authority–East is being represented in its litigation by the law firms Jones,

Swanson, Huddell, and Garrison, LLC, of New Orleans;
Fishman Haygood Phelps Walmsley Willis & Swanson, LLP,
of New Orleans; and Veron, Bice, Palermo & Wilson, LLC, of
Lake Charles, La.

TAGS: Big Oil, Clancy Dubos, coastal restoration, Gladstone N. Jones III, John M. Barry,
Mark Schleifstein, Southeast Louisiana Flood Protection Authority–East
http://www.leveesnotwar.org/louisiana-flood-protection-agency-sues-big-oil-to
-repair-wetlands/

BP Found Grossly Negligent in Deepwater Horizon Spill

SEPT. 6, 2014—The fire you see here may be BP's capital reserves going up in flames.

A federal judge has ruled that BP was "reckless," grossly negligent, and primarily to blame for the April 2010 blowout of the Deepwater Horizon oil rig that killed 11 workers and sent untold millions of gallons of crude oil gushing into the Gulf of Mexico. In New Orleans on Thursday Judge Carl J. Barbier of the District Court for the Eastern District of Louisiana apportioned to BP 67 percent of the responsibility, 30 percent to Transocean (which owned the rig), and 3 percent to Halliburton, the cement contractor on the well. Only BP was found to be grossly negligent.

Throughout the legal proceedings, BP has maintained that it is not primarily responsible, but that Transocean and Halliburton are mainly to blame. (In related news, earlier this week BP asked a federal judge to remove oil spill claims administrator Pat Juneau for "conflicts of interest"—i.e., he would be too generous to Louisiana residents, too expensive for BP.)

By finding BP grossly negligent rather than merely negligent (a critical legal distinction), Judge Barbier ratcheted up the possible financial cost to BP to as much as $18 billion in new civil penalties, "nearly quadruple the maximum Clean Water Act penalty for simple negligence and far more than the $3.5 billion the company has set aside" for fines, according to *The New York Times*. Under the Clean Water Act, *The Times-Picayune* explains, "the penalty for each barrel of oil spilled is up to $1,100 if a polluter is found to be negligent. That increases up to $4,300 per barrel with a finding of gross negligence or willful misconduct."

BP, which has consistently downplayed its responsibility and the severity of the catastrophe, claims that 2.45 million barrels of oil were spilled into the Gulf, while U.S. Justice Department attorneys calculate the amount as 4.2 million barrels.

Halliburton has already agreed to pay $1.1 billion in damages to property and the commercial fishing industry, though that settlement has yet to be approved by the District Court for the Eastern District of Louisiana.

In a sternly worded, 153-page ruling that includes a detailed timeline of events, Judge Barbier described a "chain of failures" that led to the explosion and oil spill. *The New York Times* summarizes:

> Vital seals and stoppers were left leaky along the casing of the well, the judge found, while BP then skimped on tests that might have shown the problems caused by the shoddy work. When tests were run, the results were interpreted with optimism at best and dishonesty at worst, and several critical decisions made by BP were found by Judge Barbier to have been "primarily driven by a desire to save time and money, rather than ensuring that the well was secure."

Louisiana Attorney General Buddy Caldwell said in a news release, "This is an important milestone in the process of recovering the damages and penalties due to Louisiana. I will continue fighting for the recoveries Louisiana is entitled to for the damages we have sustained."

BP says it will appeal the ruling.

BP Celebrates Earth Day
with Bonfire, Oil Spill

But Seriously, Tragically,
11 Missing Workers Are Presumed Dead

APRIL 26, 2010—On Saturday, April 24, Coast Guard officials reported that the damaged Deepwater Horizon well on the seafloor in the Gulf of Mexico was leaking oil at a rate of about 42,000 gallons (or 1,000 barrels) per day—since recalculated at 210,000 gallons per day, a fivefold increase. The leak, about 50 miles southeast of the mouth of the Mississippi River, is some 5,000 feet (about a mile) below the surface. (Chris Kirkham of *The Times-Picayune* has written a detailed, illustrated report of efforts to cap the leak.) As of Monday afternoon, April 26, the Coast Guard said the oil spill measured about 48 miles by 39 miles, or 1,800 square miles, an area larger than the state of Rhode Island. John Amos of SkyTruth reports that NASA photographs taken Sunday, April 25, show that oil slicks and sheen ("very thin slick") covered about 817 square miles. Amos, who in Nov. 2009 was invited to testify at a Senate hearing on the risks posed by offshore drilling, wrote yesterday (April 25):

This is bad news—it means the blowout preventer on that well is not doing its job, and that several attempts by BP, Transocean and the Coast Guard to operate a shutoff valve on the well using a robotic ROV have failed. The oil slick has grown rapidly and now covers 400 miles.

A friend in New Orleans who is an industry insider says the Deepwater Horizon well "was as sophisticated a rig as has been built operating in the Gulf of Mexico (not a rust-bucket)." He adds:

> So far, cleanup efforts haven't done very well. 126,000 gallons of
> oil have been spilled, but only 33,726 gallons of emulsion (which
> is part water) have been picked up, and this is when conditions

are calm. If you assume a 50/50 water/oil mix (a conservative assumption, IMHO), the cleanup has only been 13% effective.

Our friend Aaron Viles of Gulf Restoration Network reports after a flyover on Sunday:

> We were shocked at what we saw. The main spill was at least 8 miles across . . . and stretching for 45 miles, in a Northeastern and Southeastern direction. The crude at the surface of the Gulf has been churned into a 'chocolate mousse' material that was easy to spot from our altitude of 4,000 feet. The mousse covered approximately 100 square miles, and then faded into a heavy, then light sheen, which faded about 20 miles from the Chandeleur Islands, critical bird nesting and migration habitat.

Well Leaks 210,000 Gallons a Day into Gulf of Mexico

It is still unclear what caused last week's explosion; eleven crew members are still missing and are presumed dead. After the explosion, the rig burned for two days, then broke apart and sank to the seafloor. The rig is owned by Transocean, which was working for BP Exploration and Production. *The Times-Picayune*'s Chris Kirkham writes that BP, as the responsible party, must pay the cost of the cleanup under the requirements of the Oil Pollution Act passed in 1990 after the *Exxon Valdez* spill in Alaska (1989). Marcus Baram of *Huffington Post* reports that relatives of missing crew members allege that BP and Transocean violated "numerous statutes and regulations" issued by the Occupational Safety and Health Administration (OSHA). Natalie Roshto, the widow of one worker, has filed a lawsuit in U.S. District Court for the Eastern District of Louisiana. The suit alleges that the defendants—including Halliburton—failed to provide safe working conditions and to properly train and supervise their employees. BP and Transocean are said to have aggressively resisted new safety regulations proposed by a federal agency last year. Baram reports that according to a study by the Interior Department's Minerals Management Service, "there were 41 deaths and 302 injuries out of 1,443 incidents from 2001 to 2007. . . . In addition, the agency issued 150 reports over incidents of non-compliant production and drilling operations and determined there was 'no discernible improvement by industry over the past 7 years.'"

It has been estimated that stopping the leak could take two to three months. The spill poses a potential ecological catastrophe and could decimate coastal wildlife and cripple the Louisiana seafood industry if oil spreads to the wetlands' delicate habitats for fish, shrimp, oysters, crawfish, and many species of waterfowl. Louisiana supplies the nation's largest bounty of shrimp, oysters, and blue crab, and almost one-third of the fish harvested in the Lower 48, with annual retail sales of about $2.85 billion, employing about 40,000 in Louisiana.

This accident occurs just weeks after President Obama announced the administration's decision to open large expanses of water along the Atlantic coast and the Gulf of Mexico to oil and natural gas drilling—some for the first time. There has been a moratorium on oil exploration along the East Coast from Delaware down to central Florida. The decision, announced March 30, was welcomed by oil companies and domestic drilling advocates but decried by environmentalists and residents of the affected states. In a related development, ExxonMobil, with a profit of $45 billion last year, paid no federal corporate income taxes in 2009. (But Exxon's not alone: the Government Accountability Office reported that between 1998 and 2005, "two out of every three United States corporations paid no federal income taxes.") According to Forbes, the oil giant Chevron, with pretax income of $18.5 billion, paid the U.S. just $200 million in income tax in 2008.

Spill, Baby, Spill

The oil industry and its supporters routinely assert that offshore drilling is "safe" and "environmentally friendly" and that offshore rigs and hurricanes coexist amicably. During the 2008 campaign and every chance she's gotten since, Sarah Palin has shrilled, "Drill, Baby, Drill!" Samuel Bodman, former energy secretary in the Bush administration, claimed in 2008 that "there was not one case where we had a situation with oil or gas being spilled in the environment" during hurricanes Katrina and Rita, a falsehood peddled to anyone with a microphone. Sadly, not true. Those two hurricanes within a month in August and September 2005 caused 595 different oil spills, totaling 9 million gallons. The U.S. Minerals Management Service documents that Katrina and Rita totally destroyed 113 oil drilling platforms, and according to press reports at the time, the hurricanes ruptured pipelines and set rigs adrift. One rig drifted 66 miles before running aground.

We are not opposed to some oil drilling, but, as with the wars the U.S. wages to secure access to global oil supplies, we want this practice to be winding down, not escalating. *Levees Not War* has been calling for increased federal investment in public transportation because the U.S. must reduce its dependence on automobiles and on importing foreign oil (and extracting it from off the Gulf Coast). Here's why: carbon emissions aggravate global warming, which intensifies hurricanes and raises sea levels. That, along with the 10,000 miles of oil industry pipelines through the Louisiana wetlands, hurts New Orleans, Louisiana, and other precious places. In addition, investment in public transportation and other infrastructure also gives more "bang for the buck" in creating jobs and providing public works of lasting value that help support the economy in a sustainable way. President Obama has often spoken of the need to shift gears toward sustainable green energy programs, but his recent decision to open formerly protected areas of the coastal United States to oil exploration is change we cannot believe in. His recent announcement with "Amtrak Joe" Biden of $8 billion in stimulus funding for 13 highspeed rail projects, however, is what America needs more of. So far, these are very modest steps. (The war in Afghanistan eats up that $8 billion every two or three months, and for what?)

Stressing Out the Planet

Coming just weeks after the Upper Big Branch coal mine disaster in West Virginia took 29 lives, the worst in four decades, the Deepwater Horizon calamity reinforces the message that the environmental consequences of harvesting fossil fuels are as unsustainable as the price paid for burning these fuels. Other nations are doing much more than the United States to shift from carbon-based fuels to recyclable, sustainable energy sources; thousands, even millions of new jobs could grow if our business leaders and elected officials would Give Green a Chance. Read these previous posts about the ecological effects of global warming, including the rising sea levels and the warmer sea waters that intensify hurricanes.

We don't know whether the unusual frequency of earthquakes this year could be related to human activity or human-caused temperature changes, or if it just feels that way. We do know that climate change is going inexorably in one direction, and the rising temperatures are threatening more than just the low-lying areas of the world. Last assignment for this session: Read Elizabeth Kolbert's *Field Notes from a Catastrophe: Man, Nature, and Climate Change.* There will be a test.

TAGS: BP Oil Flood, climate change, green jobs, Gulf of Mexico, Gulf Restoration Network, Hurricane Katrina, oil and war, oil exploration, oil spills, renewable energy, SkyTruth, U.S. energy policy, "drill, baby, drill"
http://www.leveesnotwar.org/bp-celebrates-earth-day-with-bonfire

"Oil-Spotted Dick": Cheney's Oily Fingerprints in the BP Disaster

Conservation may be a sign of personal virtue, but it is not a sufficient basis for a sound, comprehensive energy policy.
Vice President Dick Cheney, quoted in *The New York Times*, May 1, 2001

MAY 5, 2010—The good people of Great Britain have a beloved and time-honored delicacy, a steamed suet pudding known as spotted dick. Well, we Americans too have a celebrated concoction that has served as vice president and secretary of defense as well as CEO of Halliburton. And what a rare and piquant morsel is our Dick.

It's Not "Obama's Katrina"—But It's Cheney's Second

Conservative media outlets and their followers at CNN have been quick to ask in their usual accusatory way if this disaster is "Obama's Katrina" (by all means, lose no opportunity to attack!). It is probably true that the administration should have been more proactively skeptical of BP's assertions that the situation was under control. But the responsibility for the leak's happening at all lies closer to the George W. Bush administration—and to its all-powerful vice president. Halliburton was cementing the base of the well at the time of the explosion, and for its involvement in the accident the Houston-based oil services giant is named in a lawsuit filed by the widow of one of the 11 missing offshore workers. *The Wall Street Journal* reported (4/30):

> The scrutiny on cementing will focus attention on Halliburton Co., the oilfield-services firm that was handling the cementing process on the rig. . . . Halliburton also was the cementer on a

well that suffered a big blowout last August in the Timor Sea, off Australia. The rig there caught fire and a well leaked tens of thousands of barrels of oil over 10 weeks before it was shut down.

But Cheney is implicated also in the absence of a device that could have stopped the leak. *The Wall Street Journal*, *Salon.com*, *The New Republic*, and Michael Tomasky at *The Guardian* have been following the dripping trail of oil that leads to Dick Cheney's (formerly undisclosed) location.

Cheney's 2001 Energy Task Force and the Missing Shut-off Switch

Now, the still uncontrollable BP oil disaster is infuriating and heart-sickening no matter how you look at it—especially if you're a Louisiana fisherman, shrimper, or oysterman, or the widow of one of the 11 missing workers presumed dead—but what makes the catastrophe even more revolting is the news now leaking from no less a source than *The Wall Street Journal* that the spill could have been prevented if BP had used a remote-controlled shut-off device known as an acoustic switch that has been available for some 20 years or more. The acoustic switch is required by Norway and Brazil (Norway has had them on almost every offshore rig since 1993, and Royal Dutch Shell and France's Total SA often use them voluntarily), but at Cheney's secretive energy task force convened in early 2001 it was decided that requiring this $500,000 device for all offshore wells was too onerous for the oil companies. The *Journal* reports:

> The U.S. considered requiring a remote-controlled shut-off mechanism several years ago, but drilling companies questioned its cost and effectiveness, according to the agency overseeing offshore drilling. The agency, the Interior Department's Minerals Management Service, says it decided the remote device wasn't needed because rigs had other back-up plans to cut off a well.

The National Energy Policy Development Group [NEPDG] was a task force established by President George W. Bush in March 2001, chaired by Vice President Dick Cheney and staffed by high officials from the departments of

Energy, Commerce, and State. The NEP group met with representatives of major oil and energy firms; among those advising the panel were 18 of the top 25 contributors to the Bush-Cheney 2000 campaign, including Kenneth "Kenny Boy" Lay of Enron. *The Washington Post* reported on Nov. 16, 2005, that Cheney met personally with the CEO of BP:

> [A White House document from 2001] shows that officials from Exxon Mobil Corp., Conoco (before its merger with Phillips), Shell Oil Co. and BP America Inc. met in the White House complex with the Cheney aides who were developing a national energy policy. . . . In addition, **Cheney had a separate meeting with John Browne, BP's chief executive**, according to a person familiar with the task force's work. . . . [emphasis added]

Records of the task force's meetings were never disclosed despite an unsuccessful Freedom of Information Act suit filed by Sierra Club and Judicial Watch. (The NEP's report was delivered to President Bush on May 16, 2001.) It is not clear what was discussed in this meeting or any other with the oil executives, but we can be sure that requests to be spared from "burdensome" production costs and regulations would have received a sympathetic hearing.

The New Republic's William Galston in a powerful piece titled "Forget Offshore Drilling Until We Get Some Answers" delves into the mismanagement of the Minerals Management Service, the Interior Department unit responsible for offshore drilling, under Bush-Cheney. Galston notes that "after a spill in 2000, the [Clinton] MMS issued a safety notice saying that such a back-up device [the acoustic switch] is 'an essential component of a deepwater drilling system.' . . . By 2003, government regulators decided that the matter needed more study after commissioning a report that offered another, more honest reason: 'acoustic systems are not recommended because they tend to be very costly.'" After summarizing the gross and remorseless corruption of that department in the Bush years, Galston asks:

> [W]hat is responsible for MMS's change of heart between 2000 and 2003 on the crucial issue of requiring a remote control switch for offshore rigs? What we do know is that unfettered oil drilling was to Dick Cheney's domestic concerns what the

invasion of Iraq was to his foreign policy—a core objective, implacably pursued regardless of the risks. Is there a connection between his infamous secret energy task force and the corrupt mindset that came to dominate a key program within MMS? Would $500,000 per rig have been regarded as an unacceptably expensive insurance policy if a drill-baby-drill administration hadn't placed its thumb so heavily on the scale?

For more about the connection between Cheney's energy agenda and his foreign policy, see Michael T. Klare's *Blood and Oil: The Dangers and Consequences of America's Growing Dependency on Imported Petroleum* (2004; esp. ch. 3) for the links between Cheney's NEP, neocon-protégé Paul Wolfowitz's "Defense Planning Guidance" (1992), written for Cheney when he was SecDef under Bush I, and *Rebuilding America's Defenses: Strategy, Forces and Resources for a New Century* (2000), written by Wolfowitz for the Project for the New American Century (PNAC).

Environmental attorney Mike Papantonio, whose firm has filed class-action lawsuits on behalf of coastal fishermen and shrimpers, appeared on MSNBC's *Ed Show* on Friday, April 30. He told Ed Schultz:

> . . . here's what people don't know. BP didn't want to spend the money for a system. It's a fail-safe system, absolutely fail-safe. It's a device system that's used all over the world except in the United States, because we give them a free pass in the United States. . . . during the Bush deregulation years, you had the Minerals Management Service that told companies like BP that . . . we have a new policy. It's the closed-door Dick Cheney policy. That Dick Cheney program allowed the industry to bypass safe systems like the acoustics switch, and there was no need to spend $500,000 with a company that was making $40 billion. It was a complete bypass of safety. It's the most unreported part of this story out there, Ed. I don't know why the media is not talking about this. . . . Dick Cheney changed political policy with the energy industry. We all remember when he met behind closed doors with the industry. This is one of the things that came out of there.

The $500,000 remote-controlled acoustic switches were regarded as too costly, so energy giants such as BP, ExxonMobil, Chevron, and Shell, which have posted record profits over the past decade—some $656 billion during the Bush years—while other industries are shriveling and dying, are excused not only from paying much (if any) corporate income tax to the U.S. Treasury, but also from equipping their wells and rigs with available devices that would stop oil leaks of the kind that are presently spilling 210,000 gallons per day into the Gulf of Mexico and threatening flora and fauna + the livelihoods of tens of thousands along the Gulf Coast.

(Did we mention that after Hurricane Katrina struck on Aug. 29, 2005, Cheney stayed on vacation until Sept. 1, and did not tour the Gulf Coast until Sept. 8? A passerby in Gulfport, Mississippi, yelled out, "Go fuck yourself.")

How Long a Catastrophe? And What, Really, Is the Price of a Tank of Gas?

Rachel Maddow on May 4 interviewed in his laboratory LSU's Ed Overton, emeritus professor of environmental sciences, who has been analyzing the oil leaking from the Deepwater Horizon well. Dr. Overton guessed that it may be six to nine months before the well is capped. Hurricane season begins June 1 and runs through November. Of course, the oil companies insist that nothing will go wrong—the wells won't blow—so it's not necessary to worry about how hurricanes in the warming Gulf waters may complicate efforts to cap a well that won't leak. The $500,000 that BP saved on the acoustic switch has now turned to the $560 million loss of the collapsed rig (not to mention the workers' lives) plus $6 million a day that BP is now spending to combat the spill. Other costs are incalculable.

So, let's get this straight: The oil industry sells its products to the American public at escalating prices, sometimes independent of actual supply levels; enjoys minimal federal oversight of its operations; spends hundreds of millions per year in lobbying members of Congress and state legislatures for tax and regulatory "relief" and against public funding for alternative transportation as a competitor; and yet the industry pays little or no corporate income taxes to the U.S. Treasury. Therefore whenever there is an environmental disaster, any federal response is paid for by revenues other than oil companies' taxes. And, after the environmental degradation, including some 10,000 miles of pipelines through the fragile Louisiana wetlands that have resulted in a loss of 1,900 square miles since the 1930s, the "storm surge buffer" that used to protect Louisiana's settled areas from hurricane-driven flooding—after all this, perhaps the most damnable part of the oil industry's malign influence is that our soldiers fight wars to secure access to foreign oil (see "Understanding Louisiana's Environmental Crisis" above and Michael T. Klare's *Blood and Oil*). Would the U.S. Defense Department's foreign real estate holdings (including hundreds of overseas military bases) be even remotely as extensive as they are if we were not "on the march" for access to cheap foreign oil?

One last thing: Did we mention that during the Vietnam War, Dick Cheney got five deferments from military service? Rare and piquant—and slippery, too.

TAGS: BP, corporate crime, Dick Cheney, George W. Bush administration, Gulf of Mexico oil drilling, Mike Papantonio, National Energy Policy Development Group

http://www.leveesnotwar.org/"oil-spotted-dick"-cheney's-oily-fingerprints-in-the-bp-disaster/

If New Orleans Is Not Safe . . .

JUNE 15, 2007— . . . no place in America is safe. Hurricane tidal surges of 10 feet or more could swamp Houston, Charleston, Long Island . . . A tornado in Brooklyn (really), earthquakes not limited to California, an interstate bridge collapsing at rush hour into the Mississippi in Minneapolis (it didn't take an earthquake) . . . *Where will the federal government be when you're down and out?* Northeastern energy grid blackouts, hijacked planes . . . These are matters of survival that concern us all equally, regardless of residence or party affiliation. Without care and maintenance, things fall apart. Without funding, without investment, things fall apart. And the longer our so-called leaders shy away from climate change, the higher the temperature, and so with the sea level.

The collapse of the city's physical infrastructure and the hospitals and schools and the justice system after the storm—what's happening to New Orleans is taking place all across America, except perhaps in high-rises and gated communities, such as the White House.

The Lower Ninth Ward is the national predicament carried to an extreme.

TAGS: climate change, global temperature, hurricanes, Lower Ninth Ward, New Orleans not safe
http://www.leveesnotwar.org/if-new-orleans-is-not-safe/

With Superstorm Sandy on October 29, 2012, Levees Not War's "hurricane beat" expanded from the Gulf Coast to the Atlantic Seaboard. Sandy, with its destructive winds, storm surge, power outages, and flooding of low-lying parts of New York City, Long Island, and New Jersey, and swamping the New York City subway system, brought Levees Not War's mission even closer to home.

Hurricane Watch in New York City

Extreme Weather Coming Soon to an Eastern Seaboard Near You

We have a tropical hurricane merging, or folding in, with a mid-latitude weather system, one of those low pressure systems that track across the country. The two systems' dynamics are very different and when they occasionally fold together, they actually produce the worst characteristics of both. . . . This is the same thing that happened during the perfect storm of 1991 [as popularized by author Sebastian Junger], and at roughly the same time.

**Barry Keim, Louisiana State Climatologist,
quoted by Mark Schleifstein, *Times-Picayune***

Sandy also is different in its size, rivaling the largest cyclones ever recorded around the globe, Keim said, with hurricane-force winds extending outward 175 miles from its center and tropical storm-force winds extending out 485 miles.

Mark Schleifstein, *Times-Picayune*

OCT. 28, 2012—Last year when Hurricane Irene was barreling down on the East Coast—on the 6th anniversary of Hurricane Katrina, as it happened—we were (ironically) safe from the storm, attending the Rising Tide conference in New Orleans. Irene, a Category 1 hurricane when it hit the East Coast, caused over $15 billion in damage and left many in the Northeast without power for a week or more. Now a bigger and badder storm, 900 miles across, is taking aim at the Atlantic Coast, from North Carolina to Connecticut, and low-lying areas around New Jersey and New York City and Long Island are being evacuated, with warnings of dangerously high seawater. Storm surge could reach 11 feet in New York Harbor and Long Island Sound.

The New York City subway and bus system (MTA) has been shut down as of 7:00 p.m. Sunday by order of Gov. Andrew Cuomo, along with the Long Island Rail Road and Metro North Railroad. That's 468 subway stations going dark, and officials warn that trains may not run again until Wednesday. (The MTA normally moves about 8.5 million passengers a day.) Schools and offices are closed in New York City and around the metropolitan area for Monday, and we'll see about Tuesday. Evacuations have been ordered for the lowest-elevation areas. Workers are laying down plywood over subway air vents on city sidewalks to prevent or lessen flooding in the subway tunnels, many of which are below sea level—some far below.

OCT. 28 update: *The New York Times* reports that Amtrak has canceled most trains on the Eastern Seaboard. Washington, D.C., and Philadelphia mass transit systems and New Jersey Transit are also shutting down till the storm passes.

2012's Extreme Weather Triggered Decades Ago

It is often not possible to tie any given weather event directly to man-made climate change, so we cannot say at this point whether this oncoming storm is intensified by greenhouse gas emissions. But Hurricane Sandy is coming rather late in the hurricane season (June 1–Nov. 30), and it's the second hurricane in 14 months to strike the East Coast in a big way. The point of climate change is not just "global warming," but extreme weather, as in the frequent tornadoes that pummeled America's midsection in the spring of 2011 (see "Wrath of God? Global Warming and Extreme Weather").

In this year that saw widespread drought and crop failures in the United States, with over a thousand counties in 26 states declared natural disaster areas by the U.S. Department of Agriculture—the largest such designation ever—the two mainstream presidential candidates have avoided even uttering the word "environment," unless in reference to "the business environment."

Climate change denial expands (see "Ides of March" below) even as the ice caps' summer melts reach alarming new records.

[In a GOP primary debate, however, Mitt Romney said that emergency management should be handed over to the states. "Every time you have an occasion to take something from the federal government and send it back to the states, that's the right direction." Including disaster relief? the moderator asked. "We cannot . . . afford to do those things without jeopardizing the future for our kids." Historical note: It was in response to persistent pleas from state governors that President Jimmy Carter established FEMA in 1979.]

During the peak of this summer's heat blast, *New Yorker* environmental reporter Elizabeth Kolbert pointed out one of the most alarming facts about the extreme weather: As hot as it was this summer, the record-setting heat of 2012 was set in motion decades ago:

> One of the most salient—but also, unfortunately, most counterintuitive—aspects of **global warming** is that it **operates on** what amounts to **a time delay. Behind this summer's heat are greenhouse gases emitted decades ago.** Before many effects of today's emissions are felt, it will be time for the Summer Olympics of 2048. (Scientists refer to this as the "commitment to warming.") What's at stake is where things go from there. It is quite possible that by the end of the century we could, without even really trying, engineer the return of the sort of climate that hasn't been seen on earth since the Eocene, some fifty million years ago. [LNW's emphasis]

Along with the heat and the drought and the super derecho, the country this summer is also enduring a Presidential campaign. So far, the words "climate change" have barely been uttered. This is not an oversight. Both President Obama and Mitt Romney have chosen to remain silent on the issue, presumably because they see it as just too big a bummer.

And so, while farmers wait for rain and this season's corn crop withers on the stalk, the familiar disconnect continues. There's no discussion of what could be done to avert the worst effects of climate change, even as the insanity of doing nothing becomes increasingly obvious.

Beware the Ides of March

On March 15, 2011, *Scientific American* reported, House Republicans, working on legislation to prevent the EPA from regulating carbon dioxide emissions to mitigate climate change, voted down an amendment calling on Congress to acknowledge that the "warming of the climate system is unequivocal." *Think Progress* found that 50 percent of the House Republicans elected in 2010 denied the existence of climate change.

TAGS: climate change, climate denial, Elizabeth Kolbert, global warming, Hurricane Irene, Hurricane Sandy

http://www.leveesnotwar.org/hurricane-watch-in-new-york-city/

Posted about a week before the BP oil blowout on the Deepwater Horizon rig.

Something Called "Volcano Monitoring"

[The Democrats' stimulus] legislation is larded with wasteful spending. It includes . . . $140 million for something called 'volcano monitoring.' Instead of monitoring volcanoes, Congress should be monitoring is the eruption of spending in Washington, D.C.
Bobby Jindal, Governor of Louisiana, Feb. 24, 2009

APRIL 16, 2010—Remember Bobby Jindal's celebrated response to President Obama's address to a joint session of Congress in February 2009? It included some, uh, noteworthy moments, not the least of which was his sneer at such "wasteful spending" as "something called 'volcano monitoring.'" Some speechwriter was probably pleased with that line, but this was a contemptuous display of ignorance on the level of Rudy Giuliani's ridiculing "community organizer—what's that?" at the 2008 Republican National Convention, and just as deserving of a reality-based comeuppance.

The $140 million for the U.S. Geological Survey was partly intended to provide warnings of impending volcanic eruptions in the U.S. and around the world where American military bases are located. The Americans at Ramstein Air Base in Germany probably appreciate that monitoring equipment right about now.

With international air traffic to Europe disrupted for a second straight day following a massive volcano eruption in Iceland (some 17,000 flights were canceled Friday), we have to use the occasion to poke this over-ambitious governor in the eye and say: "Now do you get it?" Jindal the boy genius used to be respected for his intelligence (Rhodes Scholar) and precocious grasp of complex policy, but those days are over. He is not serving his state or the nation—and not his own career, either—by his know-nothing, anti-science statements and decisions. (See Part IV for "Mr. Jindal, Tear Down This Ambition" and "Jindal: From Rising Star to Black Hole.")

Suffering under an Ambitious, Anti-Science Governor

This mocker of investments in volcano monitoring is the same governor who (along with senators Mary Landrieu and David Vitter) filed objections with EPA administrator Lisa Jackson against proposed regulations to limit greenhouse gases, claiming that the Supreme Court–mandated standards "will certainly have profound negative economic impacts on the state of Louisiana, as well as the entire country." Not true. Actually, an analysis by the Center for American Progress and the Political Economy Research Institute found that Louisiana stands to gain billions in revenue and tens of thousands of new jobs. As reported at *Think Progress*:

> Louisiana could see a net increase of about $2.2 billion in investment revenue and 29,000 jobs based on its share of a total of $150 billion in clean-energy investments annually across the country. This is even after assuming a reduction in fossil fuel spending equivalent to the increase in clean-energy investments.

This is the same governor who also, to his shame, signed into law the Louisiana Science Education Act of 2008 (SB733) that opened the door for teaching creationism and intelligent design alongside the theory of natural selection (Darwinian evolution). Louisiana Board of Elementary and Secondary Education made adjustments strengthening the pro-creationist provisions. Back to the pre–Scopes "Monkey" Trial era with Bobby. The CEO of the American Association for the Advancement of Science wrote to Jindal urging him to veto SB733 and reminding him that in 1987 the U.S. Supreme Court in declared unconstitutional a Louisiana "creation science" law.

The way we're going to have smart, intelligent kids is exposing them to the very best science . . .
Bobby Jindal, *Face the Nation,* **June 14, 2008**

The Science Education Act of 2008 (SB733) was spoon-fed to Louisiana state senator Ben Nevers by the Louisiana Family Forum, an affiliate of Focus on the Family. The Louisiana Coalition for Science notes that SB733's phrase "academic freedom and inquiry" is "well-documented creationist code language." After this bill was signed, science groups including the Society for Integrative and Comparative Biology notified the governor's office that as long as this law remains, they will no longer hold their conventions in New Orleans (much to their members' dismay, we're sure). The group's president wrote to Jindal, "It is the firm opinion of S.I.C.B.'s leadership that this law undermines the integrity of science and science education in Louisiana."

The SICB's convention in Boston in 2009 attracted more than 1,800 scientists and graduate students for five days, *The New York Times* reported. How is SB733 working out for the Louisiana economy, Governor? How many tourism and tax dollars were lost just with this one foregone conference? You're concerned enough about the "profound negative economic impacts" of EPA regulations that are designed to reduce carbon emissions and thereby curb global warming > hurricane ferocity > sea-level rise—but how about the economic impact of lost conventions?

Something Called "Science"

Governor Jindal, we *know* that you know better. Again, your political ambition overtakes your better judgment. (We have said before that, with the mentality of today's GOP, a Republican governor with presidential ambitions is a curse that we would not wish on any state.) Now, just to refresh your memory, there is something called "science" (it's in most dictionaries) that involves impartial investigation of natural phenomena through observation, formulating and testing hypotheses for objective results—regardless of the investigator hopes to find, or believes should be found. We know you're aware that the southernmost reaches of our beloved state of Louisiana is imperiled by subsidence, encroaching sea levels, intensified hurricanes, and desperately needs both reinforced flood protection systems (hard infrastructure) and coastal restoration in the form of replanted wetlands, river diversions, and shoreline protection including rebuilt barrier islands. (See the Multiple Lines of Defense plan drawn up by John Lopez and colleagues at the Lake Pontchartrain Basin Foundation; see also the Coalition to Restore Coastal Louisiana.) All of this work depends on science—and on elected officials who believe in the value of testing, experimentation, and hard data, not wishful thinking.

Governor, we don't have time to mess around with junk science and placating the evangelicals. Every year Louisiana loses 25 square miles of land—50 acres every day. About 1,900 square miles have disappeared in the past century—more than 25 times the land area of Washington, D.C. The land loss is not only killing species of wildlife, but is taking away the buffer that protects human settlements such as the city of New Orleans and Acadiana—Cajun country—from hurricanes and the encroaching Gulf of Mexico. Valuable oil and gas and shipping infrastructure are also endangered, exposed to violent storms. Experts say if a serious, all-hands-on-deck, fully-funded federal effort is not mounted within the next five to ten years, New Orleans and Acadiana will be lost. Metro New Orleans, home to about 1.5 million, is now protected by a buffer no more than about 20 miles of wetlands. Your attempts to block the EPA regulations may please industrial interests, but surely not all of them: you all must realize that oil and gas and shipping infrastructure are also imperiled, just like everything else along the southern coast of the state.

One more question, Governor Jindal: Do you think your Exxon engineers want their children going to Baton Rouge area schools where they're taught "young Earth" theories that humans and dinosaurs may have coexisted 4,000 years ago (as Sarah Palin seems to believe)?

LSU Fires Ivor van Heerden
of LSU Hurricane Center

Director Marc Levitan Resigns in Solidarity

APRIL 12, 2009—This is definitely one for the Fresh Hell file: Just before the Easter weekend LSU notified Ivor van Heerden, deputy director of the LSU Hurricane Center, that it would not renew his contract (he is not tenured) and he will be out of a job by May 2010. The university is not saying why—not to him, and not to the public. The firing comes after the university has imposed limits on his contacts with the media, demoted him, and retracted storm surge modeling responsibilities from his direction, among other limitations. Ubiquitous on CNN and in print after Hurricane Katrina—he is reported to have Anderson Cooper's cell phone number—van Heerden is well known as a critic of the Army Corps of Engineers' design of levees and the nation's general unpreparedness for catastrophic hurricane flooding. He is also the author of the impressive and constructively critical book *The Storm: What Went Wrong and Why During Hurricane Katrina—The Inside Story from One Louisiana Scientist* (2006). (See *Levees Not War*'s interview with van Heerden below in Part VII.)

The sword of Damocles has dangled close over van Heerden's head for several years—possibly even before Hurricane Katrina. John Schwartz reported in *The New York Times* in May 2006 that van Heerden had been called in to the principal's office and told to stop talking to the media. The university administration was annoyed that the geology professor was talking about engineering matters, making the Corps look bad, and causing LSU to miss out on potential research funding.

How high up did the approval for this firing go? Did Governor Jindal give the nod? (So suggests Len Bahr, a former official in the Governor's Office of Coastal Activities and former director of Applied Coastal Research.) Was this known about by Jo-Ellen Darcy, Obama's new nominee for overseeing the Corps of Engineers? If Darcy knew about this, it would bode ill for honesty and transparency.

[Editor's Note (2015): The Times-Picayune's Mark Schleifstein reported on April 2, 2013: "Louisiana State University spent close to $1 million to wage its battle against former research geologist Ivor van Heerden over his claims that senior university officials destroyed his career after he criticized the Army Corps of Engineers for its role in the failure of levees during Hurricane Katrina, according to new documents released Tuesday by the Levees.org activist group." On April 12, 2009, Van Heerden told Harry Shearer on Le Show, *"I learned about not being deputy director through the news media. [LSU] basically didn't have the guts to tell me that to my face. . . . They couldn't tell me why and wouldn't tell me why." (See* LNW's *interviews with Van Heerden, Shearer, and Schleifstein in Part VII, Interviews.)*

An Open Letter to LSU Chancellor Mike Martin
RE: The van Heerden Affair

April 27, 2009

Chancellor Mike Martin
Office of the Chancellor
156 Thomas Boyd Hall
Louisiana State University
Baton Rouge, Louisiana 70803

Dear Chancellor Martin:

As an alumnus of LSU and as the founder of LeveesNotWar.org, I am writing to protest the "slow-motion firing" of Ivor van Heerden and the gutting of the LSU Hurricane Center and its Public Health Center. Please, Chancellor Martin, reverse these reckless acts of political retribution. (I understand you were not aware of the firing until afterward, but as chancellor you have the authority to step in and right the wrong.) Please bring back Marc Levitan, renew Dr. van Heerden's contract, restore his teaching and other former responsibilities, and give Levitan and van Heerden the leeway to revive the Hurricane Center—including the irreplaceable Public Health Center—without further delay. Hurricanes aren't going away.

As an activist group that promotes robust rebuilding of Louisiana's flood protection systems, *Levees Not War* has benefited greatly from Dr. van Heerden's guidance in conversations and interviews. He has been generous with his time—a teacher in the true sense of the word. We have come to rely on his honesty and care for his beloved state of Louisiana and its people, a devotion we share. We have also benefited from reading and rereading his book *The Storm*. Through his knowledge of geology and engineering and coastal restoration and his decades of dedication to Louisiana by serving on countless committees such as Team Louisiana he is an essential state resource, a treasury of knowledge and courage whom the state should be empowering, not punishing. In his science-based critiques of faulty Army Corps of Engineers designs (the Corps is not his only target) he is doing his duty for public safety. And how is he rewarded?

We understand a school must make some allowances for political relationships and federal funding considerations, and we know a gadfly's criticisms can be annoying. Also, *Levees Not War* is essentially friendly to the Corps—we want them to be well funded and to "be all they can be" (tho' not all-powerful). But this firing is clearly a fulfillment of former chancellor Sean O'Keefe's threat to fire van Heerden if he served as a witness in the MR-GO lawsuit. LSU had already stripped away his teaching duties, reduced his Hurricane Center responsibilities, limited his contact with the media, and publicly belittled his expertise as a critic of the Corps.

By this obviously political maneuver, LSU makes itself and the state look very "banana republic" in the eyes of the world, reversing hard-won gains in prestige and damaging the university's fund-raising prospects. (We would have expected the administration would at least respect this aspect of the affair.) If LSU drives out an internationally respected scientist and downgrades the Hurricane Center purely for political reasons, then it is not serious about being a top-tier university. Do you and your vice chancellors not realize an alarming signal this sends to all faculty and to any prospective applicants? It sounds an alarm, too, for Louisianans who expect their state's institutions to protect the public—and defend professors who call attention to risks to public safety.

The LSU Hurricane Center, too, has been an immense asset for public safety, a local complement to the National Hurricane Center. For LSU to downgrade the Center from a $1 million budget at the time of Katrina to zero today shows a shocking disregard of public safety and contempt for academic integrity.

Chancellor Martin, the university and the governor too should reward Ivor van Heerden with honors and additional funding for the LSU Hurricane Center he co-founded, rather than punish him and the Center with a relentless campaign of "death by a thousand cuts." You know, for their investigation of the levee failures in Hurricane Katrina, the University of California rewarded engineering professors Bob Bea and Ray Seed with honors and a $20 million research center. The contrast in Louisiana—the state most directly affected by Katrina—is heartbreaking and truly makes us fear for the future. "Shoot the messenger" is not a prescription for survival or for academic excellence.

Mr. Martin, please put public safety before politics: Bring back Dr. Levitan, retain Dr. van Heerden, and restore and expand the Hurricane Center to meet the perils facing Louisiana and the Gulf Coast. Lord knows we need all the help we can get.

Yours sincerely,

Mark LaFlaur
Founder, LeveesNotWar.org

cc: David Constant, Dean of the College of Civil and Environmental Engineering
    Charles A. Wilson, Executive Vice Chancellor and Vice Provost
    Brooks Keel, Vice Chancellor, Research and Economic Development
    Robert R. Twilley, Associate Vice Chancellor, Research and Economic Development

    Bobby Jindal, Governor of Louisiana
    Mary L. Landrieu, Senator of Louisiana
    David Vitter, Senator of Louisiana
    Garret Graves, Governor's Office of Coastal Activities
    R. King Milling, Chairman, America's Wetland Foundation

http://www.leveesnotwar.org/lsu-fires-van-heerden-of-lsu-hurricane-center
http://www.leveesnotwar.org/an-open-letter-to-lsu-chancellor-mike-martin

Diagnosis of a
Stressed-Out Planet

OCT. 29, 2007—Climate change is a central concern here at *Levees Not War*—it keeps us up late at night. The reasons are obvious: As we've said before, even Category 5–strength flood protection is useless if global warming raises sea levels by 10 or 20 feet or more, as scientists have warned may happen in this century. The trend can be slowed, and eventually reversed, by massive coordinated—and sustained—effort.

Some alarming trends—along with proof that human efforts can make a positive difference—can be seen in the Global Environmental Outlook (GEO-4) released last week by the United Nations Environment Program (UNEP).

UNEP's executive director, Achim Steiner, said in a press conference on Thursday, "[W]e are coming literally to the brink where things will happen that either we cannot any longer control or that trying to reverse has both economic, social and environmental challenges that are extremely difficult to cope with. . . . The world is becoming more vulnerable almost daily . . ."

Jeffrey Sachs, director of the Earth Institute at Columbia University, added, "What the Outlook says in essence is that every part of the earth's system [is] under unique stress right now. Whether it's a terrestrial habitat, water, climate, air—we have multiple stressors and worldwide problems . . ."

The New York Times reported on Monday, Oct. 29 ("U.N. Warns of Rapid Decay of Environment"), "population growth combined with unsustainable consumption has resulted in an increasingly stressed planet where natural disasters and environmental degradation endanger people, plants and animal species."

Among the Outlook's salient points—both scary and encouraging:

- Over the last two decades, world population has increased by almost 34 percent, from 5 billion to 6.7 billion, and may reach 9 billion by 2050.
- Parts of Africa and India and China are at risk of environmental tipping points that could result in disappearance of arable land (Africa) and adequate water supply (Asia).
- Through a treaty to reduce the hole in the earth's ozone layer, international cooperation has phased out of 95% of ozone-damaging chemicals.

Jeffrey Sachs said on Thursday: "I think it's an extremely important report. I hope it's read in the White House, in Downing Street, and in other places of leadership in the world because actually this is the main true geopolitics of our age. . . . [S]ustainable development is at the very center of the true geopolitics of the world, whether we're going to have peace, whether we're going to have viable economies, whether we're going to be able to get on top of critical problems like climate change."

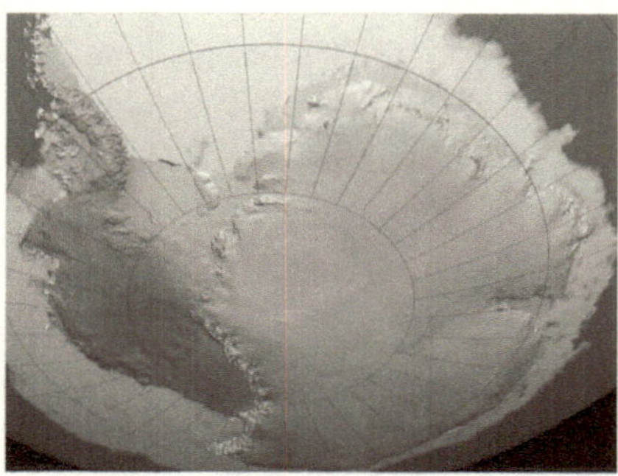

Penguins Are Melting

JAN. 23, 2009—A new report published in *Nature* suggests that overall, Antarctica is warming, and at about the same rate as the rest of the planet ("Warming of the Antarctic ice-sheet surface since the 1957 International Geophysical Year"). The study, by Eric J. Steig of the University of Washington and colleagues, analyzes temperature data over a fifty-year span. On average,

Antarctica warmed by 0.5°C between 1957 and 2006—especially on the western side near the peninsula—while on average the earth has warmed 0.6°C.

The illustration above shows the "hot spot" where temperatures have risen most compared to the rest of Antarctica. Temperatures on the West Antarctica ice sheet, colored brightest red, are rising faster than in other parts of the continent. The West Antarctica ice sheet, a stretch larger than California, Texas, and Alaska combined, includes the Antarctic peninsula, which points toward South America. The Wilkins Ice Sheet, part of the peninsula, is said to be "hanging by a thread"; a collapse of the West Antarctica ice sheet would cause global sea levels to rise. (It has been estimated that seas could rise by 23 feet if Greenland melts, and by 38 feet if Greenland and Antarctica melt.)

David Vaughan of the British Antarctic Survey, who was not involved in the study published in *Nature*, observes, "Antarctic ice shelves are breaking up because of rises in sea surface temperatures, not air temperatures." This is worrisome for two reasons: evidence of warming seas bodes ill for areas susceptible to tropical storms (warm water intensifies hurricanes), and rising sea levels obviously threaten low-lying areas such as New Orleans.

This is why *Levees Not War* regularly brings global warming matters to our readers' attention. Environmental threats are all interconnected. What good are Category 5–strength levees when the sea levels are rising to dangerous heights? (Some scientists project sea-level rises of more than 10 feet, possibly over 20, in the next century!) As President Obama noted in his Inaugural Address (2009), energy use affects climate. Energy use also leads to war. War leads to death and other bad things, including a shortage of funds for pressing needs at home, such as reinforced levees, coastal restoration, rebuilt schools and public housing, and so on.

TAGS: Antarctica, climate change, Global Environmental Outlook, global temperature, global warming, hurricanes, hurricanes and the environment, Jeffrey Sachs, United Nations Environment Program (UNEP)

http://www.leveesnotwar.org/diagnosis-of-a-stressed-out-planet/

http://www.leveesnotwar.org/penguins-are-melting/

Wrath of God? Global Warming and Extreme Weather

MAY 24, 2011—In response to our recent post* about Christian fundamental-ists' unconcern with the present danger of global warming, our good friend David in Berkeley, a former editor at Sierra Club Books, had this to say:

> I've been wanting to tell the rapturists et al.: Maybe the tornadoes, hurricanes and flooding in places they didn't use to happen—and the fact that they're ten times worse than usual—is god's way of yelling, screaming, and shaking his fists at you that climate change is real. Duh!
>
> P.S. And for you true believers in Oklahoma: Maybe god's also letting you know what he thinks about your voting for James Inhofe! D'oh!

James Mountain Inhofe (R-OK), of course, is the ranking Republican member of the Senate Committee on Environment and Public Works who has called global warming "the greatest hoax ever perpetrated on the American people."

David also sent along a link to a fine *Washington Post* op-ed by Bill McKibben (author of *The End of Nature*), "A Link Between Climate Change and Joplin Tornadoes? Never!"

We agree entirely, and so might many who are freaked out by the ter-rifying tornadoes that ripped through Joplin, Missouri, and north of Minneapolis on Sunday, and through central Oklahoma on Tuesday, and in Alabama in April. Verily, it is like unto a plague of extreme weather. There

---

* "World Survives to Be Raptured by CO2 Poisoning and Believers' Negligence" (5/22/11), about the end of the world, scheduled for Saturday, May 21, at 6:00 p.m.

have been so many tornadoes and super-tornadoes this year it's become impossible to remember them all. (Oh, and then there's the recent/current Mississippi River flooding caused by excessive rainfall in April.) *The New York Times* reports about Joplin: "More than 116 people were killed in a tornado outbreak on May 22, bringing the year's total to over 480 and making it the deadliest year since 1953, when 519 people were killed."

Andrew C. Revkin of the *Times* reports in "Tornado Outbreak Possible in Kansas and Oklahoma" that the Storm Prediction Center of the National Weather Service "has issued a blunt warning to Kansas and Oklahoma and adjacent regions to be prepared for the worst on Tuesday."

Revkin adds that the 2011 hurricane season begins June 1. The National Oceanic and Atmospheric Administration (NOAA) is warning that the hurricane season in the Atlantic Ocean should be more intense than normal. Further, NOAA warns, "Sea surface temperatures where storms often develop and move across the Atlantic are up to two degrees Fahrenheit warmer-than-average."

But back to David's point about extreme weather events in places where they didn't used to happen, we recall quite vividly the freakish tornado storm that unleashed micro-bursts of tree-toppling winds of 60 to 80 mph in Queens and Brooklyn in Sept. 16, 2010. New York City is not anywhere near Tornado Alley (Oklahoma and Kansas). Not normally.

And yet the fervent faithful may still prefer to believe—as Jerry Falwell and Pat Robertson have so often warned—that natural disasters are signs of God's wrath about abortions or the "homosexual agenda" and so on. (*"Still a man hears what he wants to hear and disregards the rest . . . la la la . . ."*)

The correlation between global warming and extreme weather is almost never simple and clear-cut, but it is demonstrable, and intensifying. It is known, for example, that warmer sea waters fuel more intense hurricanes. Global warming does not necessarily "cause" more hurricanes, but increases the likelihood that those that do arise will be more ferocious. Such was the case with Hurricane Katrina.

For science-based reporting and commentary on climate change we recommend Andrew Revkin, a science and environment writer for *The New York Times* who blogs at DotEarth (NYT). We also highly recommend Elizabeth Kolbert's excellent *Field Notes from a Catastrophe: Man, Nature, and Climate*

Change and her excellent reporting on climate and environment for *The New Yorker*. See for example "Uncomfortable Climate" on what the new Republican majority in the House of Representatives means for the earth's climate (*The New Yorker*, Nov. 22, 2010).

Faith-Based Environmental Policy Won't Save Us

The May 2011 calendar of the House Committee on Energy and Commerce, which deals with—or ignores—environmental matters, is absolutely blank.

In "Uncomfortable Climate," Elizabeth Kolbert quotes John Boehner, now House Speaker, as having said to ABC's George Stephanopoulos, "The idea that carbon dioxide is a carcinogen, that it is harmful to our environment, is almost comical." At the time of the article, one of the contenders for the chairmanship of the House Committee on Energy and Commerce was John Shimkus of Illinois. "At a congressional hearing in 2009, he dismissed the dangers of climate change by quoting Genesis 8:22: 'As long as the earth endures, seedtime and harvest, cold and heat, summer and winter, day and night will never cease.' He added, 'I believe that's the infallible word of God, and that's the way it's going to be for His creation.'" Today, May 24, under "What We're Working On," he tweets on the House Energy and Commerce a passage from Matthew 8:12: "Jesus said, 'I am the light of the world . . .'" File under God Help Us.

Kolbert writes:

> To be sure, even before the midterm elections, the prospects for meaningful action on climate change in Washington were dim. In June of 2009, the House approved the American Clean Energy and Security Act, also known as the Waxman-Markey bill, which would have imposed a nationwide cap on emissions. The bill was convoluted in all the usual, special-interest-driven ways, and not nearly ambitious enough to produce the emissions cuts that are needed. Even so, Waxman-Markey was too demanding for the Senate. After months of posturing and further concession-making, Senate Democrats failed to come up with a bill that they were willing to bring to the floor. While the Senate dithered, President Obama was silent. He did nothing to rally public

opinion on the issue, and what he did do—open up new areas to offshore oil drilling, for example—only undermined the negotiations.

Still, the recent election represents a new low. . . .

Meanwhile, as John Boehner chortles about the dangers of CO2, the world keeps heating up. According to the National Oceanic and Atmospheric Administration, the first half of 2010 was the warmest January to July on record. And this is just the beginning. Owing to the inertia of the climate system, the warming that we're experiencing is only a fraction of the temperature increase that's already guaranteed.

Indeed, a *Scientific American* headline from March—"House Repubs Vote That Earth Is Not Warming"—summed up the party's vision, and pretty much the entirety of congressional action we can expect from them on this issue.

"Death Panels" Are Real . . . and Democrats Ain't Helpin', Neither

To be brief and blunt, the only way—the *only* way—the United States will ever move seriously to mitigate the dangerous climate catastrophe that is already well under way is by electing no more Republicans to any office whatsoever. Down to their DNA, they are constitutionally averse to taking environmental matters seriously if they have the least impact on corporate earnings. A vote for Republicans is a vote for more extreme weather, more denial of reality.

Even more immediately, it's a vote for denial of emergency relief. No. 2 House Republican Eric Cantor says that the federal government cannot afford disaster relief for tornado, flood, and hurricane victims unless it finds comparable savings ("offsets") elsewhere in the budget. Similarly, on May 11 Mississippi Gov. Haley Barbour notified his citizens that they were on their own against the floodwaters of the Mississippi River.

Furthermore, Democrats—except for some admirable exceptions like congressmen Ed Markey (Mass.), Henry Waxman (Calif.), and Senator Barbara Boxer—have to be badgered and whipped repeatedly to press for environment-protecting legislation. President Obama, too, must be pressed upon to fulfill campaign pledges to protect the earth. The *Los Angeles Times* opined in a tough editorial that "the environment and public health will be thrown under a bus for the sake of his reelection in 2012." Obama's regrettable appointment of Ken Salazar as Interior secretary and his opening of offshore oil drilling—just weeks before the BP Earth Day oil blowout in April 2010—show a lack of environmental seriousness and continue a too-corporate-friendly way of doing business. See *Rolling Stone* political writer Tim Dickinson's powerful article, "The Spill, The Scandal and the President" (June 8, 2010).

We are not comforted by Congressman Shimkus's quotation of Genesis, "As long as the earth endures, seedtime and harvest, cold and heat, summer and winter, day and night will never cease." What guarantees that the earth *will* endure? And what extremes of "cold and heat," etc.?

TAGS: Andrew C. Revkin, Bill McKibben, climate change, climate denial, Elizabeth Kolbert, global warming, greatest hoax, House Committee on Energy and Commerce, hurricane season, James Mountain Inhofe, Ken Salazar
http://www.leveesnotwar.org/wrath-of-god-global-warming-and-extreme-weather/

Here Comes the Flood

National Assessment Finds Climate Change "Has Moved Firmly into the Present"

The effects of human-induced climate change are being felt in every corner of the United States. . . . If greenhouse gases like carbon dioxide and methane continue to escalate at a rapid pace, [scientists] said, the warming could conceivably exceed 10 degrees by the end of this century.

"U.S. Climate Has Already Changed, Study Finds,
Citing Heat and Floods," *New York Times* (5/7/14)

Melting of West Antarctic Ice Sheet "Has Passed Point of No Return"

Scientists say that the melting will continue as long as the heat-trapping carbon dioxide in the atmosphere increases. Even if carbon dioxide and temperatures stabilize, the melting and shifting of glaciers will continue for decades or centuries as they adjust to the new equilibrium.

"The Big Melt Accelerates," *New York Times* (5/20/14)

MAY 23, 2014—Two major reports released in recent weeks state emphatically that dramatic changes in climate are under way in the United States and globally, with a 10-degree average temperature rise in the U.S. possible by 2100, and world sea levels likely to rise by 4 to 12 feet or more by the end of the century. Perhaps most ominous of all, according to papers published last week in Science and Geophysical Research Letters, the melting of the West Antarctic Ice Sheet has already "passed a point of no return," which will lead to alarming sea level rises that will imperil—or render uninhabitable—coastal and low-lying cities around the planet: New Orleans, New York, Miami, Boston, Venice, Shanghai, Mumbai . . .

A good summary by NASA of the Science and Geophysical Research Letters papers' findings, along with an explanatory video, can be found at "Decline of West Antarctic Glaciers Appears Irreversible," May 16, 2014 (http://earthobservatory.nasa.gov/IOTD).

More Intense, Frequent Extreme Weather Projected for U.S.

The National Climate Assessment, released by the White House on May 6, was conducted by a team of more than 300 experts guided by a 60-member Federal Advisory Committee and reviewed by the National Academy of Sciences. Among the Assessment's many noteworthy findings: "The intensity, frequency, and duration of North Atlantic hurricanes, as well as the frequency of the strongest hurricanes, have all increased since the early 1980s. Hurricane intensity and rainfall are projected to increase as the climate continues to warm."

The Assessment also projects increases in extreme weather generally, both in intensity and frequency: heat waves, droughts, wildfires, along with (in other places) excessive rainfall, flooding, tornadoes "and other severe thunderstorm phenomena," etc.:

> The number of extremely hot days is projected to continue
> to increase over much of the United States, especially by late
> century. Summer temperatures are projected to continue
> rising, and a reduction of soil moisture, which exacerbates heat
> waves, is projected for much of the western and central U.S. in
> summer.

In a good summary of 12 points the Obama administration wants the American public to understand from the Climate Assessment, Grist .org includes one point (among others) that this blog takes very seriously:

"Infrastructure is being damaged by sea level rise, heavy downpours, and extreme heat; damages are projected to increase with continued climate change."

The Climate Assessment's findings on sea level rise make for chilling reading:

> The oceans are absorbing over 90% of the increased atmospheric heat associated with emissions from human activity. Like mercury in a thermometer, water expands as it warms up (this is referred to as "thermal expansion") causing sea levels to rise. Melting of glaciers and ice sheets is also contributing to sea level rise at increasing rates.
>
> Recent projections show that for even the lowest emissions scenarios, thermal expansion of ocean waters and the melting of small mountain glaciers will result in 11 inches of sea level rise by 2100, even without any contribution from the ice sheets in Greenland and Antarctica. This suggests that about 1 foot of global sea level rise by 2100 is probably a realistic low end. On the high end, recent work suggests that 4 feet is plausible. ... some decision makers may wish to use a wider range of scenarios, from 8 inches to 6.6 feet by 2100.

West Antarctic Melting "Appears Unstoppable"

A study led by NASA finds that major glaciers in the West Antarctic Ice Sheet—which alone contain the equivalent of 4 feet of sea level rise—appear to have become destabilized beyond repair; their collapse "appears unstoppable." Researchers find "continuous and rapid retreat"—two glaciers there have receded some 22 miles since 1992—and authors of the study see "no [major] obstacle that would prevent the glaciers from further retreat." (Antarctica holds 90 percent of the world's ice; a complete meltdown—not inconceivable—would raise global sea level by some 215 feet.)

The NASA press release says the West Antarctic glaciers "have passed the point of no return." The video above illustrates the big melt. The process may take several hundred years, or a millennium, but there is no comfort in the potential slow motion: Recent studies have found scientists' earlier predictions have often proved too cautious (they try not to be alarmist; see below), and many climatic changes have been accelerating faster than originally feared.

> Scientists said the ice sheet was not melting because of warmer air temperatures, but rather because relatively warm water that occurs naturally in the depths of the ocean was being pulled to the surface by an intensification, over the past several decades, of the powerful winds that encircle Antarctica. (*NYT* 5/12/14)

(It is warmer water, by the way, that intensifies the power of hurricanes; such was the case with Hurricane Katrina. Climate change does not necessarily cause hurricanes, per se, but when tropical storms do arise the warmer seawater turbocharges them.)

The National Academy of Sciences says that the earth's major ice sheets—the poles and Greenland—hold enough frozen water to raise sea levels by some 200 feet. The ice melt from Greenland alone has raised global sea levels by more than a quarter-inch since the early 1990s. In previous years only limited parts of Greenland melted in summer; now there is no part of Greenland that does not melt to some extent. Greenland holds 10 percent of the world's ice, enough to raise the sea level some 23 feet. An additional worrying factor is that the many wildfires made more common by climate change release soot into the atmosphere, which settle on the ice and darken it, reducing the ice's reflectivity and, in effect, causing the ice to absorb more sunlight thus melt faster.

This Is Not an "Alarmist" Exaggeration

Some science writers note that, far from being "alarmist," scientists tend to understate the severity of the earth's environmental predicament. As *The New Yorker*'s Elizabeth Kolbert observes,

> *The unfortunate fact about uncertainty is that the error bars always go in both directions. While it is possible that the problem could turn out to be less serious than the consensus forecast, it is*

equally likely to turn out to be more serious. In fact, it increasingly appears that, if there is any systemic bias in the climate models, it's that they understate the gravity of the situation.

Elizabeth Kolbert, "The West Antarctic Ice Sheet Melt:
Defending the Drama" in *The New Yorker* (5/13/14)

Fear Not—Organize
(or, Despair Is Not the Right Response)

The scientists' projections are serious, dire, and depressing—no question about it. But the right response—the honorable and moral response—is not to give up hope and succumb to defeat, but rather to summon courage and try to resist and press local, state, and national officials and businesses to mend their ways as rapidly and thoroughly as possible. We can limit the damage. All is not lost. For example, *The New York Times* reports (5/22/14) that billionaire environmental activist Tom Steyer of California is promising to spend $50 million of his own fortune and his super-PAC NextGen Climate in the 2014 congressional elections to make sure climate change is a prominent issue, and to assist the campaigns of environmentally serious candidates.

Most Republicans are ideologically unwilling or unable to face reality, but one, Jon M. Huntsman Jr. of Utah, a former ambassador to China and the GOP's most admirable candidate in the 2012 primaries, recently wrote an Op-Ed for *The New York Times* arguing that Republicans must no longer ignore climate change as a scientific fact: "Our approach as a party should be one of neither denial nor extremism. Science must guide sensible policy discussions that will lead to well-informed choices, which may mean considering unexpected alternatives." Huntsman then quotes the great Republican conservationist of a century ago, Theodore Roosevelt:

To waste, to destroy our natural resources, to skin and exhaust the land instead of using it so as to increase its usefulness, will result in undermining in the days of our children the very prosperity which we ought by right to hand down to them amplified and developed.

We could not agree more, and we feel very strongly that how the American public responds to this challenge—or not—and how the humans of Planet Earth organize and force governments and businesses and all the powers that be to mend our ways will be our legacy to coming generations of humanity, and other living things. The Industrial Revolution began about 250 to 300 years ago, and it has not taken humankind—or at least its industrial, carbon-producing elements—long to bring the planet to the brink of ecological destruction and mayhem.

We asked Mark S. Davis, former director of the Coalition to Restore Coastal Louisiana and now Senior Research Fellow and Director of the Institute on Water Resources Law and Policy at Tulane University, for his thoughts on what the reports mean for New Orleans, Louisiana, and the Gulf Coast and the U.S. generally (admittedly a tall order). He replied:

> We [in Louisiana] have some land-building and sustaining capacity but we also need to start managing to reduce subsidence (we are not alone in that), and factoring in potential sea level rise scenarios. We do that some, but not enough; the predictions keep getting worse . . . Since most public and private risk management decisions are made with a pretty short horizon in mind, I don't expect a really glum forecast for 100 years out to change much behavior today—however much I might advise otherwise. Most people, firms, and governments have real trouble planning for things more than five years in the future. Thirty years—the length of a mortgage—is almost an eternity, which explains a lot when you think about it.

Unfortunately, at the moment we are acting out our hopes more than we are acting on what the facts are telling us. Ignoring this information and what it portends may well be our defining act of ignorance and arrogance.

McKibben's Call to Arms

Grist reports that environmental activist and author Bill McKibben, author of *The End of Nature*, is organizing "A Call to Arms: An Invitation to Demand

Action on Climate Change" for September 20–21 in New York City when the delegates to the United Nations assemble for the UN's annual proceedings. McKibben writes in *Rolling Stone*:

> My guess is people will come by the tens of thousands, and it will be the largest demonstration yet of human resolve in the face of climate change. Sure, some of it will be exciting—who doesn't like the chance to march and sing and carry a clever sign through the canyons of Manhattan? But this is dead-serious business, a signal moment in the gathering fight of human beings to do something about global warming before it's too late to do anything but watch. You'll tell your grandchildren, assuming we win. So circle September 20th and 21st on your calendar . . .
>
> Here's a banner I know you'll see in the streets of New York: CLIMATE/JOBS. TWO CRISES, ONE SOLUTION.

PART II

'I' Is for Infrastructure

A modified version of this piece appears at Next New Deal, *the blog of the Roosevelt Institute, under the title "Memo to Chris Christie and Other Budget Cutters: Infrastructure Projects Benefit Everyone," posted March 8, 2011.*

Public Works in a Time of Job-Killing Scrooges

MARCH 3, 2011—Last week we went to a panel discussion on public works and infrastructure at the Museum of the City of New York: "Roads to Nowhere: Public Works in a Time of Crisis," part of the museum's ongoing Urban Forum series on infrastructure in New York. The discussion focused on NYC and environs, but has implications for public works—infrastructure and transportation—around the nation, including levees and flood control projects in coastal Louisiana, this blog's primary concern. The same pressures affecting public works funding (or slashed funding) in New York hold for the U.S. generally.

The distinguished panel—moderated by Michael M. Grynbaum, transportation reporter for *The New York Times*—were Dr. Michael Horodniceanu, president of the Metropolitan Transportation Authority Capital Construction Company (MTACC); Joan Byron, Director, Sustainability and Environmental Justice Initiative at Pratt Institute; Denise M. Richardson, Managing Director, General Contractors Association of New York; and Jeffrey M. Zupan, Senior Fellow for Transportation, Regional Plan Association. The panelists' collective expertise was most impressive, almost *formidable*, and quite to the liking of the near-roomful of about 150 transportation and public works geeks.

What the experts did *not* discuss to our satisfaction was *the political dimension* to the "Time of Crisis": Why are there budget shortfalls? Which political party is doing most of the canceling of projects, and why? What wouldn't be possible if the rich and corporations paid their fair share of taxes? And why, we keep wondering, aren't the president or congressional Democrats pushing for anything like the WPA & CCC programs that rebuilt America and employed millions in the last big depression? More about these questions below.

Michael Grynbaum began by reading quotations from a report on how the building of the Second Avenue subway line in Manhattan was affecting local East Side businesses, parking, etc. A spokesman from the Metropolitan Transportation Authority (MTA) estimated that work would be completed on the long-planned line in 10 years. Date of article: 1977. Status of project: still ongoing. Audience response: pained laughter, chagrin. If we didn't laugh, we'd cry.

Hanging over the whole discussion, Grynbaum noted, was the shocking, job-killing decision by New Jersey governor Chris Christie in October 2010 to pull the state out of the ARC (Access to the Region's Core) project—a new train tunnel under the Hudson River linking New Jersey and Manhattan— because, in Christie's view, New Jersey was having to pay too much, more than originally budgeted. The cancellation outraged local officials and the public generally, and the Obama administration sought to negotiate a compromise, but Christie rejected the offers. Two tunnels, built about a hundred years ago, are currently N.J. Transit's only way in and out of New York City.

Denise Richardson said that Christie's cancellation of this project that would have provided public benefits for at least a century to come—not to mention easier commutes and less auto traffic—would immediately cost about 6,000 direct jobs at a time when unemployment among contracting workers is already at 30%. (The blog *2nd Avenue Sagas* says the cancellation means $478 million flushed down the drain for New Jersey alone.)

Grynbaum pointed out that not only Christie but other Republican governors across the United States—in Wisconsin, Ohio, Florida—have been rejecting federal appropriations for high-speed rail. (Or, in Louisiana governor Bobby Jindal's case, not even applying for the funding.) Many of the same job-killing GOP governors who publicly reject stimulus money as "wasteful federal spending" quietly take the money anyway and have their pictures taken handing out checks to constituents. (See "Republicans Secretly (Seriously) Like the Stimulus" below.)

What can be done in a time of budget shortfalls and critical needs for repair and expansion of public transit and other infrastructure? The public can and should individually and collectively demand generous funding for these projects—through letters to the editor, letters and phone calls to elected officials, whatever it takes. We must also help educate our fellow citizens that the benefits are not for a few (such as those who don't drive cars) but for all.

Panelists generally agreed that transportation and public works supporters must do a much better job of communicating to the public the benefits of public works and transportation and mass transportation in particular. The public does not want to have to pay any higher taxes, understandably, but often the benefits of the public works programs are not evident and the support is lacking.

Hey Obama, Congress: Where's the WPA for *Our* Depression?

Michael Horodniceanu said that it is difficult to spread the view of public works as beneficial to all the public amid the pervasive anti-government rhetoric spread by conservative politicians. The tax on gasoline is too low to fund mass transit expansion, and would be voted down. He contrasted the widespread American view (and unwillingness to pay for public transportation) with the French readiness to embrace and pay for public works. He cited a field trip of a group of French students to see building of the trans–English Channel tunnel popularly known as the Chunnel, while across the Channel a group of British citizens were protesting the "eminent domain" taking of wheat fields to be used for the building of the tunnel and rail line into London. The implication was that the American attitude is more like the British than the French.

Denise Richardson lamented that the U.S. has lost the concept of the public good, of having to pay for travel. With the great U.S. interstate highway system launched by President Eisenhower in the mid-1950s being free, without toll fees, the public has grown accustomed to expecting something for nothing.

Jeffrey Zupan of the Regional Plan Association said that supporters of public works must communicate their support to state representatives in Albany. Even though the common view upstate is that only New York City benefits from the public works projects in the greater metropolitan area, in fact the city's health is a matter of survival for the entire state. Three-quarters of the state's tax income is received from the greater New York City area: that revenue feeds services in Buffalo, Syracuse, and so on; it's in those residents' interest to ensure that New York City and environs has a healthy, robust transportation infrastructure.

Zupan listed a "dirty dozen" reasons why public works have lost ground, or public support. Among the factors making it more difficult for public works projects to gain support or be completed are • the multiplicity of agencies involved • capital programs of limited duration compared to the length of the work to be done • unexpected cost overruns • environmental impact statements, which could be a variant of the "paralysis of analysis" • competition with backlog of maintenance needs (Horodniceanu agreed that there is always competition between "state of good repair" and necessary new projects) • public unwillingness to pay taxes and expectation of something for nothing • and an absence of professionalism in agencies: a profusion of political appointees and a shortage of professionalism (engineers, etc.).

As mentioned above, the panelists did not discuss the political, partisan angle to the predicament: the widespread Republican antipathy to any public spending. All panelists live in a primarily Democratic city and state and, aside from Grynbaum's mention above about the rejection by governors of the stimulus funding for high-speed rail projects, they did not discuss why, politically, public works and transportation projects are in such a predicament. There was no discussion of insufficient taxation—except possibly by one audience member during the too-brief question-and-answer period.

A very good account of the panel discussion—more detailed than this one—by Noah Kazis can be found at *Streetsblog*. Public works enthusiasts should also check out *Infrastructurist*, *Building America's Future*, *Building Green*, *America 2050*, and others on our Infrastructure blogroll.

It's Not "the Economy, Stupid"—It's the Evil "Starve the Beast" Agenda

This blog insists that the (unnecessary) budget crises are caused in large part by a massive redistribution of wealth to the top 1 and 2 percent of the population, especially the top sliver of the upper 1 percent. The near-meltdown of September 2008 had a devastating effect on state and municipal funds, to be sure, but it's the tax evasion by the wealthy and corporations that is driving the budget shortfalls that are crippling local, state, and federal appropriations. Pulitzer Prize–winning *New York Times* reporter David Cay Johnston, author of *Perfectly Legal: The Covert Campaign to Rig Our Tax System to Benefit the*

Super Rich—and Cheat Everybody Else, explains that not only are corporations getting subsidies and tax breaks, but the IRS and state auditors are told to lay off the corpos and focus on middle-class individuals. And in "The Tax-Cut Con," a comprehensive article in *The New York Times Magazine* in 2003, Nobel Prize–winning economist and columnist Paul Krugman explained the "starve the beast" strategy of deliberately curtailing revenue so that programs conservatives never wanted anyway can no longer be afforded.

This is the situation we're in now. But we don't have to take it—just look at Wisconsin's union members and supporters fighting back against Governor Scott Walker and his henchmen in the legislature—and we *can* do something about it. One step at a time, one day at a time, joining with others, organizing, keeping the pressure on elected officials, through letters to the editor, and political talk show and public affairs producers. If you have ideas, let us know.

TAGS: infrastructure, job-killing, Museum of the City of New York, public transit, public works, Second Avenue subway, trains are cool, unnecessary austerity, We Want FDR Again, "starve the beast"
http://www.leveesnotwar.org/public-works-in-a-time-of-job-killing-scrooges/
http://www.nextnewdeal.net/memo-chris-christie-and-other-budget-cutters
-infrastructure-projects-benefit-everyone

Framing the Case for Infrastructure Investment, Taxing the Rich

Attn.: Pro-Infrastructure Activists and Democratic Strategists

FEB. 7, 2012—In a Feb. 4 letter to the editor of *The New York Times*, Rick Stone of Madison, Wisc., makes a point that more of us should heed:

> If the wealthy knew with certainty that their increased taxes would make the roads they drive safer, resistance might be less. Yet higher taxes have generally not been framed as such, but rather as a fairness issue—that you make too much, so we'll take some of yours to give to others.

He is responding to an op-ed piece by Cornell University economics professor Robert H. Frank titled "Higher Taxes Help the Richest, Too," a somewhat abstruse argument that takes about 900 words to make a rather simple point about why the wealthy resist tax increases. Still, we agree with the basic point, perhaps best summarized in the final sentence: "When the anti-tax wealthy make campaign contributions, they are buying only the deeper potholes and dirtier air that inevitably result when tax revenue is low."

Earlier in his letter, Rick Stone cites the "behavioral economics concept of loss aversion—the idea that people strongly prefer avoiding losses to acquiring gains." The impulse to avoid losses can best be countered by showing what the tax increases could make possible. And then—he doesn't say this, exactly, but we do—change the discourse from a scarcity and austerity framework to a maldistribution-of-wealth argument.

Naomi Klein on *The Rachel Maddow Show* in October praised the genius of the "We Are the 99%" slogan and said the Occupy Wall Street activists were smart to take the protest to "the source of maximal abundance," to put the lie to the discourse of scarcity. "It's not a scarcity problem," she said, "it's a distribution problem."

Mr. Stone of Madison is not talking specifically about reinforced levees or expanded public transportation, but his point applies there as well. When we push for raising taxes on the under-taxed Upper 1 or 2 Percent (and we do); when we try to generate support for what even sympathetic politicians timidly call "revenue increases," we must show specific examples of what the revenues would pay for: stronger levees, repaired roads, expanded rail service, schools and post offices that are allowed to remain open, and so on.

We agree that arguments for higher taxes should be framed in terms of what they would make possible—that is why we are calling attention to this letter—but if Mr. Stone is saying that calls for higher taxes should not be framed as a fairness issue, then we disagree. He's probably right that the benefits to the public (including the wealthy) should be at the forefront, but fairness should certainly be part of the argument.

What Would George Lakoff Say?

We have quoted before the advice given to us by U.C. Berkeley linguist and political analyst George Lakoff. He said that in promoting investment in infrastructure and other public goods, Democrats should not try to imitate Republican appeals to self-interest (and certainly not appeals to fear), but rather should argue for doing what is morally right. People will warm to the moral argument if it is presented simply and directly. It is right and fair for a government to collect some portion of people's income to pay for the building of schools and roads and for monitoring food safety, etc. As we wrote in a piece on the social contract posted in September 2009:

> [Professor Lakoff] said the moral appeal is always the best. It's
> honest and it is more persuasive. Democrats and progressives, he
> said, always fall for the "Enlightenment fallacy," the naïve belief
> that if you simply present the facts, people will see the light and
> support your cause. Not so simple. . . . Democrats should never
> try to imitate Republican appeals—it's never believable. Instead,
> use the moral argument (the golden rule)—It's the right thing to

do. Expanding health care coverage, protecting our cities from hurricanes with reinforced flood protection is the right thing to do, morally and ecologically.

Lakoff said Democrats and progressives are never persuasive with the appeal to self-interest—they can't compete on that turf with Republicans. Part of the weakness of the self-interest approach is that it is fragmented, does not show how the various parts are connected, and therefore lacks a cohesiveness and persuasive force. To be convincing, what we must do is show how seemingly disparate phenomena are related. Show, for instance, how the nation's dependence on oil and the ravaging of the wetlands are connected; how the 10,000+ miles of oil and gas canals through the Louisiana wetlands destroy the storm-surge buffer that protects us from hurricanes, while the carbon emissions aggravate global warming, which intensifies hurricanes and raises sea levels, and so on.

(See "Does Believing in Social Contract Make Us Socialists? Then So Be It" on page 160.)

Thanks to Rick Stone of Madison for taking the time to write the letter, and our best wishes for the people of Wisconsin—especially the embattled public employees and union members there. We stand with Wisconsin.

TAGS: George Lakoff, infrastructure, Naomi Klein, Occupy Wall Street, social contract, tax, taxation, We Are the 99%, Wisconsin
http://www.leveesnotwar.org/how-to-call-for-infrastructure-investment-tax-increases/

Infrastructure, Baby, Infrastructure!
A Defense of Stimulus Investments

APRIL 9, 2010—Joe Conason, a stalwart defender of infrastructure, has written a strong column defending the stimulus money dedicated to repairing America's aging roads, levees, bridges, transit systems, schools, and other essential components of our nation's physical framework. (The American Recovery and Reinvestment Act is working and America needs more of it.) Conservatives, says Conason, habitually decry federal stimulus spending as "pork barrel waste" and claim the stimulus failed and created no jobs; they insist Washington should cut taxes and not spend at all. ("Starve the beast.") They say it's wrong to burden the next generation with debt (an argument we never hear from the GOP concerning war spending). Well, friends, think of infrastructure spending as an investment, akin to paying college tuition. Here are some portions from Conason's "Rebuilding an American Legacy":

> What would be left to future generations if the public functions
> symbolized by stimulus spending simply disappeared? What
> will the future be if government doesn't repair and transform the
> roads, bridges, sewers, power grids, reservoirs, levees, airports,
> railways, subways, schools, parks, colleges and hospitals that we
> are leaving to our children in much worse shape than they were
> left to us? How will those facilities serve the future if they are
> disintegrating today? . . .
>
> President Barack Obama's stimulus legislation appropriated
> nearly $100 billion for highways, transit, schools, parks,
> water and other public facilities, but its real purpose was
> to stoke immediate economic activity rather than long-
> term infrastructure improvements. The aim was to create

and save jobs right away and to provide relief to state and
local governments and working families. Its provisions for
infrastructure hardly began to address actual needs—as the
president would certainly acknowledge.

. . . To keep roads and bridges in decent repair . . . we would
have to spend $166 billion a year for the next five years. . . .
To improve transit sufficiently to meet increasing demand in
a carbon-choked world, we should spend an additional $25
billion every year.

. . . the politicians and television personalities who rant
constantly against government insist that tax cuts are the only
priority and oppose every attempt to restore the very things
that laid the foundation of our prosperity are worse than
irresponsible. They are like termites, gnawing away at the
remarkable legacy left to our generation, one which we must
pass on. They are willing, even eager, to squander trillions of
dollars on wars abroad, no matter how dubious, and then
waste trillions more on "defense" pork that benefits only
their donors.

(Speaking of the Republican gluttony for tax cuts, their cure for every ill,
read *New York Times*'s columnist Bob Herbert's "The Same Old Song" [Jan. 26,
2009] about congressional Republicans' demands for further tax cuts in early
2009 when Obama was prescribing a healthy dose of stimulus spending to
revive the traumatized economy—and was offering one-third of the stimulus
bill in the form of tax cuts in the vain hope of attracting some GOP support.)

As we noted in our April 3, 2010, post on employment gains, "the American
Society of Civil Engineers gives the U.S.A. a D grade and estimates a five-year
investment of $2.2 trillion is needed to get the nation back in shape." For
names and contact info of congressional friends of infrastructure, see "Get
Congress on Track to Stimulate Mass Transit" (Jan. 25, 2009).

What's in It for Levees and Flood Protection?

ProPublica.org, which has been keeping an Eye on the Stimulus, reported last
year that the allocations for the U.S. Army Corps of Engineers construction

($2 billion), Mississippi River and tributaries ($375 million), and operations and maintenance (nearly $2.1 billion) add up to nearly $4.5 billion. Another $25 million was allocated for Corps investigations, $25 million for the Corps regulatory program, and $100 million to the Corps for "formerly utilized sites remedial action program." By our count this is $4.6 billion for the Corps of Engineers. Not bad. For comparison, bear in mind that until November 2007 when the newly Democratic-controlled Congress overrode George W. Bush's veto and at long last passed the Water Resources Development Act (WRDA), there had not been a water projects bill in seven years, when in normal conditions water projects bills are passed every two years. (Read our post "Good News for Water Works!" [Nov. 7, 2007] for more about the 900 projects WRDA funded after a long, war-weary drought.)

Republicans Secretly (Seriously) Like the Stimulus

AUG. 20, 2011—Here's the best new idea we've heard in a long time (h/t to Rachel Maddow): When *HuffPo*'s Sam Stein reported that "Michele Bachmann Repeatedly Sought Stimulus, EPA, Other Government Funds," Steve Benen of *Washington Monthly* thought of something politically savvy that could jump-start new job creation:

> How about a new stimulus package focused on granting Republicans' requests for public investments?
>
> Here's the pitch: have the White House take the several hundred letters GOP lawmakers have sent to the executive branch since 2009, asking for public investments, and let President Obama announce he'll gladly fund all of the Republicans' requests that have not yet been filled.
>
> This is especially important when it comes to infrastructure, a sector in which GOP members have pleaded for more investment in their areas. When pressed, these same Republicans will offer an explanation that "sounds like something out of the mouth of a Keynesian economist, rather than the musings of a congressman who proudly touts his support from the Tea Party movement."
>
> So, how about it? If these Republican lawmakers have identified worthwhile projects in need of government spending, which they themselves insist will boost the economy, why not start spending the money GOP officials want to see spent?

Steve Benen, this is brilliant. It could work.

Never Mind the Hypocrisy—Just Get It Started.

What Sam Stein found through a Freedom of Information Act request for federal records was that Michele Bachmann (R-MN), who poses as a fiscal conservative and has publicly denounced the "orgy" of federal spending and called the 2009 American Recovery and Reinvestment Act "fantasy economics," has asked the federal government for financial help for her district on at least 16 occasions. Well, we can't blame her: she knows that federal spending does create jobs by funding projects to build roads and bridges, hire teachers and police officers, and so on. Louisiana governor Bobby Jindal knows it, too.

Steve Benen's bright idea—and we should all push the White House (202-456-1111; comments@whitehouse.gov) and Congress to put this into action immediately—is to approve all the requests by congressional Republicans for federal funding of projects in their districts. Never mind the hypocrisy. This should come very easily to this president, who can't seem to say no to Republicans anyway.

Obama should call in the press as he approves the projects in batches, day after day. He can use a big rubber stamp and say, "Yes to Republican Representative Bachmann who asked for funding for the Trunk Highway 36 bridge project over the St. Croix River to produce 1,400 new jobs. Approved. Yes to Republican Senator Jeff Sessions of Alabama who asked for stimulus money for an ethanol plant to create 750 jobs. Approved . . ." And then, after illustrating the point day after day, move on to approve Democrats' requests.

'S' Is for Stimulus—But Call It Whatever You Want

On *The Rachel Maddow Show*, Steve Benen said that it doesn't matter whether we use the term "stimulus" or "jobs program," which Republicans hate, or whatever. Just do it.

> If this is a list that Republicans came up with, saying these
> are things that they believe will create jobs in their own
> communities, their own districts, their own states, then at a
> minimum, if Democrats want to make these investments and
> create jobs, then just start here. Now, one might say, well, at that

point, you might look at job opportunities in blue districts and blue states. But fine, we can get to that later. If we just want to . . . inject capital into the system, create jobs right away, we want to create demand in this economy, we can start with the list Republicans came up with and make an immediate difference. . . .

[Bachmann] is one of many who have requested public funds . . . but then publicly rail against public spending. . . . So, to a certain extent, she's not unique. But at the same time, she is uniquely brazen. She . . . requested funding from the EPA, the Environmental Protection Agency, for her district despite the fact that she doesn't believe the EPA should even exist, and she actually wants to eliminate the agency altogether. And so, . . . trying to communicate to Republicans the importance of these kinds of projects, Democrats are in a position to say, well, [if] even Michele Bachmann believes that all this public spending can create jobs and help the economy, then other Republicans can certainly go along because she's to their right.

Mr. President, Don't Wait for Congress to Act. FDR Established the WPA by Executive Order, Employed 8.5+ Million

As we wrote to President Obama (and to Democratic members of Congress in similar letters) during the debt ceiling crisis in July:

The millions who voted for you are begging you to address the nation's real crisis and launch an ambitious WPA-style jobs program and lower the eligibility age for Medicare and Social Security to 55. That would restore public and investor confidence, and would invigorate this lame, sucking economy. If tax rates were fair, this wealthy nation could afford it. You could help make it happen.

Your reelection would be less in doubt if you gave America's 15+ million unemployed and the nation's crumbling infrastructure a comprehensive WPA-style jobs program at least 10 times as aggressive as the ARRA stimulus: public works, transportation (not just high-speed rail), public housing, environmental conservation (think CCC), schools, hospitals. Franklin Roosevelt didn't wait for Congress: he established the WPA in 1935 by executive order. You could do the same.

TAGS: American Recovery and Reinvestment Act, Bobby Jindal, CCC, infrastructure, jobs, Rachel Maddow, Sam Stein, Steve Benen, stimulus, WPA
http://www.leveesnotwar.org/republicans-secretly-like-the-stimulus-seriously/

Barack, You're Totally Our Infrastructure Hero!

FEB. 14, 2008—At a General Motors plant in Janesville, Wisc., on Feb. 13, Barack Obama "turned it down a notch" and gave a major policy address that laid out a broad agenda for reinforcement of the American economy. The plan would restore a measure of economic balance and stability, create infrastructure and renewable-energy jobs, and many other necessary and ambitious undertakings. The speech is substantive and shows Senator Obama's seriousness and grasp of economic reality and possibility. Optimism and realism together. We're delighted to see at least one of the three major candidates offering serious solutions to infrastructure and environmental degradation (as John Edwards also did). See excerpts from Obama's speech below.

Obama, in Wisconsin, Calls for $60 Billion National Infrastructure Investment Bank

Hillary Clinton and John McCain pick at Obama for being all rhetorical "airy nothings" and no substance. Well, what new proposals do they have to show? If they're all about experience, let them experience some new ideas. Let us experience their proposals. (Watching them, in contrast to Obama's energy, it's like watching machines, dead candidates walking.)

The Republican National Committee has rolled out an "Obama Spend-o-Meter" (seriously) to calculate the cost of the programs the Illinois senator is proposing. It's too cute. It's also instructive, in a dimly lit way, to see how the RNC views Obama's plans. RNC spokesman Alex Conant says Barack Obama's policy initiatives are "the same old tax-and-spend liberal dogma." Well, sure. Politicians of both parties tax and spend. The question is, what do they buy? Some invest in new bridges and new classrooms and fiber-optic cables, others deficit-spend on new wars, surveillance systems, missiles, and tax cuts.

But the Republicans don't just tax and spend—they borrow and spend. If they want to talk about spending, we would point them to the $12 billion the Iraq War is costing every month. We would point to 2008's $677 billion in defense spending ($196b for Iraq and Afghanistan + the Pentagon's $481b). We would point them to a good War Spend-o-Meter through our friends at the National Priorities Project.

The budget Bush has proposed for 2009, the first ever to exceed $3 trillion, asks for $514.4 billion for the Pentagon, along with deep cuts from Medicare and Medicaid. The 2009 defense budget does not include the supplemental $70 billion spending the Pentagon will request to carry the Iraq and Afghanistan wars into the early months of 2009. This is all deficit spending for the next president (and each one of us) to inherit, and every year the costs keep going up.

Obama has some great ideas for the economy, the nation's infrastructure, and environmental protection. But if he is elected, we the people will have to keep after him, as we would with any other president, to deliver on the promises.

Excerpts from Barack Obama's Economic Policy Address

General Motors
Janesville, Wisconsin
February 13, 2008

Today, I'm laying out a comprehensive agenda to reclaim our dream and restore our prosperity. It's an agenda that focuses on three broad economic challenges that the next President must address—the current housing crisis; the cost crisis facing the middle-class and those struggling to join it; and the need to create millions of good jobs right here in America—jobs that can't be outsourced and won't disappear.

For years, we have stood by while our national infrastructure has crumbled and decayed. In 2005, the American Society of Civil Engineers gave it a D, citing problems with our airports, dams, schools, highways, and waterways. One out of three urban bridges were classified as structurally deficient, and we all saw the tragic results of what that could mean in Minnesota last year. Right here in Wisconsin, we know that $500 million of freight will come through this state by 2020, and if we do not have the infrastructure to handle it, we will not get the business. . . .

For our economy, our safety, and our workers, we have to rebuild America. I'm proposing a National Infrastructure Reinvestment Bank that will invest $60 billion over ten years. This investment will multiply into almost half a trillion dollars of additional infrastructure spending and generate nearly two million new jobs—many of them in the construction industry that's been hard hit by this housing crisis. The repairs will be determined not by politics, but by what will maximize our safety and homeland security; what will keep our environment clean and our economy strong. And we'll fund this bank by ending this war in Iraq. It's time to stop spending billions of dollars a week trying to put Iraq back together and start spending the money on putting America back together instead. . . .

My energy plan will invest $150 billion over ten years to establish a green energy sector that will create up to 5 million new jobs over the next two decades—jobs that pay well and can't be outsourced. We'll also provide funding to help manufacturers convert to green technology and help workers learn the skills they need for these jobs.

TAGS: bailout, General Motors, infrastructure, infrastructure investment bank, Barack Obama

http://www.leveesnotwar.org/barack-you're-totally-our-infrastructure-hero/
http://obama.3cdn.net/8f478c5e1bb07ca0b1_sh1umv2zy.pdf

A Reply to "Obama Our Infrastructure Hero": Letter from a New Orleans Engineer/Blogger

FEB. 15, 2008—In reply to "Barack, You're Totally Our Infrastructure Hero," our friend Tim Ruppert of *Tim's Nameless Blog* points out that in fact the infrastructure part of Obama's economic agenda doesn't appear till near the end of the plan. Also, the senator doesn't mention the words "Katrina," "levees," "flood," "Corps of Engineers," etc. (Tim Ruppert is a New Orleans–born engineer at the Corps of Engineers, N.O., and a past president of the Louisiana chapter of the American Society of Civil Engineers.)

> I've said it before and I'll say it again: Politicians will say whatever they think they must say to win the election. When Obama was in New Orleans [2/7/08] his proposals were all centered on rebuilding the Gulf Coast. Once he left Louisiana air space—nary a mention. In the subject policy paper the following words appear ZERO times: levees, flood, hurricanes, Katrina, Corps of Engineers, Gulf Coast . . .
>
> Obama may very well be the best man for the job, but these broadside, laundry-list, promise-everything-to-everybody speeches count against him in my estimation. I want a candidate who will give the virtually the same speech to all Americans. If you believe in something, stand up and fight for it, don't hide it or show it selectively.

Stand up and fight, indeed. Ruppert's right that infrastructure is too important to be left to page 6 of an 8-page program. And it's true that healthy infrastructure is something every state needs, whether it's well-maintained bridges and tunnels or reinforced levees, and the candidates should be talking it up everywhere they go. We fully agree, and it's up to Us the People to keep the politicians focused. As we said at the end of "Infrastructure Hero": "Obama has some great ideas for the economy, the nation's infrastructure, and environmental protection. But if he is elected we the people will have to keep after him, as we would with any other president, to deliver on the promises."

On Feb. 7, the day of Obama's appearance at Tulane University, Tim Ruppert posted an open letter thanking the senator "for taking a strong stand in support of building significantly improved hurricane protections around the New Orleans area." Tim also clarified the technical meaning of the term "100-year storm," often used but little understood. This was one of the topics of his PowerPoint presentation "In Levees We Trust" at the Rising Tide conference of Katrina bloggers in New Orleans last August in which Tim, speaking as a citizen not a Corps man, gave an excellent overview of repairs since Katrina and to come by 2011.

TAGS: Infrastructure, infrastructure hero, Katrina bloggers, NOLA bloggers, Tim Ruppert
http://www.leveesnotwar.org/a-reply-to-'obama-our-infrastructure-hero/

American-Made:
A WPA History for Our Time

*All work undertaken should be useful—not just for a day,
or a year, but useful in the sense that it affords permanent
improvement in living conditions or that it creates future new
wealth for the Nation.*

Franklin D. Roosevelt, second State of the Union address (1935)

*You can start out from Baton Rouge in any direction and pass
through town after town which has water facilities or sewer
facilities or roads or streets or sidewalks or better public buildings,
which it would not have had but for the Works Progress
Administration.*

**WPA administrator Harry L. Hopkins, dedication of addition to
Tiger Stadium, Louisiana State University, Baton Rouge, Nov. 28, 1936**

MARCH 4, 2009—*Levees Not War* has been recommending a Civilian Conservation Corps for Louisiana coastal restoration for some time now,* and here is more encouragement in that direction.

From his first days in office, Franklin Roosevelt worked to establish relief programs to ease the pain of 25 percent unemployment nationwide, with some 15 million men, or 60 million Americans, having no income whatsoever. But it was not until his third year in office that Roosevelt launched the Works Progress Administration, the famous jobs and public works program that is one of the hallmarks of the New Deal. Other public assistance and jobs programs had come before—FDR's beloved CCC was created in his first month—but the WPA took relief to a whole new level: practical, rewarding, enduring.

Yesterday we went to the 92nd Street Y–Tribeca to hear Nick Taylor speak about his book *American-Made: The Enduring Legacy of the WPA: When FDR Put the Nation to Work* (2008). Mr. Taylor began research for the book in 2001, and its publication could hardly be more timely: lucky for the book's sales and for American readers. *American-Made* is an engaging account of the Roosevelt administration's Works Progress Administration (1935–43), the nationwide jobs and public works program that put 8.5 million Americans back to work (enrollment peaked at about 3.3 million in 1938) in building roads and bridges, tunnels and airports, producing plays and painting murals, serving millions of hot lunches, sewing clothes and repairing toys, and many more useful and entertaining works.

Louisiana benefited from the WPA statewide, from Chalmette to Monroe, Opelousas to Vidalia—but especially in New Orleans and Baton Rouge. Employing tens of thousands of Louisianans on jobs recommended by local officials, the WPA completed the seawall along Lake Pontchartrain and developed Pontchartrain Park and the Crescent City Golf Course at City Park; and at LSU, WPA workers built the Ag Center, a physics and math building, and a U-shaped addition to the north end of Tiger Stadium that combined seats above and dorms below. Across the state, WPA projects repaired or constructed 221 school buildings, 5 college dorms, 10 stadiums, 8 auditoriums; ran a free lunch program and an adult education program (385 teachers and over 15,000 students in 1937); and a bookbinding program paid workers to mend worn books, saving the state textbook purchasing costs. The WPA's Federal Writers Project also collected life histories in an oral history project and wrote the popular *WPA Guide to New Orleans.*

Beyond *American-Made's* full coverage of the WPA, this big book is also an overview of the Great Depression, easily readable with its short chapters and well populated with lively anecdotes and engaging characters, particularly the driven, impatient WPA director Harry Hopkins ("Hell," he snapped at critics of relief work for white-collar workers, "they have to eat like everybody else"). Taylor tells about the Negro Theatre's Harlem production of a "voodoo *Macbeth*" set in Haiti, directed by Orson Welles and featuring an authentic witch doctor. *Macbeth* was a popular success; the one critic who panned the production, however, was dead of pneumonia within a week of his review.

In its review, *The New Yorker* said, "The WPA . . . returned to the nation what FDR called 'the joy and moral stimulation of work.' Taylor's book is both a paean to American resourcefulness and a staunch defense of the New Deal." Now in paperback, *American-Made* is a handbook and model for today's activists, city planners, and policymakers. Nick Taylor has already put one in the hands of his former boss, Congressman John Lewis of Georgia (yes, *the* John Lewis), who we're hoping might loan it to his friend the president.

We hope *American-Made* will be read closely by Team Obama—and receptive members of the Jindal administration. Perhaps Lieutenant Governor Mitch Landrieu and his sister, Senator Mary Landrieu, would be more receptive. Taylor's book instills pride in our nation's past and hope for America's present and future. We hope our readers will buy a copy today. Better yet, buy two, and give one to the elected official of your choice. (Put our policy makers to work—reading this book!) In our time we need jobs—there is so much work to be done and so much talent available—and we need what FDR called "bold, persistent experimentation . . . above all, try something."

———

* (See Mark LaFlaur's guest article at *LaCoastPost*, "Why Not Institute a 'Green' Corps for the Coast?" [Nov. 18, 2009], http://lacoastpost.com/blog/?p=15876.)

TAGS: American-Made, Civilian Conservation Corps, CCC, federal relief agencies, Great Depression, Nick Taylor, WPA
http://www.leveesnotwar.org/"american-made"-a-wpa-history-for-our-time-"yes-we-can"-do-it-again/

FDR, Treehugger-in-Chief, Inspires Hopes for Coastal Conservation Corps

JUNE 23, 2010—This past weekend we went to the 7th annual Roosevelt Reading Festival at the Franklin D. Roosevelt Presidential Library and Museum in Hyde Park, New York, that featured 21 authors of such works as *FDR's Alphabet Soup: New Deal America 1932–1939* (Tonya Bolden), *Beyond the Bonus March and GI Bill: How Veteran Politics Shaped the New Deal Era* (Stephen R. Ortiz), and *The Sound of Freedom: Marian Anderson, the Lincoln Memorial, and the Concert That Awakened America* (Raymond Arsenault), topped off with a keynote address by the eminent historian Alan Brinkley, author of a new biography, *Franklin Delano Roosevelt*.

"I Propose to Create a Civilian Conservation Corps . . ."

The author we most wanted to see—introduced by FDR's grandson David M. Roosevelt—was Neil M. Maher, author of *Nature's New Deal: The Civilian Conservation Corps and the Roots of the American Environmental Movement* (Oxford, 2008). Maher, an environmental historian at the New Jersey Institute of Technology, explained that Franklin Roosevelt's conservationist credentials were strong even before he was governor of New York (1929–1932) and president of the United States; fittingly, while governor he was also president of the Boy Scout Foundation of Greater New York.

As a young man, Franklin Delano Roosevelt became concerned about erosion on his family's Hudson River estate, Springwood, and became "a tree-planting fiend" to prevent further soil loss and degradation and to restore his family's farm to its former abundance. Roosevelt was stunned to learn that in the 1840s his ancestors had grown prizewinning corn; in the years since, the formerly rich topsoil had washed away. In the 1920s FDR launched an aggressive soil restoration program, directing the planting of about 20,000 to 50,000 trees per year on his estate. So committed was Roosevelt to trees' restorative powers that once in the '20s when he went to vote, he listed his occupation as "tree farmer."

Only weeks after taking office, Franklin Roosevelt said in his "Relief of Unemployment" message to Congress on March 21, 1933:

> It is essential to our recovery program that measures
> immediately be enacted at unemployment relief. . . . The first
> step is the enrollment of workers now by the federal government
> for such public employment as can be quickly started. . . . I
> propose to create a Civilian Conservation Corps to be used in
> simple work, not interfering with normal employment, and
> confining itself to forestry, the prevention of soil erosion, flood
> control, and similar projects . . .

Roosevelt signed the Civilian Conservation Corps into law in March 1933. The new president saw the CCC as a practical solution to two urgent crises, economic and environmental. Unemployment in 1933 was about 12 million—or 25 percent of the American workforce. Young, unmarried men between 18 and 25 who were on relief rolls were eligible to enlist. About 200 men lived at each camp, many of which they built themselves—eventually there were some 5,000 across the U.S.—and room and board were provided. The men were paid $1 per day; they could keep $5 per month, but had to send $25 back home to their families, an invigorating stimulus to depressed local economies. The CCC sorted seeds, planted trees (seedlings), fought forest fires, and built fire lookout towers. At night the men could take courses to learn to read, type, and to study practical crafts and trades such as stonework, carpentry, and automotive repair. Maher writes in *Nature's New Deal*:

> The more than 3 million young men who joined the CCC
> between 1933 and 1942 . . . [planted] 2 billion trees, slowing soil
> erosion on 40 million acres of farmland, and developing 800 new
> state parks.

The terrible Dust Bowl of the mid-1930s, whose rust red dust clouds blew from the Great Plains as far as Hyde Park, New York, would have been even worse if not for the remediation work of the CCC, including tree plantings and contour plowing. Later in the decade, work on state and national parks included picnic shelters, hiking trails, bridges, dams to form swimming lakes, etc. Between 1933 and its closure in 1942, "Roosevelt's Tree Army" planted some 2.3 billion trees in the United States. Many "veterans" or "graduates" of the CCC went on to pursue careers as forest rangers and environmentalists, in engineering, agronomy, botany, chemistry, and related fields. Many took jobs with federal conservation bureaus such as the Soil Conservation Service or worked in the U.S. Forest Service.

The Conservation Corps' Legacy Lives On

In 1965 Lyndon Johnson created Job Corps, which was administered by a former CCC enrollee and housed its own young enrollees in abandoned CCC camps that were named Civilian Conservation Centers; in 1971 Richard Nixon signed an act establishing the Youth Conservation Corps; and in 1977 Congress initiated the Young Adult Conservation Corps. President Bill Clinton followed suit in 1993 with AmeriCorps, which according to one newspaper reporter "considers itself the 'grandchild' of the original CCC [and] routinely does much of the same type work its 'grandparent' did." —*Nature's New Deal* (p. 215)

In addition to AmeriCorps, there is still today a Corps Network, "strengthening America through service and conservation," that is active in 45 states with some 30,000 members aged 16 to 25, active in conservation, infrastructure improvement, and human service projects.

Maher says that a present-day, "new and improved" Civilian Conservation Corps could hire young people to plant trees, set up windmills across the former Dust Bowl and solar energy panels in the Sun Belt, and help cultivate energy-efficient biofuels throughout the U.S. He has written that "While Roosevelt funded the New Deal's CCC with federal dollars, public spending for Obama's new program could be greatly reduced through market mechanisms like those embraced by Brazil . . . by collecting carbon vouchers and water-use fees from the new program's reforestation efforts, and by selling clean, green energy generated from new windmills, solar panels, and biofuels."

We had a chance to talk with Maher after the presentation, and he likes the idea of a Coastal Conservation Corps that *Levees Not War* and *LaCoastPost.com* have promoted. He says that for greatest impact a new CCC should probably be federally administered and funded (perhaps with additional contributions from friendly private firms). If a state already has its own CCC (California, for example), the state's CCC could partner with the national organization.

In Louisiana the America's Wetland Conservation Corps (AWCC), sponsored by America's Wetland: The Campaign to Save Coastal Louisiana, with funding from AmeriCorps, functions on a similar model: it is administered jointly by Louisiana State University's Ag Center and the lieutenant governor's office, and participates in the national AmeriCorps program. (Each state's AmeriCorps program is administered by the lieutenant governor's office—in Louisiana, the guiding office is called Louisiana Serve.) Louisiana's AWCC has some 30 full-time and part-time members who for the past three years have been working on wetlands restoration projects (such as planting cypresses in St. Bernard Parish) and outreach education projects on wetlands and environmental conservation.

We also spoke briefly with Mr. David B. Roosevelt, a grandson of FDR, who wrote a concept paper based on the CCC for the Clinton Administration, an outline that eventually became the National Civilian Community Corps department of AmeriCorps. As a consequence Mr. Roosevelt was appointed to serve on the national board for the National Civilian Community Corps. He recommends the California state CCC as a model of how a state civilian conservation corps should be organized.

By the way, we took an Amtrak train from Penn Station in New York City and we were pleased to see that the Poughkeepsie station is being renovated with funds from the American Recovery and Reinvestment Act [ARRA], better known as the stimulus bill of February 2009. Our tax dollars at work!

TAGS: CCC, coastal Louisiana, Coastal Conservation Corps, David B. Roosevelt,
   FDR, Neil Maher, New Deal, WPA

http://www.leveesnotwar.org/fdr-treehugger-in-chief-inspires-hopes-for-coastal
-civilian-corps/

Neil M. Maher, "Is It Time for a Green New Deal?" (*NJIT Magazine*, Fall 2009)
http://magazine.njit.edu/2009/fall/green-new-deal.pdf

PART III

War and Peace and War

Photograph by Tim Hetherington/Magnum Photos

Eisenhower on the Opportunity Cost of the War Machine

Every gun that is made, every warship launched, every rocket fired signifies, in the final sense, a theft from those who hunger and are not fed, those who are cold and are not clothed. This world in arms is not spending money alone. It is spending the sweat of its laborers, the genius of its scientists, the hopes of its children. The cost of one modern heavy bomber is this: a modern brick school in more than 30 cities. It is two electric power plants, each serving a town of 60,000 population. It is two fine, fully equipped hospitals. It is some fifty miles of concrete pavement. We pay for a single fighter plane with a half million bushels of wheat. We pay for a single destroyer with new homes that could have housed more than 8,000 people. This is, I repeat, the best way of life to be found on the road the world has been taking. This is not a way of life at all, in any true sense. Under the cloud of threatening war, it is humanity hanging from a cross of iron. . . . Is there no other way the world may live?

Dwight D. Eisenhower, "The Chance for Peace," address to the American Society of Newspaper Editors, April 16, 1953

Obama Has Plans for ISIS; Now Congress Must Vote.

Our objective is clear: We will degrade, and ultimately destroy, ISIL through a comprehensive and sustained counterterrorism strategy.

Statement by the President on ISIL, Sept. 10, 2014

SEPT. 11, 2014—Happy 9/11, everyone, on the centennial of the outbreak of the war to end all wars.

We listened closely to President Obama's speech last night, we have read the transcript, and, like many around the world, we are profoundly uneasy. It is clear that this president is seriously reluctant to get the United States re-involved in Iraq and to start anything with Syria. He and his national security team have drawn up a four-part plan "to degrade and ultimately destroy the terrorist group known as ISIL."

The Guns of August, September, October . . .

We are nervous, with a sense of dread, at the prospect of more war in the Middle East. We support the president's preference for diplomatic solutions, for involving as many neighboring countries as possible, and assembling a coalition at the recent NATO summit meeting. It is right to push the Iraqi government to be more inclusive of Sunnis and Kurds (as the previous, U.S.-backed prime minister Nuri Kamal al-Maliki, a Shiite, was not). It is right to involve neighboring countries in the counterterrorism fight against ISIS; this cannot be the U.S. against ISIS. (That is what they want.)

> . . . this is not our fight alone. American power can make a
> decisive difference, but we cannot do for Iraqis what they must
> do for themselves, nor can we take the place of Arab partners in
> securing their region.

But when the president says "we will not get dragged into another ground war in Iraq," we have no confidence that the situation is controllable (see "dogs of war" below). With the new deployment of 475 more service members to Iraq, there will be 1,500 soldiers in Iraq (there were none in early June). As we wrote in mid-June, it's beginning to smell like early Vietnam. Drone strikes and aerial assaults alone will not suffice, and the troops we're supposedly partnering with, even the Kurdish pesh merga, are less than reliable. ISIS has captured serious military hardware from the Iraqi army that dropped its arms and fled. Anti-aircraft weaponry could be part of their arsenal. If one of our planes is shot down, and if the crew are taken prisoner, what happens then? The U.S. won't abandon them on the battlefield.

ISIS's videos of beheading American journalists have (predictably) made the public revolted and angry—even individuals who a month earlier were not inclined to support any more U.S. military involvement anywhere. Now, most Americans say "We've got to do something"—and we agree—but it is important not to respond emotionally. We must not go into war angry. ISIS wants to provoke the U.S. into a fight—so did al Qaeda—and this is where the president's patient assembling of a coalition of neighbors of Iraq and Syria is essential; this must not be a U.S. vs. ISIS (or Muslim) fight. It was good that President Obama made clear, early in his speech, that "ISIL is not 'Islamic.' . . . It was formerly al Qaeda's affiliate in Iraq. . . . ISIL is a terrorist organization, pure and simple."

And, let's not forget, contrary to the neocons' assertions, there was no al Qaeda in Iraq before the U.S. invasion in 2003. (Al Qaeda hated Saddam, a secularist too cozy with the West.) ISIS's commanders include former generals from Iraq's army that was disbanded, along with Saddam's Baath Party, in 2003 by Coalition Provisional Authority Administrator Paul Bremer, with disastrous results. These are among the reasons why we feel the U.S. is obligated to try to help clean up the mess—very carefully.

Congress Must Vote on This

Congress must step up and vote on whether to authorize additional force against ISIS. We want to see some "profiles in courage." There is not a single member of Congress—Democrat, Independent, or Republican—about whose reelection hopes and job security we frankly give a damn; we want to see them do their jobs and fulfill their constitutionally required responsibility to declare war (or authorize the use of force). Per Article I, Section 8, Clause 11 of the Constitution:

> [The Congress shall have Power . . .] To declare War, grant
> Letters of Marque and Reprisal, and make Rules concerning
> Captures on Land and Water;

Further, the congressional Republicans who have blocked votes on more than 40 ambassador nominations—to Turkey, among other nations—should end their dangerous games and vote already. The diplomatic angle of the anti-ISIS struggle will not work without Turkey's cooperation; we must have an ambassador now. (For much of this year—this year of all years—the U.S. did not have an ambassador to Russia because of GOP stonewalling. "Country first.")

Senator Bernie Sanders makes an excellent point: that ISIS must be resisted, but we have severe problems here in the U.S. that must be tended to—a collapsing middle class, veterans from the Iraq and Afghanistan wars who are not being taken care of by an underfunded Veterans Administration, and much more. National security begins at home.

Iraq War Is Already Costing $3 to $5 Trillion

Nobel Prize–winning economist Joseph Stiglitz and Harvard professor Linda J. Bilmes estimated the Iraq war would ultimately cost the United States some $3 trillion when all health care costs over the soldiers' lifetimes are factored in. In 2008 they raised their estimate to $4 or $5 billion.

As noted by *New York Times* columnist Charles Blow, Jason Fields of Reuters has reported that the American airstrikes against ISIS (150 and counting) are destroying millions of dollars' worth of military equipment the U.S. gave to the Iraqi army—the army we trained for years ("As Iraqis stand up, we will stand down," said George W. Bush), the one that melted before the ISIS onslaught this year. Worse, Fields writes,

> Now, U.S. warplanes are flying sorties, at a cost somewhere
> between $22,000 to $30,000 per hour for the F-16s, to drop
> bombs that cost at least $20,000 each, to destroy this captured
> equipment. That means if an F-16 were to take off from Incirlik
> Air Force Base in Turkey and fly two hours to Erbil, Iraq, and
> successfully drop both of its bombs on one target each, it costs
> the United States somewhere between $84,000 to $104,000
> for the sortie and destroys a minimum of $1 million and a
> maximum of $12 million in U.S.-made equipment.

Because the escalated, re-upped war is being waged in part to make business and shipping conditions safe for the oil industry in and around the Persian Gulf, we want ExxonMobil and all the other U.S.-based oil companies doing business in the Middle East to pay higher corporate taxes—at least, say, 25 to 50 percent higher—and for the Internal Revenue Service and the Justice Department to enforce timely payment to the U.S. Treasury. The five largest oil firms doing business in Iraq are BP, Exxon Mobil, Occidental Petroleum, Royal Dutch Shell, and Chevron.

On paper, statutorily, corporations are supposed to pay a tax rate of 35 percent. A 2011 study by Citizens for Tax Justice found that, over 2008–2010,

> Exxon Mobil paid an effective three-year tax rate of only
> 14.2 percent. That's 60 percent below the 35 percent rate that
> companies are supposed to pay. And over the past two years,
> Exxon Mobil's net tax on its $9.9 billion in U.S. pretax profits was
> a minuscule $39 million, an effective tax rate of only 0.4 percent.

There is very much we do not know, but, as far as we can see, the Obama administration has been careful and methodical about using diplomacy, preferring to withdraw troops (not precipitously), not rushing into conflict, and judicious and cautious regarding the super-complicated, internecine snake pit of the Syrian civil war. Just because the president is not exaggerating the threat ISIS poses to the Homeland; just because he is (apparently) not lying to us as some presidents have done (weapons of mass destruction, 2003; Gulf of Tonkin, 1964), does not mean that the renewal of war in Iraq won't go badly out of control. They cannot tell us how this will end.

We worry, as does David Corn at *Mother Jones*, whether the dogs of war can be controlled once they are unleashed. This new escalation of the counter-terrorism fight against ISIS is likely to last years, into the next administration. We worry when we consider that the U.S. does not always have a president with the patience for deliberation that the current president has. Just look at the attention span and patience exhibited by Obama's predecessor, and the consequences thereof.

Now, tell us again about the guns of August . . .

TAGS: al Qaeda, Bernie Sanders, Iraq War, ISIS, Islamic State of Iraq and Syria, Barack Obama, Syria, U.S. foreign policy
http://www.leveesnotwar.org/obama-has-plans-for-isis-now-congress-must-vote/

As "End" of Iraq War Is Announced, U.S. Digs In, Warns Iran

Where's That "Mission Accomplished" Feeling?

In August [2002] a British official close to the Bush team told Newsweek: "Everyone wants to go to Baghdad. Real men want to go to Tehran."

Paul Krugman, "Things to Come," *New York Times*, **March 18, 2003**

OCT. 30, 2011—On Friday, Oct. 21, President Obama announced that "as promised," by the end of this year, 2011, the last remaining U.S. forces (about 39,000) will leave Iraq and be home in time for the holidays.

> A few hours ago I spoke with Iraqi Prime Minister Maliki. I reaffirmed that the United States keeps its commitments. He spoke of the determination of the Iraqi people to forge their own future. We are in full agreement about how to move forward. So today, I can report that, as promised, the rest of our troops in Iraq will come home by the end of the year. After nearly nine years, America's war in Iraq will be over.

The U.S.–Iraq status of forces agreement (2008) worked out between Iraqi prime minister Nouri al-Maliki and the George W. Bush administration had provided for continued U.S. military presence of some 50,000 "advise and assist brigades" for security and training until the end of 2011, with a possible extension if negotiated.

As WhiteHouse.gov puts it, "President Obama Has Ended the War in Iraq." Some 90,000 American combat brigades were withdrawn between early 2009 and August 2010 (see "As Combat Troops Leave Iraq, Where's Our

National Security?"); many were redeployed to Afghanistan. On Sept. 1, 2010, Operation Iraqi Freedom ended and Operation New Dawn commenced.

This month Prime Minister Maliki decided to have all U.S. troops leave by Dec. 31, 2011. By doing so, he would remove a political liability for himself and a social and political irritant, but would also forgo a potential stabilizing force in case of an outbreak of civil war—or of invasion by a foreign power, such as Iran. But the Americans are already negotiating to send a new round of military trainers to Iraq in 2012, along with equipment specialists for the weapons systems the U.S. hopes to sell, and to base a large contingency force nearby in Kuwait (see below). Thus the New Dawn.

Republican reaction to the president's Oct. 21 announcement was mixed: G.O.P. presidential candidates and senators McCain and Graham denounced the withdrawal; other Republicans expressed approval, relief, or said nothing. (McCain this month recommended U.S. military action against Syria, like that against Libya, "to protect civilian lives.") For an Iraq war veterans' perspective on the announced withdrawal, see the statement from Paul Rieckhoff, founder and executive director of Iraq and Afghanistan Veterans of America.

Now that the "cakewalk" we were promised in 2003 is ending, we have to ask of the George W. Bush foreign policy team (many of whom Mitt Romney wants to hire) and in particular those in Congress who voted to authorize military force against Saddam Hussein in October 2002: Where's that "Mission Accomplished" feeling?

And where is our national security? How's that workin' out?

And to what kind of economy and job prospects are these soldiers returning—those who don't have to turn right around and go fight in Afghanistan? What "job creators" will hire them? While they were risking their lives amid hardships and dangers that most of us can hardly imagine, what has become of their One Nation Under God? Fortunately for some of them, Michelle Obama and Dr. Jill Biden are leading a Veterans Jobs initiative to press the private sector to commit to hiring 100,000 veterans and their spouses by the end of 2013. That's not very many jobs, but if it succeeds at all, it will help.

The Freedom and the Damage Done

Regrettably, even though it has been announced that some 40,000 troops like Stratego game board pieces will be returned to home base for a while, and despite the claims of a White House in reelection mode, we and many others do not see The War as ending. Iraq is, or was, only one theater—a particularly misguided, costly, and tragic one—in the larger War on Terror that has in effect already expanded into Pakistan and—hey, why not?—threatens Iran ("Tensions Flare As G.I.s Take Fire Out of Pakistan" and "Iran Reacts to Pressure from America," *New York Times*, Oct. 16, 2011). The United States is not moving from its strategic positions in the Middle East and Central Asia. And the financial costs to the United States, which may reach $3 to 5 trillion, are still being paid, and will paid for decades to come.

Indeed, beyond the financial cost, the damage done to the American economy, the psychic harm to our citizens, both combatant and noncombatant, and to the nation's culture and political system, are incalculable. If you close your eyes and listen with your heart in the way a psychic or a shaman is able to listen, you might hear a great howl of agony resounding from the nation's soul, a scream or roar as of a wounded giant that shakes the forests and mountainsides and echoes down the skyscraper canyons of Wall Street, bouncing off the concentric rings of the Pentagon, from all the needless pain inflicted, from the death groans of shattered, burned, eviscerated soldiers who will never come back, and those who are damaged for life, inside and out, in the veterans' hospitals. And though we turn our iPods or TVs up to full blast, the roars and screams of pain could not be drowned out. If, that is, we could hear them at all. That we cannot hear the howls and cries doesn't mean they're not there to be heard.

And then, even harder for us to imagine, is all the pain and destruction suffered by the people of Iraq, the bereft families of the more than 100,000 killed; the massive destabilization of political systems and relations in the Middle East; and the shattering of the ancient social systems, culture, and archaeological heritage, all symbolized by the looting of the National Museum and the torching of books and Korans in the National Library in Baghdad ("stuff happens," shrugged Donald Rumsfeld), plus the damage to the archaeological heritage in Nineveh, Ur, Babylon, and other sites of irreplaceable relics of the cradle of human civilization around the Tigris and Euphrates with an archaeological record going back 7,000 years that includes the cultures of the Sumerians, Akkadians, Babylonians, Assyrians, Chaldeans, Persians, Greeks, Romans, Parthians, Sassanids, and Muslims. (See Chalmers Johnson, "The Smash of Civilizations," and Frank Rich, "And Now: 'Operation Iraqi Looting.'")

A Post-Iraq Presence to Protect Persian Gulf from "Outside Interference"

A week after the president's announcement of the troop withdrawal, *The New York Times* (Oct. 30) reports that the Obama administration "plans to bolster the American military presence in the Persian Gulf. . . . That repositioning could include new combat forces in Kuwait able to respond to a collapse of security in Iraq or a military confrontation with Iran." The plans, says the *Times*, have been under discussion for months. At least.

"Back to the future." Maj. Gen. Karl R. Horst, Central Command's chief of staff "said the command was focusing on smaller but highly capable deployments and training partnerships with regional militaries. 'We are kind of thinking of going back to the way it was before we had a "boots on the ground" presence,' General Horst said. 'I think it is healthy. I think it is efficient. I think it is practical.' "

> *We will have a robust continuing presence throughout the region, which is proof of our ongoing commitment to Iraq and to the future of that region, which holds such promise and should be freed from outside interference to continue on a pathway to democracy.*
>
> **Secretary of State Hillary Rodham Clinton**

"Outside interference"? Might that refer to neighboring Iran? And the United States is, what, local?

Since the American invasion of Iraq in 2003, Iran's influence in the region has grown while Iraq, once a counter-balancing power, was crushed by Operation Iraqi Freedom. (Nice work, neocons.) Sunni Muslims, including Saddam Hussein and most of the Ba'ath Party he led, were a minority in Iraq but ran the government. Now they are out of power there, as they are in Afghanistan, and 90% majority Shiite Iran has benefited from the American invasions on both its eastern and western borders. The "war on terror" thus far has only strengthened Iran, which has a larger economy than Saudi Arabia or Egypt.

But the United States has plans for Iran and the region generally.

Juan Cole, whose blog *Informed Comment* is indispensable for understanding the U.S. role in the Middle East, writes in "US Out of Iraq, But Peace Remains Elusive" (Oct. 22, 2011):

> The US is entering an age of perpetual drone wars. The US is hitting targets in Yemen and the tribal belt in Pakistan. . . . The US is also arming Israel to the teeth and stoking an arms race in the Middle East. . . .
>
> US sanctions on Iran are becoming so severe as to constitute a blockade, which in international law [is] an act of war. The war party in the US is salivating for that war with Tehran, which is halfway begun as we speak, and it is freely acknowledged as a goal by most Republican presidential candidates.

Robert Dreyfuss reports in *The Nation* that from the president, secretary of state, and defense secretary on down, "U.S. officials are unanimous in declaring that they intend to go back to the negotiating table to make sure that the United States can send some military trainers and equipment specialists to Iraq in 2012, to help Iraq learn how to use the high-tech weapons Washington hopes to sell to Iraq in the future."

Secretary of State Hillary Clinton had a blunt message for Iran:

> Iran would be badly miscalculating if they did not look at the entire region and all of our presence in many countries in the region, both in bases [and] in training, with NATO allies, like Turkey.

Defense Secretary Leon Panetta—or is he still CIA director?—added for Iran's consideration the fact that the U.S. has normal, friendly (i.e., arms sales and military training) relationships with many nations in the Persian Gulf region:

> . . . when we talk about normal relationships in that part of the world, we have a number of them in the region, and they vary in number. For example, in Bahrain I think, you know, we've got

almost 5,000 troops that we have in Bahrain. We've got . . .
almost 3,000 in the UAE [United Arab Emirates] and about
7,500 in Qatar.

Since at least this summer Panetta, who became SecDef July 1, 2011, has also been warning Iran not to interfere with Iraq, and has been blaming the Iranians for the rise in violence in Iraq. On a visit to Iraq in early July, he said the U.S. is "very concerned about Iran and the weapons they are providing to extremists here in Iraq." More recently (Oct. 11), the U.S. is accusing Iran (accurately, it sounds like) of plotting the assassination of the Saudi ambassador to the United States, Adel al-Jubeir. Steve Clemons of *The Washington Note* blog, a sober, reliable source who is well plugged in to foreign affairs in Washington and not prone to exaggeration, writes, "This is a serious situation—and this kind of assassination is the sort that could lead to an unexpected cascade of events that could draw the U.S. and other powers into a consequential conflagration in the Middle East."

The New Hundred Years' War Is Still Young

Regarding the departure of U.S. forces from Iraq, we would like to hear a similar announcement about the 100,000+ troops and contractors in Afghanistan, where the U.S. has been at war since October 2001. But even if massive numbers of troops are one day pulled out of that quagmire, the U.S. presence from the Persian Gulf to Central Asia will remain, for geostrategic reasons—as a bulwark against expansion by China or Russia or both toward the oil and natural gas reserves in Central Asia. Burgeoning India, too, needs fuel. The War on Terror is a Hundred Years' war, at least—if the U.S. can sustain it that long.

Readers of this blog know that we have been opposed to war on Iraq since the very beginning—before the beginning. We joined hundreds of thousands of anti-war protesters in marches in New York City and Washington in 2003, 2004, 2005 . . . and as recently as this month, where many signs at the Occupy Wall Street march called for an end to the wars, and all the war spending, so that, at long last, after so many billions (mis)spent, national security can begin here at home through reinvestment in jobs programs, social services, infrastructure, etc. But that use of the federal treasury does not seem to be on the agenda.

The national treasury—*individual* taxpayers' dollars, that is, while corporations evade taxation to an unpatriotic extent—will continue to be redirected away from investment on Americans' education, housing, health care, infrastructure. The U.S. armed forces will continue to serve as bodyguards for the interests of U.S.-based multinational corporations such as ConocoPhillips and ExxonMobil (which, like many other American corporations, do not pay taxes to the U.S. Treasury).

This is how the future looks from here. The citizens of the United States are war-weary, exhausted by economic anxiety, turned off by toxic bickering between the two major political parties—paralyzed, impotent, and unresponsive to people's needs—and have little confidence in their own government or economy ("New Poll Finds a Deep Distrust of Government").

Is it any wonder, then, that Occupy Wall Street / 99 Percent protests have sprung up all over the nation, and that related protests have taken place in over 900 cities on four continents? "Almost half of the public thinks the sentiment at the root of the Occupy movement generally reflects the views of most Americans," according to a new *New York Times*/CBS poll, which found "Americans' distrust of government at its highest level ever." Pollsters found that "89 percent of Americans say they distrust government to do the right thing, . . . 74 percent say the country is on the wrong track and 84 percent disapprove of Congress."

> *Everything is for the wealthy. This used to be a lovely country,*
> *but everything is sliding.*
> **Jo Waters, 87, of Pleasanton, Calif.**

The war is ending (so to speak) and everyone is too tired, or too skeptical, to celebrate. Or too busy, working too many jobs, trying to make ends meet, or too busy looking for a job, or too tired of finding no job. Or more interested in protesting economic inequality by taking to the streets, the public parks. The Occupy movement is not going to be dispersed, not by the Oakland police or any other force. Maybe the troops coming home can be rehired as cops (not if Republicans can help it) or as private security forces to protect the banks. We expect, however, that more of the veterans are likely to be in the streets and parks with their fellow 99 percenters—such as (USMC) Sgt. Shamar Thomas of New York, the big, angry Iraq war vet who yelled at about

30 uniformed cops near Times Square for the NYPD's having used excessive force on unarmed Occupy Wall Street protesters toward the end of the Oct. 5 march from City Hall to Zuccotti Park.

> *It doesn't make you tough to hurt these people! . . . Leave these people alone! They're U.S. citizens. Stop hurting these people! . . . This is not a war zone! . . . These cops are hurting people that I fought to protect.*

TAGS: Afghanistan War, Central Asia, corporate tax evasion, Iraq War, John McCain, Juan Cole, military-industrial complex, Occupy Wall Street, oil and war, Paul Rieckhoff, Steve Clemons, War on Terror

http://www.leveesnotwar.org/as-end-of-iraq-war-is-announced-u-s-digs-in-warns -iran/

As Combat Troops Leave Iraq, Where's Our National Security?

AUG. 19, 2010—The last combat troops have left Iraq, as a convoy of the 4th Stryker Brigade rumbled in the wee hours of August 19, 2010, from Iraq toward U.S. bases in Kuwait. At the end of August, Operation Iraqi Freedom will end and 50,000 advisory and security troops will remain in Iraq until the end of 2011 for a new phase to be known as Operation New Dawn.

Michael Gordon of *The New York Times* reports here on how the U.S. State Department, with about 2,400 civilian employees protected by up to 7,000 private security guards, will continue the training of Iraqi police and assist with political stabilization and other functions—including counterterrorism—in an effort to help Iraq rebuild without the presence of U.S. combat troops. The 2,400 civilian State Department employees will work at the Baghdad embassy and regional outposts in Mosul, Kirkuk, and at consulates in Erbil and Basra. Gordon writes:

> The startup cost of building and sustaining two embassy branch offices—one in Kirkuk and the other in Mosul—and of hiring security contractors, buying new equipment and setting up two consulates in Basra and Erbil is about $1 billion. It will cost another $500 million or so to make the two consulates permanent. And getting the police training program under way will cost about $800 million.

So, the combat forces are withdrawing, returning to the Homeland. Some soldiers will get to rejoin their families after a long time away—we wish them well—and others will have to redeploy in maybe six months to Afghanistan, where Obama's surge continues.

Where's That "Mission Accomplished" Feeling?

It is a good thing that the combat forces are withdrawing from Iraq, but why don't we feel any pleasure or pride? What has been accomplished, aside from doubling the price of a gallon of gas and making Iran the main power in the region? The soldiers themselves surely feel some pride and relief, and after all their hard work and the dangers they've passed, they deserve more than a good cigar. But what have we gained? The United States is immeasurably poorer, more weak and divided than when this war began—economically, socially, politically. As of this writing, 4,415 American soldiers are dead; tens of thousands are wounded, many critically, missing limbs, and some with unimaginable brain and neurological injuries, and alarming numbers have committed suicide: 27 in July alone, 32 in June. (In addition to all the Iraqi dead—estimates are around 100,000—there have been 179 British dead and 139 from other Coalition nations.) And then there's the psychological, soul damage the soldiers suffer, and the broken marriages, the frayed family relationships, the children who have grown from infants to eight- and ten-year-olds hardly even knowing their fathers or mothers who have been away on multiple deployments and come home virtually strangers with scant job prospects here in the Homeland. But Saddam Hussein is no longer in power, so maybe it's all worthwhile.

Meanwhile the war in Afghanistan—the one that began in October 2001—goes on and on, with 2,005 dead and casualties increasing in frequency, while General David Petraeus with tacit administration backing begins a P.R. campaign to tamp down expectations of withdrawal from that war despite the president's promise—or strong suggestion, sort of—that U.S. forces would begin pulling out of that interminable war by July 2011. (At the same time, Aug. 17, professional alarmist and provocateur John Bolton—whom George W. Bush saw fit to appoint as U.N. ambassador—warns ominously that Israel has "only eight days left" in which to strike Iran's Bushehr nuclear facility to stop Iran from acquiring the capacity to build a nuclear plant. This neocon campaign will go on . . .)

Frayed Flags

The wars since 2001 have cost over $1 trillion, with over $740 billion spent in Iraq and $325 billion in Afghanistan. Nobel Prize–winning economist Joseph

Stiglitz has estimated that the Iraq War will ultimately cost $3 trillion when all health care costs over the soldiers' lifetimes are factored in. The continuing cost of the State Department's mission in Iraq was hinted at above, but how much more will the U.S. spend on that nation? How many more lives will be lost, and how much more national wealth that could be spent on jobs programs for the millions of unemployed and the rebuilding of America's crumbling infrastructure?

One positive sign of increasing congressional unwillingness to continue funding the wars was seen in the recent vote on $59 billion in appropriations for the Afghanistan and Iraq wars. On July 27 the House of Representatives voted 308 to 114 (148 Democrats and 160 Republicans in favor, and 102 Democrats and 12 Republicans opposing). Last year the "no" votes came from 32 Democrats, so opposition has increased by 82 votes and is becoming bipartisan. Please go to our POLITICAL ACTION page and contact your members of Congress to urge them to wind down the wars and appropriate your tax dollars for use here at home for the public good. National security begins at home.

We welcome the troops back from Iraq, and hope that most of them will get to stay home and build good relations with their families and communities. We hope the U.S. government—through a functioning, better-funded Veterans Administration—will give them the health care and psychological counseling they need and deserve. And we hope a good many of them will join us in the anti-war movement to bring the Afghanistan war to a close so we can begin to rebuild our own war-torn land. As President Obama said at West Point last December when he announced the 30,000-troop increase, "we must rebuild our strength here at home . . . . the nation that I'm most interested in building is our own."

Let's hold him to that pledge—and his promise to begin withdrawing troops from Afghanistan in mid-2011.

TAGS: $3 trillion war, Afghanistan, Iraq War, National Security Begins at Home
http://www.leveesnotwar.org/as-combat-troops-leave-iraq-where's-our-national
-security/

Ten Years of U.S. War in Afghanistan

While post-9/11 veterans are more supportive than the general public, just one-third (34%) say that, given the costs and benefits to the U.S., the wars in Afghanistan and Iraq have both been worth fighting.

Pew Research Center, "War and Sacrifice in the Post-9/11 Era," Oct. 2011

OCT. 8, 2011—Is it a rule of the age of the War on Terror(ism) that no armed conflict the U.S. enters ever really ends? Is that what the Defense Department was signaling when it came up with the name Operation Enduring Freedom?

With all the attention this week to Occupy Wall Street and, sadly, the death of Steve Jobs, it was almost possible to not notice the tenth anniversary of the U.S. war in Afghanistan that began on Oct. 7, 2001. But, as we said this past September 11, we're not forgetting.

This war has been the longest in American history for over a year: the milestone was passed in June 2010 when the war entered its 104th month. U.S. involvement in Vietnam is reckoned at 103 months long. U.S. participation in World War II was only 44 months. The Afghan war is now in its 120th month, and the Obama White House and Pentagon see our forces there well into 2014 and beyond.

A majority of the American public has long said this war is not worth fighting. A Pew Research Center poll in June found 56% of Americans—an all-time high—want the U.S. to pull troops out of Afghanistan as soon as possible. Veterans are usually the segment of the population most supportive of military engagements, but a new Pew Research poll, "War and Sacrifice in the Post-9/11 Era," finds that only one-third of post-9/11 veterans say that, "given the costs and benefits to the U.S., the wars in Afghanistan and Iraq have both been worth fighting." *Only one-third of veterans.*

And what is Congress doing? What are we telling Congress to do? How do we get their attention? Do they ever read their mail?

The White House issued a quiet statement (no graphic pictures of burned or bloody shredded bodies of nineteen-year-olds) noting the sacrifice of some 1,700 American service members in this war, to "honor the memory of the nearly 1,800 American patriots, and many coalition and Afghan partners, who have made the ultimate sacrifice in Afghanistan for our shared security and freedom." The statement hits all the right notes, if you believe in that kind of thing.

End It Now. Quietly. Steadily.
Reinforce the Diplomatic Corps.

What we believe is that the war in Afghanistan is not one that can ever be won. The best that can be done is not through arms but through quiet steady accelerated withdrawal of armed forces and the intelligent application of diplomacy along the lines the late envoy Richard Holbrooke was attempting. Try to forge agreements or alliances between the numerous tribes and ethnic groups and factions within them to provide for their living together with as little violence as possible. Accept the necessity of some diplomatic presence and some foreign aid, with as little interference as possible from neighboring interests (Pakistani, Iranian).

A precise prescription for a diplomatic resolution is beyond our pay grade, to put it lightly—and for all we know it may not be possible even for a diplomat / peace broker of Richard Holbrooke's or George Mitchell's capabilities—but we do know the costly military operation is unaffordable for a nation as cash-strapped by under-taxation of its wealthy individuals and effectively non-taxation of its corporations. (Far from the traditional approach of raising taxes during wartime, the Republican-driven U.S. government has been slashing revenues since the Afghan war began.) The United States has already spent some $462 billion in the Afghanistan war, more than 1,700 soldiers have died, and over 14,000 have been wounded in action. The war is approaching a half trillion dollars—a figure that would surely be higher had not the Bush administration siphoned off a great proportion of U.S. "resources" toward the invasion of Iraq from 2003 until they were redirected back to Afghanistan by

President Obama in 2009. The war in Iraq has cost $800 billion by the time you read this. And already the Iraq war alone is estimated by Nobel Prize–winning economist Joseph Stiglitz to eventually cost the U.S. $3 trillion.

The present Obama plan announced in June is to wind down the Afghan war by 2014, when the U.S. role will change "from combat to support." But what does "wind down" mean? How many soldiers will still be stationed there? How many are presently in Iraq? How many military contractors will still be in Afghanistan and Iraq by 2014, and at what cost? The projected reductions will only bring us back to the roughly 65,000 troops that were stationed in Afghanistan when Obama announced the surge. As we pointed out in June,

> we still have 85,000 active duty military personnel stationed in Iraq at a monthly cost of about $4 billion. For that matter, U.S. military personnel number some 50,000 in Germany, 35,000 in Japan, and 25,000 in South Korea. How long does the government intend to keep this going? ("Obama's Troop Drawdown Is Little, Late, But a Start," 6/23/11)

Everything But War Is on the Chopping Block, Including "the Blessings of Freedom and Security"?

Every day members of Congress, most often Republicans but often Democrats too, and allegedly serious economists and members of conservative think tanks and policy groups, say with a straight face that the budget deficit is so deep and threatening to the nation's well-being that Washington can no longer continue its "out-of-control spending." Therefore social benefits such as Social Security and Medicare, unemployment benefits and health care and education programs must all be "on the table," by which they mean the chopping block.

The Obama statement concludes with these fine-sounding words: "As we reflect on ten years of war and look ahead to a future of peace, Michelle and I call upon all Americans to show our gratitude and support for our fellow citizens who risk their lives so that we can enjoy the blessings of freedom and security."

The "blessings of freedom and security"? Increasingly little of the American population even believes in such anymore. Look at the Occupy Wall Street signs—they're in cities all over America now. Businesses are not hiring, and the federal government is paralyzed by deliberate partisan gridlock. They tell us there is no money to invest in this country anymore. We must first draw down the deficit—the deficit caused by the tax breaks to the wealthy that cannot be ended and by the endless wars. This is a lie, and we and thousands of others are trying to change the discourse from one of scarcity to one of possibility if only the nation changes its priorities. Speaking to Rachel Maddow, author Naomi Klein praises the "organizing genius" of the "We Are the 99%" slogan and taking the protest to Wall Street, "the source of maximal abundance," to put the lie to the discourse of scarcity. "It's not a scarcity problem," she says, "it's a distribution problem."

So, with at least 15 million unemployed, countless millions under-employed, and millions more having given up even looking for a job, how's that "blessings of freedom and security" thing workin' out for us? Think we can do better?

Want contact info for representatives in Washington, D.C.? Let 'em hear from you. Run for office. Take to the streets. Or all of the above.

TAGS: Afghanistan war, cost of war, diplomacy, Iraq War, Occupy Wall Street, Operation Enduring Freedom, Richard Holbrooke, War on Terrorism
http://www.leveesnotwar.org/ten-years-of-u-s-war-in-afghanistan/

In September 2010, Levees Not War raised the question of whether Hurricane Katrina was a more significant catastrophe than 9/11, more emblematic in terms of chronic ills afflicting the United States. Now the question is raised whether the nation faces internal political and economic dangers more pernicious and destructive than Osama bin Laden, lethal as he was, ever posed.

Mission Accomplished: Bin Laden Is Dead. Now Focus on Threats Closer to Home.

MAY 2, 2011—Well, this ought to change the subject from royal weddings and presidential birth certificates for a few days.

It is a good thing that Osama bin Laden is dead, and good that it was U.S. forces that killed him. There is a certain (long-delayed) revenge satisfied in that, shared pretty much equally across the nation. It is also good for this president—politically and for his standing within the military and foreign policy establishment—that his promise to bring bin Laden to justice—to death, that is—has been fulfilled.

Much will be said and written by better-informed and deeper-thinking authorities, but on this important occasion we wanted in our own modest way to offer a few observations we think worth keeping in mind.

First, Americans must not gloat about the killing of this enemy. It's done. It's good that it's done. Any loud grandstanding or other exploitation of this event for political or commercial self-promotion should be avoided. It should not be an occasion to further insult Arabs and Muslims. There was and is an enormous sense of injustice, impoverishment, and wounded pride among Muslims that bin Laden was able to exploit for his own purposes against the West, the U.S. in particular. No good will come from any further demonization of Arabs and Muslims. Instead we should hope that the independence movements in the Middle East will succeed, as peacefully as possible, in the Egyptian model.

Next, we hope that this "mission accomplished" will energize the antiwar movement (such as it is) and hasten the de-escalation of the wars in Afghanistan/Pakistan and in Iraq and Libya. Much of the justification—the figurehead or "poster child" of the terrorist enemy—is now removed. Can we get back to rebuilding the United States?

No, of course not. The war machine, we fear, will grind on. (Defense appropriations are higher than they ever were during the Cold War against the Soviet Union.) There will be calls from the likes of John McCain and other neocon "security" promoters to identify new threats that call for ever-expanding aggressions overseas. Verily, with only a few exceptions, we tend to see these forces as greater threats to peace and national security than anything outside our borders.

The personal attacks on this president and demonization of new enemies will go on. We expect that within days—on Fox News it's probably already under way—fresh insults and unfounded accusations and outright foolishness will prevail. Sometimes it seems the United States—or the far right, so-called conservative dimension of the national psyche—cannot exist without an enemy, whether in the form of despised immigrants, anarchists, communists, socialists, minorities, etc.

Pardon our pessimism, but aside from the brave working people's resistance movement in Wisconsin and elsewhere in the Midwest where labor rights are under assault, there's been little to inspire confidence in improvements. The long-awaited killing of bin Laden is not going to change the agenda of Grover Norquist, Karl Rove, the Koch brothers, FreedomWorks, or Americans for Prosperity—nor will it infuse fresh adrenaline into the hearts of Democrats. The far-right corporatists of the Republican party will continue slashing away at the social safety net, insulting workers and the unemployed alike. And, very likely—unless the public forcefully demands that they stand up and fight—the timid centrist-corporatists known as congressional Democrats will continue to allow the savaging of Medicare, Social Security, and any semblance of health care reform and financial regulation. (We use the word "corporatist" because the radical extremists running amok in Washington and statehouses across the nation have nothing to do with conserving.)

What About the "Inside Job" Enemies?

(No, this does not refer to 9/11 as an inside job.)

One last thought: We recall a scene from a certain well-publicized film released in 2004 [*Fahrenheit 9/11*] in which a man describes to the film's narrator his desolate, eviscerated neighborhood in a former industrial town in the Midwest. Street after street of abandoned homes, shut-down restaurants and barbershops, broken windows, torn screens flapping in the wind. There's no one around. The man says, "You want to talk about terrorism? Osama bin Laden didn't do this to us."

Every year, more Americans die from lack of access to doctors and medication than died on September 11, 2001. In 2010, New Jersey governor Chris Christie killed 6,000 direct jobs in a swipe when he pulled his state out of the Trans-Hudson Passenger Rail Tunnel (ARC) project designed to link New Jersey and Manhattan—6,000 jobs when unemployment among contracting workers is already at 30% (see "Public Works in a Time of Job-Killing Scrooges," Part II). Other assaults on the American people are going on all the time, day by day, under the guise of "balancing budgets" and "reforming a broken system" and other lies and euphemisms. We could also point to the catastrophic damage done worldwide by the 2008 financial meltdown ignited by greedy and reckless insiders.

Now, we're not claiming that Christie's killing of contracting workers' jobs is exactly equivalent to the horrible death by burning and crushing of 3,000 lives in the World Trade Center and Pentagon. But we do definitely assert that Osama bin Laden was only one enemy. Focusing on this one "evildoer" has distracted our national attention for too long. Who has been "brought to justice" for the 2008 financial crisis? Who has paid a price for the 1999 act of Congress that repealed the Glass-Steagall Act and deregulated the banking industry? (See Robert Scheer, *The Great American Stickup*.) Who has been brought to justice for BP's infamous "Earth Day" blowout and three-month pollution of the Gulf of Mexico by the Macondo well, or for the Department of the Interior and Minerals Management Service's lax oversight of offshore drilling?

There are other enemies among us who seek to dismantle some of the best parts of America: the social services that protect the very young, the elderly, the sick and the very poor. Rather than make up for the revenue deficit caused by undertaxation of the wealthy and corporations, elected officials are seeking to shut down the agencies that protect the public from tainted food, unsafe working conditions, from mechanical failures on airplanes. These and a million other aspects of civilized living conditions are under assault by highly paid lobbyists and corporatist politicians, mainly of one major party but with "bipartisan" assistance from the other. (Ed. Note: See Hedrick Smith, *Who Stole the American Dream?* [2013])

Osama bin Laden did terrible damage and it's good he's gone, but pernicious threats remain—often with much lighter skin clothed in $1,000 suits and covered by premium health insurance funded by the taxpayers. And while they are well paid on a regular basis from the public treasury they are voting to cut unemployment benefits, insulting the jobless as lazy, scheming to eviscerate the social safety net, to shut down schools, to let bridges crumble and levees erode—whatever it takes to cut budgets without letting a single tax increase even be proposed, much less voted upon and enacted. All of this after pushing like hell to extend a high-end tax cut that will add $700 billion to the deficit over the next 10 years, and pushing for a war of choice that will ultimately cost the U.S. around $3 trillion.

Well, these are a few of our thoughts on this day after the killing of Osama bin Laden. See why we're not much relieved by the elimination of this one particular evildoer? We were not among the crowds shouting "U.S.A.! U.S.A.!", though we can understand why many thousands were.

As ever, there's a bit more work to be done. And we're not talking about second amendment remedies, but by concerted democratic action—like the kind admirably acted out in Cairo and in Madison. We believe in the people. And we hold this truth to be self-evident: national security begins at home.

And finally . . . just for fun,

Imagine a *Democratic* President Getting Away with Saying This:

I don't know where bin Laden is. I have no idea and really don't care. It's not that important. It's not our priority.
George W. Bush, March 13, 2002

*On President Obama's decision in December 2009 to send 30,000 more
troops to Afghanistan.*

Deeper into Afghanistan:
360 Degrees of Damnation

*We must rebuild our strength here at home . . . . The nation that
I'm most interested in building is our own.*
President Obama, Dec. 1, 2009

DEC. 10, 2009—We wanted to take time to try to make sense of President
Obama's speech at West Point last week in which he announced his decision to increase U.S. troop levels in Afghanistan by 30,000 over the next six
months. We pray he knows what he's doing. We can only imagine the risks
and variables he has been weighing. Because he is a peaceful man by nature
(the Nobel may have been awarded at the wrong time but it was not given to
the wrong man), we are inclined to give him the benefit of the doubt. And
yet, even though he knows more than we're privy to, we are still skeptical.
Our favorite lines in the address were those quoted above. Perhaps the most
painful part of the speech is its overall contrast with and cancellation of those
fine-sounding sentiments.

A Surge for Afghanistan

There are truly no good options—all are fraught with unacceptable consequences: 360 degrees of damnation—and yet we feel the president has made a
tragically wrong decision. Even though we were impressed by his methodical
and deliberative approach to a maddeningly complex issue, and even though it
is theoretically possible that with unlimited time, money, and the blessings of
fortune this new "Way Forward" can work, we do not believe it will. There is
too much reliance on military force, too many moving parts that have to come
together just so. (There is a saying that whenever you have two Afghans, you
have at least three factions.) Of course the generals say they can do it—give 'em

enough troops and they'll promise you anything. Hendrik Hertzberg writes in *The New Yorker* that Obama would have faced "a probable Pentagon revolt" had he chosen to withdraw starting now, and if such a decision had been followed by a large-scale terrorist attack he would face "savage, politically lethal scapegoating." Very likely. This is the situation we're in. Nicholas Kristof observes in his *New York Times* column that amid all the president's consultations of experts, one important set of players not consulted were the tribal elders of Afghanistan. Without their cooperation, nothing will work.

After all the president's careful deliberation and his public explanation, we remain unconvinced. We still want U.S. forces to withdraw from Afghanistan (as well as from Iraq) as soon as possible, leaving only a small counterinsurgency force, a well-staffed diplomatic corps (the Foreign Service), Peace Corps–like builders of schools, hospitals and other constructive works (Kristof says that "for the cost of deploying one soldier for one year [estimated at about $1 million], it is possible to build about 20 schools"). And yes, the U.S. should (and of course would) retain the capability for drone attacks as used in Somalia and other places inhabited by al Qaeda. We also would like to know what Vice President Biden and National Security Adviser General Jim Jones recommended (General Jones said in October that at a maximum there are probably fewer than 100 al Qaeda operatives in Afghanistan); both were reported to have been uneasy with the idea of a large troop increase, as was U.S. ambassador to Afghanistan Karl Eikenberry.

A 35-Year-Long Civil War

One of the principal reasons why we lack confidence in the Obama administration's decision is that the U.S. government has failed to level with the American public regarding the nature of the conflict in Afghanistan and what would constitute "success" (much less "victory"). For one thing, they're not acknowledging that the U.S. is mired in a civil war that has been going on for some 35 years—and, as in Vietnam, we're backing a side that lacks popular support. The U.S. has been involved in this conflict since 1979 at least, covertly supplying arms to the mujahedin "freedom fighters" (remember *Charlie Wilson's War*?) and, along with Saudi Arabia, encouraging the spread of Islamic fundamentalism as a bulwark against Soviet communism. How well has that worked out?

> *. . . the reality, secretly guarded until now, is . . . [that] . . . it was July 3, 1979 that President Carter signed the first directive for secret aid to the opponents of the pro-Soviet regime in Kabul. . . . That secret operation was an excellent idea. It had the effect of drawing the Russians into the Afghan trap. . . . The day that the Soviets officially crossed the border, I wrote to President Carter. We now have the opportunity of giving to the USSR its Vietnam war. Indeed, for almost 10 years, Moscow had to carry on a war unsupportable by the government, a conflict that brought about the demoralization and finally the breakup of the Soviet empire. . . . What is most important to the history of the world? The Taliban or the collapse of the Soviet empire? Some stirred-up Moslems or the liberation of Central Europe and the end of the cold war?* —Zbigniew Brzezinski, national security adviser to President Jimmy Carter; interview with *Le Nouvel Observateur*, Jan. 15–21, 1998

Afghanistan's civil war is a conflict between secular, modern, urban elites (such as Hamid Karzai, a former Unocal consultant, and his cronies) and the rural, traditional and religious Pashtun tribes. The so-called Taliban and insurgents, many of them, are not ideologically opposed to the West but simply want the foreign troops to leave their land. (Former Foreign Service officer Matthew Hoh calls them "taliban with a small t.") The murky, multi-layered role of Pakistan is another complicating factor that also was not addressed candidly in the president's speech—and likely could not have been without causing a diplomatic row.

We definitely do not relish the prospect of a nuclear-armed Pakistan being overtaken by al Qaeda or other extremists—of course, no one does—but why are China and Russia not actively involved in making sure this does not happen? Just as Russia has reasons to cooperate with the U.S. in trying to dissuade Iran from developing nuclear weapons, so it should be actively concerned about Pakistan's arsenal. And China helped Pakistan develop its nuclear program—why are they not worried? Is there something China knows that we don't? Are these two powerful nations letting the U.S. do the policing for them? Is this part of what the U.S.'s indebtedness to China entails? How deep a hole are we really in? Those who know aren't saying.

A further dismaying aspect of Obama's decision is the almost immediate reversal of the president's statement that the new strategy should allow the U.S. to hand over responsibility to Afghan forces and to begin withdrawing our troops by July 2011: within days his Defense and State department officials were tamping down expectations of early departure. And Hamid Karzai has said that Afghanistan will need U.S. help for the next 15 to 20 years. This depressing prospect has to be even more anguishing for the soldiers and their families, especially for those who are facing their third, fourth, or fifth deployments. Ready to get your PTSD on, soldier?

Read Steve Coll and Listen to Matthew Hoh

Two of the most trustworthy authorities we've found on Afghanistan are former Marine captain Matthew Hoh, who resigned from the Foreign Service in Afghanistan in September, and Steve Coll, author of *Ghost Wars: The Secret History of the CIA, Afghanistan, and Bin Laden, from the Soviet Invasion to September 10, 2001* (a book Obama is said to have read) and a writer for *The New Yorker*. In September Matthew Hoh wrote a powerful four-page letter of resignation from the Foreign Service, for which he had been a senior civilian representative in Zabul Province, lamenting, "I fail to see the value or the worth in continued U.S. casualties or expenditures of resources in support of the Afghan government in what is, truly, a 35-year-old civil war. . . . Like the Soviets [in the 1980s], we continue to secure and bolster a failing state, while encouraging an ideology and system of government unknown and unwanted by its people."

In his *New Yorker* blog published the day after the president's West Point speech, Steve Coll wrote:

> One problem was that the line of Obama's argument suffered
> from its embedded and deliberately constructed contradictions.
> We are going in but we are going out; we are fighting to defend
> a vital national interest, but only to the extent that we can afford
> to do so. We must prevail in this struggle, but we must recognize
> that we have other challenges that are perhaps more important.

Speaking of being able to "afford to do so": We acknowledge the potential risks of not "getting it right" in the war in Afghanistan and Pakistan—we were in Manhattan on September 11—but we also see the damage done here at home by long neglect and cost-cutting and underfunding. (Funding for the flood protection system around New Orleans, for example, was cut by the Bush administration and shifted instead to the wars in Afghanistan and Iraq.) It seems deficit spending is acceptable for war but never for health reform or jobs programs. The additional $30 billion increase in military spending that the president projects for the Afghan war next year could pay for some mighty fine flood protection and coastal restoration for southern Louisiana. The American Society of Civil Engineers gives the United States a D in infrastructure and calls for a five-year investment of some $2.2 trillion to restore the structural integrity of the nation's roads, bridges, levees, schools, transit systems, etc.

Even if the president's careful deliberations resulted in a master plan for winning the Afghan/Pakistan war—by 2011 or any other year—we still would say no, it's not worth it. By the time we win this war, or extricate what's left of our military, there will be nothing left to live in here in the United States that they are supposedly fighting to protect.

What We Are *For*

So, to repeat: What we do want in Afghanistan and Pakistan is continued diplomacy and aid based upon consultation with local tribal elders—after all the time our officials have been in Afghanistan, there are some trusting relationships—and maintenance of ability to strike at confirmed al Qaeda targets if we know they are plotting or posing a clear and present danger to the U.S. mainland. We also hope the wise elders in Washington will work diplomatically with Iran as well as Pakistan and other neighbors of Afghanistan to resolve long-term strategic issues. Russia and China should be in the loop, as well; these closer neighbors have a clear interest in regional stability.

What we want for America is a wiser, more sustainable level of public spending that benefits the people who pay the taxes. We want our fellow citizens in great numbers to realize, before it is too late, that this nation simply cannot afford to prolong this war. Opinion polls currently suggest that such understanding is not imminent. After eight years in Afghanistan, and more than six years in Iraq, and approaching $3 trillion in costs, and with soldiers committing suicide and killing one another and civilians here at home—what columnist Bob Herbert calls "Stress Beyond Belief"—how much more can this nation take? Is it time to take Congressman Charles B. Rangel up on his idea for reinstating the draft? Maybe it is as logical an idea under Obama as it was under Bush. And is it time, finally, to raise taxes to pay for the wars, as the United States has always done until this decade, and as recommended by Senator Carl Levin, chairman of the Senate Armed Services Committee? These and other sacrifices also went unmentioned in the president's address.

These, then, are our thoughts on the president's decision. We would have made these arguments directly to the commander in chief, but, mysteriously, our invitation to participate in the president's strategy review sessions did not arrive in time.

In Honor of Veterans

In Flanders fields the poppies blow
Between the crosses, row on row . . .
"In Flanders Fields," by Lt. Col. John McCrae (1915)

A Salute to the Living and the Dead

NOV. 11, 2011—Today—the eleventh day of the eleventh month of the eleventh year—we pause to honor the veterans of wars, especially Americans in uniform since the Great War, World War I, whose ending at 11:00 a.m. on November 11, 1918—the eleventh hour of the eleventh day of the eleventh month—was commemorated one year later with the first Armistice Day (armistice = 'stopping hostilities', or, loosely, 'a farewell to arms'). Armistice Day became a national holiday in 1938, and was renamed as Veterans Day in 1954 to honor those who had served in all U.S. wars.

We also call upon the "job creators"—especially those in the uppermost One Percent—to hire veterans and pay them well. Hire them and give generously to their medical and mental care and rehabilitation.

Although *Levees Not War* opposes the wars of the War on Terror(ism), that does not mean we don't respect and honor the men and women who serve in the U.S. military. We know that this less-than-one-percent of the American population is being called upon—even in a nominally "all-volunteer army"—to undergo harsh, grueling, too often deadly conditions that we civilians can only imagine, if we dare.

Today we have joined Iraq and Afghanistan Veterans of America (civilian membership), and made a contribution to IAVA. We also contributed to Iraq Veterans Against the War in the name of Scott Olsen, the U.S. Marines veteran of the Iraq war who on Oct. 25 was struck in the head by a tear gas canister or smoke canister fired by an Oakland police officer during a crackdown on Occupy Oakland protesters. Suffering a fractured skull, Olsen was hospitalized in critical condition.

See our blogroll, under "Anti-War," for links to IAVA, IVAW, and other organizations that work for veterans and their families. If you can, please make a contribution today.

TAGS: Iraq and Afghanistan Veterans of America, Iraq Veterans Against the War, Occupy Oakland, Scott Olsen, Veterans Day
http://www.leveesnotwar.org/in-honor-of-veterans/

Jobs, Jobs . . . Senate Republicans Keep Vets Unemployed

This Congress let partisan bickering stand in the way of putting thousands of America's heroes back to work. Lowering veteran unemployment is something both parties should be able to agree on—even in an election year.

Paul Rieckhoff, Iraq and Afghanistan Veterans of America

Where is our honor? Where is our valor? Where is our sacrifice?

Senator Tom Coburn (R-OK), leading opposition to Veterans Jobs Corps Act

I care deeply about the veterans. I care deeply about housing and helping the veterans who have fought for their country.

Senator Rand Paul (R-KY), assisting the opposition

SEPT. 25, 2012—The next time you hear Republican politicians praising "our brave men and women in uniform," remember that *all but 5* G.O.P. senators voted No on the Veterans Jobs Corps Act of 2012. The bill failed, 58–40, on a procedural vote, just two votes short. This bipartisan bill would have provided $1 billion over five years to help up to 20,000 veterans find work in their communities. All Democrats voted for the bill. The Republicans who voted Aye are Lisa Murkowski (AK), Olympia Snowe and Susan Collins of Maine; Scott Brown (MA); and Dean Heller (NV). Two Republicans did not vote. (In the Obama years, 51 votes is no longer a majority. Because the G.O.P. filibusters all legislation, 60 votes are needed.) Now the Congress is on recess till after election day—the earliest pre-election vacay since 1960—and Republicans will be busy blaming Obama and the Democrats for the underperforming economy.

Now, in the federal budget, $1 billion is not a large amount, and, in our humble opinion, even as a down payment this would be a pathetically small investment when the unemployment rate of veterans is officially 10.9% (certainly higher in fact). Further, this money would have been "paid for": it would not have added to the federal debt because Senator Patty Murray (D-WA) ensured that funding would have come in part from Medicare providers and suppliers who are delinquent on their tax bills. Remember also that during the George W. Bush years, the enormous costs of the Iraq and Afghanistan wars were never part of the official budget of the United States, but were routinely allocated through "emergency supplementals." According to the National Priorities Project, costs of these two wars so far total $1.38 trillion (with Iraq at $807.4 and Afghanistan at $570.9 billion). But $1 billion for job training that would help 20,000 veterans, said Republican senator Tom Coburn, was a mere "political exercise" and a waste of time, as the House of Representatives would not pass it anyway.

According to the Iraq and Afghanistan Veterans of America:

> In addition to creating jobs for veterans as police officers, firefighters, first responders, and restorative conservationists, the Veterans Job Corps Act would have also extended the critical Transition Assistance Program (TAP). TAP provides employment, education and entrepreneurship advice for troops separating from the service, and to veterans and their spouses after they've left the military. The VJC would also require states to consider military training and experience in granting credentials and licensure for EMTs, nursing assistants and commercial driver's licenses.

A *New York Times* editorial in favor of the bill pointed out:

> The bill gives priority to those who served on or after 9/11, with good reason: the jobless rate for veterans of Iraq and Afghanistan hit 10.9 percent in August, compared with 8.1 percent nationally. This is a time of persistent homelessness and unemployment among veterans, and record suicides among veterans and active-duty service members, many of them

stressed by the burdens of two long wars. *It makes sense for the 99 percent of Americans to find new ways to pay their debt to the 1 percent who serve in uniform.* [LNW's emphasis]

To most people, Senator Murray's bill would seem like one decent way to do that. But not if you're one of those Republicans in Washington who thinks it's more important in an election year to deny Democrats a success or accomplishment of any kind.

For the last word here, let's listen to the occasionally candid and revealing Senate Minority Leader Mitch McConnell (R-KY), as he gives away the game just before the 2010 mid-term elections:

The single most important thing we [congressional Republicans] want to achieve is for President Obama to be a one-term president.

TAGS: budget deficit, Iraq and Afghanistan Veterans of America, Republican fiscal stewardship, unemployment, Veterans Jobs Corps Act of 2012
http://www.leveesnotwar.org/jobs-jobs-senate-republicans-keep-vets-unemployed/

Grinch Wins Plastic Turkey Award: Pentagon Demands Repayment of Disabled Vets' Signing Bonuses

NOV. 19, 2007—Remember the Commander's surprise Thanksgiving visit to Baghdad in 2003, when the perfectly Norman Rockwell turkey that he held on a platter turned out to be plastic (supplied by a contractor)? In the spirit of Thanksgiving, we propose a new use for that fake bird: As an award for bureaucratic idiocy + callous penny-pinching. (We thought Rumsfeld had left the Pentagon, but the following story makes us think the streamlining, privatizing CEO–SecDef is still in the bunker.)

Pittsburgh's KDKA reports that the Defense Department is demanding that thousands of disabled U.S. soldiers return parts of their signing bonuses because they are unable to serve out their commitments. They had to go and get blown up so bad the army couldn't patch them up well enough to push 'em back out on the streets of Baghdad as they do with other wounded soldiers. It is well known that the army has had to resort to signing bonuses of up to $30,000 to attract new soldiers to an increasingly unpopular war (though the army continues to fall short of its recruiting goals).

This latest twist is sure to make an impression on would-be recruits. Step right up . . .

Naturally, Republicans will blame the "obstructionist Democrats" for stiffing the troops by not passing the President's 2008 military budget request ($481 billion for DoD + $196 billion for Iraq+Afghanistan = $677 billion.)

Stinginess is business-as-usual for the administration's treatment of military personnel. In June 2003, about three months into Operation Iraqi Freedom, the Democratic staff of the House Appropriations Committee, reviewing Bush's 2004 budget, pointed out that he was cutting $1.5 billion from military housing and slashing $14.6 billion over 10 years in benefits paid through the Veterans Administration. The president's $674 billion tax cut of 2003—three-fifths of which went to the top 10% of taxpayers—neglected to extend a tax credit to nearly 200,000 low-income military personnel. The 2004 budget also cut $200 million from the program that helps fund public schools serving military bases, hitting especially hard the children of soldiers in Iraq. (And this was before the 2006 revelation of disgusting conditions at the Walter Reed Army Medical Center—squalor resulting from Bush Inc.'s privatizing of as many formerly government functions as possible: in this case, IAP Worldwide Services, Inc.)

Talking Points Memo's Muckraker reports that Rep. Jason Altmire (D-PA) has introduced a bill, the Veterans Guaranteed Bonus Act, that would require the Pentagon to pay bonuses to wounded vets in full within 30 days after discharge for combat-related wounds.

The DoD's statement demanding reimbursement—it looks like a printout from the IRS—gives a number phone number in case the recipient has questions. We have a few questions, too, and will be calling 1-800-967-0648. We urge our readers to do the same—and say, along with us, "WTF?! With a $500+ billion-per-year budget, DoD has the gall to demand that disabled troops *give back their signing bonuses*?" Then we'll call the White House at 202-456-1414. (The bonuses, of course, come from our April 15 tax dollars.) Demand that disabled soldiers be guaranteed medical care *for life*—and while we're on the subject, Mr. President, there are more than a few other citizens who could use a checkup . . .

Since well before the Iraq War was launched, we have opposed the war these soldiers have been sent to fight, and we will keep working to end the war till the troops come home. In the meantime, in this Thanksgiving season we want all U.S. military personnel to know we at *Levees Not War* sincerely pray for their quick, safe return to their families. Happy Thanksgiving, with real turkey (or other authentic food), wherever in the world you may be stationed.

TAGS: Defense Department, House Appropriations Committee, Iraq War,
     Walter Reed Army Medical Center
http://www.leveesnotwar.org/grinch-wins-plastic-turkey-award-pentagon
-demands-reimbursement

Approaching Five Years in Iraq, 4,000th U.S. Fatality

I think [the war will] go relatively quickly. . . . Weeks rather than months.

Vice President Dick Cheney, March 16, 2003, on CBS's *Face the Nation*

. . . could last six days, six weeks. I doubt six months.

Defense Secretary Donald Rumsfeld, February 7, 2003, at Aviano Air Base, Italy

MARCH 11, 2008—We don't know how this will play out, but we can be sure that while the Clinton and Obama campaigns sharpen their knives against each other, American troops in Iraq and Afghanistan will keep on killing and being killed—for what?—and the U.S. will still be borrowing billions monthly for those insatiable wars.

And New Orleanians once able to afford rent or mortgage payments before the federal levees broke will still be homeless, encamped near City Hall and under the Claiborne Street overpass, and the U.S. Army Corps of Engineers will still be late with its plan for Category 5–strength hurricane protection for New Orleans and vicinity.

Five Years Ago We Were Promised "a Cakewalk"

March 19 will mark the fifth anniversary of the invasion of Iraq, and will roughly coincide with the 4,000th death of an American soldier in that war. What brave soldier will win the distinction of being No. 4,000? As of this writing, the official U.S. troops fatality count is 3,973.

The U.S. is deficit-spending $12 billion per month for this war. John W. McCain with all his vaunted experience actually believes this is a sustainable expenditure. Hillary W. Clinton hammers away at Obama, trying to raise doubts about his ability to answer a telephone at 3:00 a.m., but she won't account for her vote in October 2002 to authorize the use of military force against Iraq.

- If the U.S. can borrow $12 billion a month for the Iraq War—
- If the president and Congress can find $720 million a day—
- If we can deficit-spend $500,000 a minute on this war—

—then let's go even deeper into debt so we can also have $12 billion a month's worth of medicine and schooling and housing. Give us $720 million a day for a serious climate change initiative. We want $500,000 a minute to develop alternative energy sources, hybrid and electric cars, billions for mass transit, restoring the railroads, and shifting from coal to clean, safe, French-style nuclear energy plants. (Coal-burning has got to go: with all its carbon emissions, it's like a cigarette habit, and it's killing us.)

While we're sending our candidates money by credit card, we can also press their campaigns to tell us specifically what they're planning to do to reinvest in America, in schools and health and rebuilding infrastructure and storm protection and training for emergency preparedness. What are their plans for housing displaced people, and how will they help people in disaster-stricken cities to afford rents, or help country people rebuild their homes? Keep pressure on the news media, too, to focus more on issues than on the horse race. It's a constant struggle to keep them tuned in to what matters.

It is up to Us the People to keep the pressure on Congress and the White House—to the extent that they are still functioning as governing institutions—to demand an end to war and a redirection of our tax dollars to uses that actually benefit us taxpayers. The federal government will ignore these questions as long as it can. If anything positive is to happen, it will only be because we keep organizing and pressing Congress and the White House by phone and by fax, no matter who's in office or which party's dominant, not letting them forget how and where we want our tax dollars spent. Otherwise, how soon they forget.

Omigod! Infinite Iraqi Freedom!
We're Never Leaving!

APRIL 7, 2008—As reported in *The Guardian* (UK), which has seen a confidential draft agreement covering the future of U.S. forces in Iraq, the U.S. has plans for an indefinite stay there. The agreement is intended to replace the existing UN mandate and authorizes the U.S. to "conduct military operations in Iraq and to detain individuals when necessary for imperative reasons of security" without a time limit.

It is not just a war, it is an occupation, so we have to decide that there is not going to continue to be an occupation. There is going to be a withdrawal. This is broader than just Iraq. We need to demand a Middle East–wide withdrawal of military forces from Iraq and Turkey and Qatar and what remains in Saudi Arabia and possibly Jordan and so on. We need to realize *our presence there is an irritant that will always be resisted*—and we'll call that resistance "terrorism."

Naomi Klein and Jeremy Scahill write in *The Guardian* that anti-war campaigners have to change tactics. As the Bush administration is impervious to public opinion, we have to go after the Democratic candidates. While Obama and Clinton are battling it out, we have a perfect opportunity to let them compete for the most serious stand against U.S. occupation of Iraq—including private contractors that Scahill and Klein have written about in their books (*Blackwater* and *The Shock Doctrine*, respectively):

> This is exactly where we want the candidates: outdoing each
> other to prove how serious they are about ending the war. That
> kind of issue-based battle has the power to energize voters and
> break the cynicism that is threatening both campaigns.

We urge our readers to demand answers from the Senate Armed Services and Foreign Relations committees: When General Petraeus appears before the committee on Tuesday and Wednesday, please do not waste time with fine-sounding speeches, but grill the man relentlessly with tough, realistic questions about withdrawing, about the $12 billion the U.S. is currently spending in Iraq every month, about the extreme wear and tear on the armed forces that military officials have been publicly decrying for years now. What are they going to do about the current DoD policy of relentlessly redeploying soldiers on exhausting and often fatal *fourth, fifth, sixth tours of duty*? No soldier should have to go on so many deployments. Never before in American history have soldiers been made to go back to the battlefield so many times. This is a cost of empire. And less than 1 percent of the U.S. population is currently serving in the (all-volunteer) military. How does Petraeus justify this policy?

Make General Petraeus and the Armed Services and Foreign Relations committees *deal with* the arguments compiled by Iraq Veterans Against the War:

- The Iraq war is based on lies and deception.

- The Iraq war violates international law.

- Corporate profiteering is driving the war in Iraq.

- Overwhelming civilian casualties are a daily occurrence in Iraq.

- Soldiers have the right to refuse illegal war.

- Service members are facing serious health consequences due to our Government's negligence.

- The war in Iraq is tearing our families apart.

- The Iraq war is robbing us of funding sorely needed here at home.

- The war dehumanizes Iraqis and denies them their right to self-determination.

- Our military is being exhausted by repeated deployments, involuntary extensions, and activations of the Reserve and National Guard.

TAGS: Bush administration, Foreign Relations committees, Iraq War, Senate Armed Services
http://www.leveesnotwar.org/omigod-infinite-iraqi-freedom-we're-never-leaving/

Politics, Society, and the Social Contract

Photograph by Genevieve Hafner

Posted two weeks after the fifth anniversary of Hurricane Katrina

Is Katrina More Significant
Than September 11?

Thoughts on Two American Traumas

SEPT. 11, 2010—Between 9/11 and Hurricane Katrina, which do you think gets most attention, and why?

What if the national focus on 9/11 is exaggerated and the nation should focus instead on 8/29—Hurricane Katrina—as the catastrophe that signifies the greatest threat to America? The fifth anniversary of Hurricane Katrina has received high-profile attention, marked by the release of feature films (Spike Lee, Harry Shearer), hour-long special reports (Brian Williams, Anderson Cooper), and a presidential address at Xavier University, so we're not complaining that Katrina has been ignored.

We were in Manhattan on September 11, 2001, and saw men and women in dust- and debris-covered clothing walking the streets in a daze and crossing the 59th Street Bridge into Queens as from an apocalypse. We heard distraught eyewitnesses on pay phones talking about seeing the burning, falling bodies ("Look, Mommy, the birds are on fire"); we have heard first-person accounts from survivors who were just 20 feet away when their coworkers fleeing the burning towers were crushed beneath chunks of falling metal the size of garbage trucks. We've heard accounts from neighbors who were trapped on the E train near the World Trade Center while frantic escapees pounded on the doors to get in. The haunting stories, the anguish go on and on. Many others have experienced far worse than we can ever imagine. So, the following thoughts are by no means intended to diminish the trauma of September 11 or the necessity of dealing with al Qaeda and other extremist threats. (See "We're Not Forgetting [On the 10th Anniversary of September 11]" in Part V.)

Anorexia of the Homeland: Making War While "Starving the Beast"

And yet we think maybe the challenges this nation faces are more accurately represented by the natural and bureaucratic/political disaster suffered on August 29, 2005, and in the following days, weeks, months, years. The United States is falling apart from a lack of funding of every kind of infrastructure—resulting from neglect, indifference, and a mean-spirited conservative agenda that seeks to roll back the progressive reforms of the 20th century. Our nation is in a downward spiral because of political unwillingness to protect the environment and our fellow citizens who are poor, jobless, homeless, in need of medical care and decent education. Our coasts and cities are vulnerable because of long-term environmental neglect and denial of the effects of industry—global warming, rising sea levels, intensified storms resulting from warming seas—and because corporate-captive politicians of both parties have put industrial and political interests ahead of what's best for the planet, humanity, and other life forms. Even if 9/11 had never happened, all these conditions would still threaten our way of life.

- Don't forget that in the years before Katrina, funds for reinforcing storm protection systems around New Orleans were cut off and redirected to the war effort in Iraq—the war launched on false pretenses. (Will Bunch wrote in 2005, "The Corps never tried to hide the fact that the spending pressures of the war in Iraq, as well as homeland security—coming at the same time as federal tax cuts—was the reason for the [severe reduction in federal appropriations for flood control projects].")

- Don't forget that FEMA's resources were systematically whittled down and made impotent (despite the protests of former FEMA administrator Michael "Brownie" Brown) by an administration obsessed with fighting terrorism and building up a security apparatus (the Department of Homeland Security) that minimized the threats posed by natural disasters.

- Remember that about one-third to half the National Guard of Louisiana and Mississippi were stationed overseas in Iraq and Afghanistan when they were needed at home to rescue their fellow citizens.

- And let it be remembered that for days after the storm, Defense Secretary Rumsfeld refused to deploy a fleet of search-and-rescue helicopters at Hurlburt Field Air Force Base in Florida—only 200 miles from New Orleans—who were waiting for go orders.

Driven in large part by politicians frightening the populace about Islamic extremists (talkin' to the likes of you, Newt "Final Struggle" Gingrich), and motivated also by enormous arms profits, this nation is hell-bent on war. Our national resources are overwhelmingly diverted to the military, to some 150 or more overseas bases to maintain strategic control on every continent, while the Homeland is being hollowed out by deliberate underfunding (a form of anorexia nervosa).

September 11 remains a potent symbol, a wound that is never allowed to heal in order to keep the public frightened and subdued in order to justify massive, ever-increasing spending on wars and weapons systems and overseas bases and other military "needs." (At the same time, this summer only 12 out of 178 Republicans in the House of Representatives voted for funding for medical treatment for Ground Zero rescue workers and residents of New York City who suffered lung ailments and other illnesses from the toxic dust and debris.)

Hope over Fear: A More Affirmative Commemoration + Commitment

We propose that in order to make the nation stronger at home—after all, national security begins at home—America's public officials, activists, volunteers, and ordinary citizens who pray and work for the common good should regard 8/29 as the event that calls us to say Never Again. By all means let's remember what happened on September 11, and let us honor the courage and sacrifice of those who risked their lives to save others. Surely they have a special place in heaven. But at the same time, let the disaster of Katrina—the man-made disaster resulting from flawed engineering and cheap-ass construction and stingy congressional appropriations—let this be the event that motivates our work to repair and rebuild this self-crippled but still salvageable nation. As we've written before, if New Orleans is not safe then no place in America is safe. What's happened to New Orleans is happening to the entire country. The Lower Ninth Ward is the national predicament carried to an extreme. But it doesn't have to be this way.

9/11 is something foreign enemies did to the United States.

8/29 is what America did to itself, with a little push from nature.

"Kill the Bill" vs. "Stop the War": A Tale of Two Protests

APRIL 11, 2010—Has anyone besides us found it kind of odd that there's been so much fire and brimstone about the health care reform bill compared to Bush's Iraq War?

The first thing we'll say about the violence and threats following Congress's passage of the Patient Protection and Affordable Care Act is that right-wing politicians and radio/TV hate-spewers have stoked outrage among their followers and are still fueling the flames. They thrive on conflict; it boosts ratings and fund-raising. The second observation, which we find more intriguing, is that there is a shocking disparity between the opponents of Obama's health care reform and the anti-war protesters who opposed Bush's drive to invade Iraq in 2003. Both presidential "initiatives" have been controversial, but the temperament and character of the public protests of each are different in the extreme. It is more than a little disconcerting that a push to expand public access to health care is more violently opposed than a determined march to a war of choice. Look at the aims, the purposes underlying the two initiatives, and think about which warrants the more passionate support, and which the stronger opposition.

Maybe the different responses are not so surprising, though, when you consider the traditional American readiness to wage war (as long as we personally don't have to fight it, or have our taxes raised to fund it), and our reluctance to spend money on (rather, to be taxed for) public health, education, or other social programs. The Pentagon has the credit card.

"Break Their Windows. Break Them Now."

In recent weeks millions of Americans have been alarmed by the death threats and bricks through office windows of Democratic members of Congress, the spitting and ugly slurs at the Capitol when the House of Representatives was debating the health care bill. Americans have been troubled, too, by the silence of the Republican leadership, who have opened their mouths only to say that "the American people have a right to be angry"—then to claim *the Democrats* are to blame for the threats and violence against Democrats. (This is akin to Iowa Rep. Steve King's combining a near-justification of Joseph Stack's flying his plane into a Texas federal building in Austin in February with self-promotion of his own calls to abolish the IRS. If only we'd listened!)

As the health care reform bill neared a vote on the weekend of March 20–21, GOP House members stood on the Capitol building porches waving "Don't Tread on Me" flags and egging on the Tea Party protesters down below as they shouted "kill the bill!", spit on Emanuel Cleaver (D-Mo.), and used racial slurs against civil rights hero John Lewis (D-Ga.) and similar hateful language against openly gay Barney Frank (D.-Mass.), chair of the House Banking Committee. When protesters in the visitors' gallery of the House chamber caused an uproar during Sunday's debate, Republicans cheered their disruptive behavior as the protesters were escorted out by Capitol police. Later that evening Rep. Randy Neugebauer (R-Tex.) shouted "baby killer!" at Bart Stupak (D-Minn.) in the House chamber shortly before the House voted to approve the bill.

More recently a man has been arrested by the FBI for making repeated and obscene death threats against Senator Patty Murray of Washington; there have been threats against other members of Congress, too, including House Speaker Nancy Pelosi. The Capitol's sergeant-at-arms says lawmakers reported 42 threats in the first quarter of 2010, compared to 15 in the last quarter of 2009. (Not all threats have been against Democrats: one Norman Leboon was arrested for threatening, in YouTube videos, to kill Republican Rep. Eric Cantor of Virginia (who is Jewish); Leboon has since been declared psychologically unfit to stand trial.) Then, adding more creepiness to the already anxious atmosphere (like sprinklings of anthrax in the weeks after 9/11), in Michigan on the weekend of March 27–28 the FBI arrested a strange band of "Christian militia" calling themselves the Hutaree. These events, along with the alarming threefold increase of hate groups since 2008, are of a piece with Sarah Palin's "Don't retreat, reload" rhetoric, the rifle crosshair symbols on her Facebook page indicating office locations of Democratic members of Congress, and the always unhinged rhetoric of Minnesota GOP Rep. Michele

Bachmann ("I want people in Minnesota armed and dangerous on this issue of the energy tax because we need to fight back"). Where are the responsible, adultlike Republican leaders when such things are said and done?

Some of the brick-throwers were incited to violence by a government-hating blogger in Pinson, Alabama, named Mike Vanderboegh, a former militiaman and self-described "Christian libertarian" living on Supplemental Security Income checks issued by the government that he professes to despise, paid for by the income taxes of his fellow citizens, presumably not all of whom share his anti-government views. But, he urges readers of his blog, *Sipsey Street Irregulars*, "To all modern Sons of Liberty: THIS is your time. Break their windows. Break them NOW."

Brick-Throwers, Too, Will Be Covered by Health Care Reform

What strikes us is the extreme contrast in behavior between protesters of a health reform bill designed to extend protection in case of illness to some 32 million people—including the very people throwing bricks—and the reaction of another segment of the population when George W. Bush was pushing the nation to war in 2002 and 2003 against the popular will (including international opinion), and at a velocity that troubled such seasoned Republican stalwarts as Chuck Hagel, Brent Scowcroft, and Colin Powell, who for their pains were derided in a *Weekly Standard* editorial as "The Axis of Appeasement." (Going to war in Afghanistan was logical and widely supported, but what was the sudden fixation on Iraq? Former Treasury Secretary Paul O'Neill claimed that discussions about invading Iraq—not whether to but when and how— were commonplace in the administration's first months, well before 9/11. Former counter-terrorism adviser Richard A. Clarke told *60 Minutes* that on 9/12 Bush directed him to find a link between 9/11 and Saddam, even though it was known that the attack came from al Qaeda.)

So, let's review the two administrations' "initiatives" that aroused public protest.

Aside from the 2001 and 2003 tax cuts (mainly benefiting the rich) that increased federal deficits by about $1.7 trillion between 2007 and 2008, the Iraq War was George W. Bush's central accomplishment. His administration sold a war by cultivating public fear through rhetoric of "mushroom clouds" and weapons of mass destruction and incessant linkages of 9/11 and al Qaeda with the regime of Saddam Hussein (never mind the fact that Osama bin Laden despised Saddam as an apostate, a secular unbeliever). The Bush White House and Pentagon directed the invasion of a sovereign nation that had not attacked the U.S. Eight years later, U.S. troops still number over 100,000, at a cost so far of some $716 billion (not counting the war in Afghanistan).

The Obama administration, on the other hand, soon after signing the American Recovery and Reinvestment Act (the stimulus bill) of 2009, launched a campaign to reform America's health care system and massively expand public access to medical care and control costs. The president explained that the current system was leaving too many people behind; the rate of health insurance premium increases was unaffordable for individuals and businesses; and the escalating costs were making it impossible for American firms to hold their own with foreign competitors who benefited from national health systems. What turned out to be the Patient Protection and Affordable Care Act, although imperfect and passed only through much wrangling and deal-making, includes many originally Republican ideas and was designed to expand access to health care for those who lack insurance and improve its performance for those with policies. Major reforms include:

- Small business owners will receive tax credits to purchase health insurance
- No child will be denied coverage because of a preexisting condition
- Insurance companies will not be able to drop your coverage because you get sick (so-called rescission, or rescinding coverage)
- Insurance companies will be required to offer free preventative care to their customers
- No more lifetime limits or restrictive annual limits on benefits
- Seniors "in the donut hole" will receive $250 to help them pay for drug prescriptions
- A new independent appeals process will ensure a hearing for customers when their insurance company denies a claim

Now, About That Splendid Little War . . .

Before March 2003, public support for war with Iraq was quite low, and varied depending on how the questions were framed. In the fall of 2002, a CNN/ *USA Today* poll found support at 33% for a war that would incur 5,000 casualties. (To date there are nearly 4,300 U.S. dead, and 30,180 wounded.) The White House pushed hard on the WMD and nuclear threats and the falsified linkage between Baghdad and al Qaeda to frighten the public into supporting an invasion. (The absence of a selective service draft also helped.) Pentagon officials, including assistant secretary Paul D. Wolfowitz, minimized costs and downplayed the number of soldiers that would be needed. General Eric Shinseki was fired for having estimated before Congress that the invasion would require at least "several hundred thousand troops," a comment Wolfowitz dismissed as "wildly off the mark" and publicly ridiculed by Defense Secretary Donald H. Rumsfeld. Shinseki is now Obama's secretary of Veterans Affairs [2009–14].

It is impossible to know what the public opinion would have been without the carefully orchestrated marketing of the war, but Bush Inc. was leaving nothing to chance. Explaining why the administration waited until after Labor Day 2002 to launch the war-promotion campaign, chief of staff Andrew Card, former CEO of the American Automobile Manufacturers Association, explained, "From a marketing point of view, you don't introduce new products in August." Although the White House insisted the president had not yet made any decisions, The War was a product that had already been designed by the White House Iraq Group (WHIG), a task force whose purpose was to "educate the public" about the "gathering threat" posed by Saddam Hussein. Among WHIG's members were Karl Rove, Karen Hughes, Mary Matalin, Condoleezza Rice, I. Lewis "Scooter" Libby (now in prison), and Stephen Hadley. The Selling of the Threat was handled by Vice President Dick Cheney starting in August 2002; President Bush at the U.N. (9/12/02) and in Cincinnati (10/7/02) and his infamous 2003 State of the Union address; Condoleezza Rice on the Sunday morning talk shows; and Secretary of State Colin Powell's February 5, 2003, address to the United Nations Security Council in which he held up a simulated vial of anthrax with CIA director George Tenet sitting just behind him. (Memories of anthrax deaths and scare stories were still fresh in the public's memory from October 2001.)

Peaceful Protests of War,
Violent Protests of Health Reform

The public's opposition to the Iraq War was angry and distressed, to be sure, and "full of sound and fury," but overall it was peaceful and law-abiding. The marches were far more populous—the anti-war rallies in New York, San Francisco, and Washington often drew 200,000 to 350,000 protesters— and generally more civil and certainly more culturally and demographically diverse and therefore more representative of the nation's general population than the anti-"Obamacare" brick-throwers. We who mobilized against the war joined in massive marches, stood on street corners with signs and banners, wrote letters to editors and congressmen and assembled phone banks to urge members of Congress to stop the war. How quaint this all seems now, how gentle. The anti–Iraq War movement was genuinely grass-roots, with mass demonstrations steered by progressive groups such as the A.N.S.W.E.R. Coalition. It was not driven by any sympathetic cable news organization or powerful lobbying group the way the anti–health reform protests have been (see below). The generally peaceable character of the anti-war rallies must have disappointed the conflict-hungry news media, and was underreported accordingly—unlike Tea Party events that sometimes draw only hundreds but seem to get unlimited, breathless coverage on cable TV. (One of the signs we recall from a massive anti-war demonstration we joined in New York City in the spring of 2003 read "CORPORATE MEDIA LOVES A WAR.")

If we had acted in the Bush years with anything like the ferocity shown by Tea Partiers and other anti-"Obamacare" protesters, given the zero tolerance of even occasional non-Republicans at Bush campaign events (search under "Denver Three, 2005" or "Republican Convention 2004 arrests"), we would have been shipped off to Guantánamo. We did not post billboards promoting "A citizens guide to REVOLUTION of a corrupt government" or advocating PREPARE FOR WAR—LIVE FREE OR DIE. You can be sure the anti-war movement would have been ten times as populous and angry had the youth of America been subject to a selective service draft as they were during the Vietnam War. Law-abiding as we were, however, opposition to the Iraq War—before and once it was launched—was denounced by the Bush administration and its supporters as treasonous. Questioning the war was vilified as anti-American (Fox News's Hannity and O'Reilly took care of that quite firmly). Now many of the same people who denounced anti-war protesters as treasonous urge the public to not cooperate with the government and talk about secession.

If you've read this far, perhaps you can see why it strikes us as paradoxical—upside down, even—that an effort to improve the public health system should trigger outrage and bricks through windows, while these same dissenters accepted largely without protest a war launched through deliberate deception that pulled hundreds of thousands into harm's way—and thousands into body bags and V.A. hospitals. Just to underscore the upside-down nature of the Tea Party / Hockey Mom public's acceptance of the Rich Man's War fought by Ordinary Folks: Bush Inc.'s ties to industries standing to profit handsomely from a war in Iraq—oil, arms, and other war infrastructure supplies—are well documented (see *Halliburtonwatch.org* and the World Policy Institute's special report *The Ties That Bind: Arms Industry Influence in the Bush Administration and Beyond* [2004]).

Anti-Government Hypocrisy: Serve Us, But Don't Expect Us to Pay for It

By the way, are these anti-government protesters so outraged by the "corrupt government" also opposed to federal air safety regulations? child labor laws? food and drug inspections? Securities and Exchange Commission oversight of Wall Street? Much of what they are protesting—aside from ethnic and cultural issues we'll address below—likely derives not from government itself but from a *failure of government* to work properly, starved and understaffed as it was during the Bush years, as exemplified by FEMA's incompetence after Hurricane Katrina. Similarly, Tea Party members in a recent poll asserted that they want a smaller government but more federal help in boosting employment and expect Washington to do a better job of reining in Wall Street excesses. One of the most delicious ironies was when attendees of the 9/12 rally in 2009—Tea Partiers and other Glenn Beck fans who feel they're "taxed enough already," and their Republican congressional supporters—griped that the Washington, D.C., Metro "did not make a great effort to simply provide a basic level of transit for them" to get them to the Tea Party rally. Just months before, Rep. Kevin Brady, a Texas Republican who complained about the inadequate service on the D.C. Metro, had voted against $150 million in emergency funding for the rail service. All right, then, walk.

Anti–Health Care Fury Stoked by Same Party That Started Iraq War

For some 40 years the Republican party has been campaigning against government itself ("government is the problem"), against "Washington" (by which they usually mean onerous corporate taxes and business regulations). In a more recent twist of the same old knife, they have served the insurance and drug industry by arousing public opposition to health care reforms, namely, limits on insurance and pharmaceutical profits. Getting the public all riled up—"Get Your Gov't Hands off My Medicare!"—has been the work of former House Majority Leader Dick Armey and David Koch's "grass-roots" FreedomWorks.org ("Less Taxes, Less Government, More Freedom") and David Koch's Americans for Prosperity Foundation, which also spreads disinformation and denial about the perils of climate change. Republicans warned that if health care reform passed, it would be "Armageddon" (House minority leader John "Hell No You Can't!" Boehner of Ohio), yet all this overheated rhetoric that stirs up the beehive ends up making it impossible for the accusers to deal with the Democrats. As Obama pointed out to House Republicans in February, they demagogue themselves into a corner. How can they turn around and negotiate with an extremist socialist who (they claim) wants to kill Grandma?

And Now About the Demographic Angle

A recent University of Washington study has found a high correlation of anti-minority sentiment among members of the Tea Party supporters. The study found that "among whites, southerners are 12 percent more likely to support the tea party than whites in other parts of the U.S." Similarly, "those who are racially resentful, who believe the U.S. government has done too much to support blacks, are 36 percent more likely to support the tea party than those who are not." Photographs of Tea Party and anti-"Obamacare" rallies show only white faces. The racial component to the attitudes and motivations is a complex matter that's beyond the scope of this survey; we simply call attention to this study's findings. (There has been no black Republican member of Congress since 2003.) To be sure, much of today's anti-government rhetoric would be the same regardless of which Democrat, of whatever color, was in the White House. Militias and hate groups swelled during the 1990s when another Democrat was president. And even if a Republican had won in 2008, there would still be enormous public outrage, understandably, at the Wall Street bailouts.

Ultimately, though, we cannot overlook the difference in the two presidents' ethnic and religious backgrounds. A white evangelical son of a Republican president versus a darker-skinned Democratic son of a Kenyan with a Muslim name who is less ostentatious about his Christian church-going? And there's more. As Charles M. Blow observed in a *New York Times* op-ed titled "Whose Country Is It?":

> Even the optics must be irritating. A woman (Nancy Pelosi)
> pushed the health care bill through the House. The bill's most
> visible and vocal proponents included a gay man (Barney Frank)
> and a Jew (Anthony Weiner). And the black man in the White
> House signed the bill into law. It's enough to make a good old
> boy go crazy.

So maybe *Times* columnist Frank Rich is right when he writes "The Rage Is Not About Health Care." Rich says the right's reaction to the health reform bill—"an unglued firestorm of homicidal rhetoric" and "a small-scale mimicry of Kristallnacht"—is less like the response to the passage of the Medicare bill in 1965 than to the Civil Rights Act of 1964.

> The real source of the over-the-top rage of 2010 is the same kind
> of national existential reordering that roiled America in 1964. . . .
> The conjunction of a black president and a female speaker of the
> House—topped off by a wise Latina on the Supreme Court and
> a powerful gay Congressional committee chairman—would sow
> fears of disenfranchisement among a dwindling and threatened
> minority in the country no matter what policies were in play.
> It's not happenstance that Frank, Lewis and Cleaver—none

of them major Democratic players in the health care push—received a major share of last weekend's abuse. When you hear demonstrators chant the slogan "Take our country back!," these are the people they want to take the country back from.

What Is to Be Done? Work for a More Perfect Union

Well, fellow Americans, we're all in this together, and the country would be a whole lot better off if more of us were moving in the same direction to push Congress to enact stronger financial reforms and really robust job-creation bills. (Our recommendation is to invest in some serious WPA- and CCC-like programs to put the unemployed back to work.) We'd be much better off if Republican leaders, who salivate at the prospect of harnessing Tea Party passion to help their electoral chances, would actually stand up on their hind legs and tell the people to calm down and be reasonable. But they will not do this. Therefore, because Republican leaders will not try to calm the waters they're busy roiling, moderates, progressives, and independents disturbed by the spread of violence and hate rhetoric must demand that Republican and Democratic leaders take a stand against intimidation (another word for terrorism). Demand that advertisers withdraw from Glenn Beck and Rush Limbaugh and other hate-spewers (many have already pulled out from Beck's show).

We would like to see fact-checking outfits such as Media Matters for America and the Center for American Progress (*Think Progress*) and Organizing for America (DNC) establish rapid-response teams to challenge and correct the fresh outbursts of falsehoods—perhaps by aiming principally at the networks that give air time to Sarah Palin and Michele Bachmann and replay the latest lies, distortions, and insults to American democracy (a Sisyphean undertaking). Bloggers should direct readers to reality-based sites such as *Think Progress* and *Media Matters*, or establish their own. Yes we can. The general public is not inclined to look things up, but folks are usually willing to listen to reason. We can help by calmly asserting the facts and disputing the lies. Keep up the pressure on Democrats and fair-minded Republicans to stand up for the truth, and call to thank them when they do.

One thing we know: No appeasement will make the ranters go away. The hard-core haters will never be satisfied. Folks, there are eliminationists out there who think Democrats and progressives should be exterminated. Limbaugh and Beck say this repeatedly. That was part of Beck's message as the keynote speaker at the CPAC convention in February—the speech in which he said that "progressive" is a euphemism for communist. It's on his chalkboard if you don't believe it.

So, only by persistently challenging falsehoods, patiently correcting the record, and presenting a compelling vision of a more humane and decent America does a more progressive, inclusive, livable United States stand a chance—an America that has a place for the supporters of the health care bill as well as for those troubled by it, for those who supported the Iraq War as well as those who opposed it, for the soldiers and their families regardless of their views on the war. It's not easy, and it may sound corny, but if we don't work for a more perfect union we may lose what the justly honored Founding Fathers sought to establish many years ago.

We'll leave the last words to our favorite Virginian ever, Thomas Jefferson:

> I know of no safe depository of the ultimate powers of the society but the people themselves; and if we think them not enlightened enough to exercise their control with a wholesome discretion, the remedy is not to take it from them, but to inform their discretion by education.

The Social Contract, Explained by Elizabeth Warren, Paul Krugman, and Robert Kuttner

*There is nobody in this country who got rich on his own. Nobody.
. . . You moved your goods to market on the roads the rest of us
paid for. You hired workers the rest of us paid to educate.*

Elizabeth Warren

SEPT. 24, 2011—Elizabeth Warren, the consumer protection reformer and
Harvard law professor who is now campaigning to represent Massachusetts
in the U.S. Senate, has given one of the most direct and cogent explanations
of the social contract we've ever heard. It's an idea that is not talked about,
or even thought of, often enough. One way of describing the social contract,
also known as the social compact, is of putting the Golden Rule into practice
in society through the agencies of government for the benefit of all: Do unto
others as you would have them do unto you. Share and share alike. It's something children can understand, but not many bankers or senators.

United We Stand, Divided We Fall

Briefly, our understanding of a social contract is of society as a kind of cooperative, a mutually beneficial system that serves both the ordinary folk and
the wealthy, and makes demands on all, a two-way street of reciprocal obligation and fulfillment. Since the days of the early colonies, the closest the U.S.
has ever come to enacting a social contract is through FDR's New Deal and
LBJ's Great Society. It is an ideal, never quite reached completely, but its essen-
tials were in place not so long ago and could be restored by determined, sustained effort. Robert Kuttner has written about how during the boom decades

after World War II a "managed, rather than laissez-faire, brand of capitalism . . . delivered broadly shared prosperity, as well as greater security for both the system and individuals" (*The Squandering of America* [2007], p. 6; more below).

Let's go straight to Dr. Warren herself.

> I hear all this, you know, "Well, this is class warfare, this is whatever."—No!
>
> There is nobody in this country who got rich on his own. Nobody.
>
> You built a factory out there—good for you! But I want to be clear.
>
> You moved your goods to market on the roads the rest of us paid for.
>
> You hired workers the rest of us paid to educate.
>
> You were safe in your factory because of police forces and fire forces that the rest of us paid for.
>
> You didn't have to worry that marauding bands would come and seize everything at your factory, and hire someone to protect against this, because of the work the rest of us did.
>
> Now look, you built a factory and it turned into something terrific, or a great idea—God bless. Keep a big hunk of it.
>
> But part of the underlying social contract is you take a hunk of that and pay forward for the next kid who comes along.

Isn't this more or less the idea behind "United we stand, divided we fall"?

As Steve Benen at *Washington Monthly* notes of Warren's remarks, "First-time candidates don't usually articulate a progressive economic message quite this well."

We have written lately about how the Democrats seriously need to sharpen and toughen up their communication skills. We hereby nominate Elizabeth Warren as one of the chief instructors and exemplars at the Democrats' School for the Mute. The school also needs a disciplinarian. The Democratic party cannot depend on the skills of Barack Obama alone—though he has lately been showing signs of improvement. Every senator, every representative who wears a D after his or her name should be in intensive training. Dr. Warren—whose talk about economic fairness prompted Jon Stewart to say, "I want to make out with you!"—is the Teacher of the Week.

We were alerted to the good professor's comments by Paul Krugman's column "The Social Contract" (Sept. 23, 2011). After explaining why President Obama is right to assert that the wealthy should bear part of the burden of reducing the budget deficit, Krugman cites the "eloquent remarks" made this week by Elizabeth Warren, now on the campaign trail in Massachusetts, countering the assertion that the rich should get to keep all their wealth. It's hardly "class warfare." Summarizing Warren's argument, Krugman writes:

> "There is nobody in this country who got rich on his own.
> Nobody," she declared, pointing out that the rich can only get
> rich thanks to the "social contract" that provides a decent,
> functioning society in which they can prosper.

This column follows several days after President Obama, in remarks in the Rose Garden (Sept. 19) on Economic Growth and Deficit Reduction, asserted with welcome clarity, "Either we ask the wealthiest Americans to pay their fair share in taxes, or we're going to have to ask seniors to pay more for Medicare. We can't afford to do both. . . . This is not class warfare. It's math."

Who You Callin' "Class Warfare"?

American Prospect co-founder and co-editor Robert Kuttner (cited above), who once worked as an investigator on the Senate Committee on Banking, Housing, and Urban Affairs, writes in *The Squandering of America* that "the social compact of a bygone era is scorned by the Right as 'tax-and-spend.'"

> Progressive taxation was once used by government to
> underwrite outlays that helped ordinary people. In its heyday,
> tax-and-spend worked, both economically and politically. People
> concluded that it was a good deal. Regulation was also part of
> the package, and it too protected citizens from the vicissitudes of
> rampant markets. (*Squandering*, 278)

The very same so-called conservatives who now decry as "class warfare" any shared responsibility for repairing the deficit are the same folks who largely built that deficit through massive tax cuts and shifted more of the tax burden onto the less fortunate.

> To wreck a politics of progressive taxation and social investment, the Right changed the terms of who was taxed and what the taxation bought. The tax load was shifted off business and onto workers and citizens. The Right deliberately used tax cuts for rich allies to create permanent deficits, as a "starve the beast" strategy denying government resources and forcing cuts in programs that people value, such as Pell Grants. What could be clearer class warfare from the top? But pocketbook issues are so depoliticized that most ordinary people don't grasp the connection, and too few Democrats help them connect the dots. (*Squandering*, 278)

Just several pages earlier, Kuttner points out that "when Democrats raised money from big business, there was an ideological disconnect. Economic populism was what had made Democrats the majority party. Yet wealthy donors, with a handful of exceptions, were paying Democrats to be less populist. They were rewarding the Democrats for deserting their natural constituency . . ."

It is our argument, yesterday, today, and tomorrow, that the Democrats must be forcibly reminded (as with skillets over the head) that they and we prosper if they stand with populist fervor and gusto for the middle class and the less fortunate; they can never out-Republican the G.O.P. and shouldn't even try. They have to trust the people, and represent the people, or we vote them out.

TAGS: Barack Obama, Elizabeth Warren, Great Society, New Deal, Paul Krugman, Robert Kuttner, Silence of the Dems, social contract, Tax the Rich
http://www.leveesnotwar.org/elizabeth-warren-paul-krugman-on-the-social-contract/

Does Believing in Social Contract
Make Us Socialists? Then So Be It.

SEPT. 6, 2009—If we're learning anything from the messy struggles for health care reform and the passage of the stimulus bill back in February (how long ago that feels!)—and it's far from clear whether anyone is learning anything—it could be that anyone seeking to improve the conditions of life for one's fellow citizens is in for a real (endless) struggle. Okay, we already knew that, but now we find that if we start getting organized and gaining any traction, we're in for a fight against not only powerful entrenched well-funded interests, but also their artificial grass-roots ("astroturf") campaigns that stir up already nervous, agitated citizens to vent outrage against socialism in the White House and government takeovers of Medicare, among other threats to the republic.

Learning What We're Up Against, and How to Carry On

This site has long advocated increased, liberal spending on hurricane- and flood-protection infrastructure and reinvigoration of social services in storm-damaged New Orleans and the Gulf Coast—including the restoration of the invaluable Charity Hospital. This is what we're here for. But sometimes your own supposed representatives act against you: In February, Louisiana's ambitious governor Bobby Jindal made a spectacle of himself through his well-publicized vow to reject some $98 million of the stimulus money that would have benefited about 25,000 unemployed. Embattled and also ambitious governor Mark Sanford of South Carolina, with an even higher unemployment rate, vowed the same. With caring leadership like this, who needs more hurricanes?

What we're finding, as though we hadn't learned the lesson well enough already, is the intensity with which fiscal and social conservatives will stand in the way of provision of funding for improvements. We now have "tenthers"—a movement of true believers in the Tenth Amendment to the Constitution of the United States who resolutely hold that anything not provided for in the first nine articles—such as the interstate highway system—is unconstitutional and shouldn't be funded by their hard-earned tax dollars. Not surprisingly, there is a populous overlap between tenthers and would-be secessionists. This is some of what we're fighting against. If they don't want to pay for the interstate highway system that they (can) use every day, how eager will they be for their tax dollars to be spent to help their fellow citizens who need a little flood protection now and then?

The conservative opposition to what used to be called "internal improvements" (in the early 1800s there were protracted struggles over plans for canals, a National Road, and other public works projects) sometimes derive from sincere principles about judicious use of public funds. For many, anything other than national defense is suspect. But it has to be borne in mind that a very powerful impetus for conservative opposition to public spending is the determination *to block any program that will warm public affection for Democrats.* This, you may recall, was one of the goals behind the push to privatize Social Security (circa 2005).

And so, when we seek to expand access to medical coverage, when we want to increase federal spending on storm-defense infrastructure and restoration of vital wetlands and other environmental protection, we face opposition from conservatives in the Deep South (never mind that hurricanes hit hard there) and elsewhere who want to block the success of any program that would redound to the benefit of what they insist on calling the Democrat party.

Lakoff Says "the Moral Appeal Is Always the Best"

We met the great U.C. Berkeley linguist George Lakoff, author of *Whose Freedom?*, at a panel discussion on political propaganda at the New York Public Library in 2007. We asked his advice on how *Levees Not War* and other advocates for more generous funding for public works and social services should try to appeal to the public and elected officials. He said the moral appeal is always the best. It's honest and it is more persuasive. Do unto others the Golden Rule, etc. Democrats and progressives, he said, always fall for the

"Enlightenment fallacy," the naïve belief that if you simply present the facts, people will see the light and support your cause. Not so simple. (Republicans, who historically represent the powerful more than the common folk, tend to appeal to fear [national security concerns], self-interest, class or racial resentment, and falsehoods and distortion about the opposition.) Democrats should never try to imitate Republican appeals—it's never believable. Instead, use the moral argument (the golden rule)—It's the right thing to do. Expanding health care coverage, protecting our cities from hurricanes with reinforced flood protection is the right thing to do, morally and ecologically. Be good stewards of the earth, etc. Improving schools and hospitals and paying the teachers and nurses well is the right and fair thing to do. It makes our country stronger and treats our neighbors with the respect they deserve, and so on.

Lakoff said Democrats and progressives are never persuasive with the appeal to self-interest—they can't compete on that turf with Republicans. Part of the weakness of the self-interest approach is that it is fragmented, does not show how the various parts are connected, and therefore lacks a cohesiveness and persuasive force. To be convincing, what we must do is show how seemingly disparate phenomena are related. Show, for instance, how the nation's dependence on oil and the ravaging of the wetlands are connected; how the 10,000+ miles of oil and gas canals through the Louisiana wetlands destroy the storm-surge buffer that protects us from hurricanes, while the carbon emissions aggravate global warming, which intensifies hurricanes and raises sea levels, and so on. (This is why we occasionally write about the coolness of public transportation—such as a train from New Orleans to Baton Rouge, for which stimulus money could be available!—which we hope Governor Jindal will begin to understand.)

Sometimes we worry that we are working on too many fronts to be effective; at other times we feel we might just be developing a sort of unified field theory of public works, social services, environmental protection, and peace-mongering. As ever, the three legs of our tripod are infrastructure, anti-war, and environmental issues as they relate to rebuilding New Orleans and the Gulf Coast. This whole venture—this thing we call *Levees Not War*— grew out of a "social contract" project, an argument for a repair of the social safety net and a more equitable distribution of wealth. We believe in a system, a government and a society, that is activist in nature and serves poor, middlin', and rich, and makes demands on all, a two-way street of reciprocal obligation and fulfillment. These ideas, these values, are at the core of our mission. Though we may sometimes appear to be wandering off the reservation, this is what we always come back to, and where we hope everyone feels welcome.

TAGS: George Lakoff, health care reform, infrastructure, public works, social contract, social services, tenthers

http://www.leveesnotwar.org/does-believing-in-social-contract-make-us-socialists-then-so-be-it/

Anti-Islamic Furor Helps al Qaeda,
Endangers America

The World Trade Center Site will forever hold a special place in our City, in our hearts. But we would be untrue to the best part of ourselves—and who we are as New Yorkers and Americans—if we said 'no' to a mosque in Lower Manhattan. . . . We would betray our values—and play into our enemies' hands—if we were to treat Muslims differently than anyone else. In fact, to cave to popular sentiment would be to hand a victory to the terrorists— and we should not stand for that. . . . there is no neighborhood in this City that is off limits to God's love and mercy.

Mayor Michael Bloomberg, Aug. 3, 2010

Congress shall make no law respecting an establishment of religion, or prohibiting the free exercise thereof; or abridging the freedom of speech or of the press; or the right of the people peaceably to assemble, and to petition the government for a redress of grievances.

First Amendment to the Constitution of the United States, 1791

AUG. 23, 2010—Ordinarily this blog would have no reason to comment on the building of an Islamic cultural center in lower Manhattan—the subject doesn't naturally pertain to our core mission of infrastructure, environment, and peace (especially for New Orleans and environs). But these are not ordinary times, and this is no longer an ordinary religious-freedom issue.

The uproar over Park51, commonly known as the "Ground Zero Mosque," has reached national security–threatening levels of madness. What we find most troubling about the furor is that the hate speech against Islam generally—blaming all Muslims, including the 5 to 7 million Muslim Americans, for the crimes of al Qaeda on 9/11—is making it easier to justify war on the Islamic world, to continue fighting in Afghanistan and Iraq and beyond. (Recall the WWII internments of Japanese-Americans and the atomic bombings made politically and morally more palatable by persistent demonization of "the Jap" as subhuman.) Most insane and threatening of all is that the broad-brush insults of Muslims validate Osama bin Laden's claims that America hates Islam and that therefore all Muslims should fight against "the Crusaders." Do Newt Gingrich and Sarah Palin really want to do bin Laden's recruiting work for him?

[The manufacture of the controversy cannot be understood without seeing *Atlas Shrugs*, the blog of author and activist Pamela Geller, executive director of a group called Stop Islamization of America ("a human rights organization dedicated to freedom of speech, religious liberty") and coauthor of *The Post-American Presidency: The Obama Administration's War on America* (foreword by John Bolton). In "How the 'Ground Zero Mosque' Fear Mongering Began," *Salon*'s Justin Elliott explains how Geller pushed Park51 from being unremarkable when announced to being suddenly seen as a dire threat to America.]

The site in question is occupied by a former Burlington Coat factory that was damaged on 9/11. The building dates back to the 1850s. The owners of the property, Feisal Abdul Rauf, a graduate of Columbia University, and his wife Daisy Khan, plan to build a Sufi Islamic cultural center—not a mosque—modeled on the (Jewish) 92nd Street Y, a prominent cultural and fitness center in New York City. (Sufis are well known as the most peaceful and "cosmic" of the varieties of Islam—they are like the opposite of extremist or violent. Think of the Persian poet Rumi.) The Park51 board includes Christians and Jews along with Muslims. The plans call for classrooms, a 500-seat auditorium, a restaurant, a memorial to the victims of September 11 (some of whom were Muslim, as were some of the first responders), a prayer room but not a mosque, and so on. Feisal Abdul Rauf, the imam of a mosque in TriBeCa for nearly 30 years, vice-chair of the Interfaith Center of New York and the author of "What's Right with Islam Is What's Right with America," has conducted "sensitivity training" for the FBI. He is famous as a peaceful moderate. His wife, Daisy Khan, runs the American Society for Muslim

Advancement, which she co-founded with Rauf. (When she appeared on Fox News in December 2009 to talk about the center, Laura Ingraham said, "I like what you're doing.") Rauf and Khan are precisely the kind of Muslims America should welcome and encourage. Harassing them and demonizing their project, telling them and others of their faith that they don't belong here sends a very bad signal to the Muslim world and reinforces their suspicion that America is at war with Islam.

Where Is George W. Bush When You Need Him?

This is precisely why President Bush was careful to clarify publicly, repeatedly, that the U.S. is fighting al Qaeda, not Islam. "Islam is peace," he said. Where is he now? Maureen Dowd writes (almost pleadingly), "W. needs to get his bullhorn back out." At the time Bush said these things, we were not confident his heart was really in it, but he was right to reinforce the message, and it would do a lot of good for America as a United States if he would resurface to try to cool the hostility. (See Joshua Holland's disturbing report at AlterNet about an epidemic of anti-Islamic hate spreading across the U.S., nearly 10 years after September 11.)

> *Muslims are as much a part of our City and our country as the people of any faith and they are as welcome to worship in Lower Manhattan as any other group.*
>
> Mayor Michael Bloomberg

What the right-wing demagogues don't seem to understand—or do they just not care?—is that in exchange for a few votes they're making things worse for the nation and for the troops they claim to support. For recruiting and hate-stimulation purposes, Osama bin Laden and al Qaeda need the United States to be seen demonizing Muslims, being at war with Islam. *New York Times* columnist Nicholas Kristof writes, "Osama abhors the vision of interfaith harmony that the proposed Islamic center represents. He fears Muslim clerics who can cite the Koran to denounce terrorism." Similarly, President Obama's speech at Cairo University in June 2009 was exactly what the al Qaeda recruiters do not want; they recruit more members (often resentful unemployed youth) when Newt Gingrich compares the builders of the

Islamic cultural center to Nazis. As Robert Scheer writes in "Ground Zero for Tolerance":

> Just ask Gen. David Petraeus, who is leading the war without
> end to win the hearts and minds of Muslims in Afghanistan,
> how helpful it is to the Taliban for American politicians to
> identify all Muslims with terrorism. Or to the theocratic leaders
> of Iran who justify their hard line with the insistence that the
> U.S. is obsessively anti-Muslim.

(About Gen. Petraeus, Frank Rich writes that no one is listening to his sales pitch as he goes from one media outlet to the next, trying to sell a longer stay in Afghanistan. "Poor General Petraeus. . . . No one was listening and no one cared. Everyone was too busy yelling about the mosque.")

Ali Soufan, a former FBI agent whose duties included interrogating suspected terrorists, writes in *Time* magazine, "From a national security perspective, our leaders need to understand that no one is likely to be happier with the opposition to building a mosque than Osama bin Laden. His next video script has just written itself."

A Question of "Sensitivity"

Now, it should be said that Park51's proximity to Ground Zero is certainly not ideal; even many supporters of the owners' right to develop the center would be happier if it were a little farther way from the sore spot. But how far? There are already several functioning mosques in the neighborhood. There are also functioning strip clubs (the Pussycat Lounge, New York Dolls Gentlemen's Club). Park Place is two blocks north of the former World Trade Center site; in Manhattan, two blocks can feel like a long distance, with every inch of real estate filled with shops, bodegas, bars, newsstands, liquor stores, parking garages, etc. Furthermore, the Landmark Preservation Commission voted unanimously to give the center the green light, and Community Board No. 1, the local council that represents the area, voted 29 to 1 to allow the building. The locals don't seem to mind. As the *New Yorker*'s Hendrik Hertzberg points out, the objections to the Islamic center seem to intensify more the farther you get from the neighborhood. (His "Zero Grounds" is one of the most fair-minded pieces we've read about the issue.) Those who assert that Imam Rauf and Daisy Khan should "show sensitivity" to the families of 9/11 victims have a reasonable point, but they should remember that Muslims, too, died at Ground Zero.

So, how far away would be far enough to satisfy the opponents? And for how many more years must "they" keep their distance from the hallowed ground? It's been nearly ten years.

We understand many people have become upset about this matter, upset and even outraged, but has it occurred to thoughtful opponents that the whole "mega-mosque" controversy is a manufactured distraction in an election year? The United States is sinking in intractable economic turmoil. One political party is trying fitfully, sometimes lamely, to pass legislation that will alleviate the suffering, while the other party is actively opposing any and all efforts to repair the damage, much of which that opposition party caused while it was in power. The nation's crises are many, and they are profound. Is a struggle against a cultural center for Muslims really what Americans need to be pouring our passions into right now? It should be clear that the right wing of the GOP (is there any other part?) encourages this hollering, expecting votes without having to offer any serious, constructive program for generating economic recovery, jobs, or helping people afford to stay in their homes or pay for their health care.

How many of the Republicans who profess undying loyalty to the sacred memory of 9/11 and its heroes voted for funding for medical treatment for Ground Zero rescue workers and residents of New York City who suffered lung ailments and other illnesses from the toxic dust and debris? *Twelve.* Twelve out of 178 Republicans in the House of Representatives. *The New York Times* reported on July 29 that "243 Democrats and 12 Republicans supported the measure; 155 Republicans and 4 Democrats opposed it."

Of course, these right-wing attacks on the mosque are also an attack on President Obama (derided by the despicable out-on-a-Limbaugh as "Imam Obama"). MediaMatters.org shows that the right-wing media are relentlessly pushing the false accusation that Barack Obama is a Muslim: more people believe this now than before he was elected president.

(To their credit, some responsible conservatives such as Congressman Ron Paul, former solicitor general Ted Olson—whose wife was onboard the plane that crashed into the Pentagon on 9/11—and New Jersey governor Chris Christie have urged their fellow Republicans to tone down the anti-Muslim rhetoric.)

In our own little house of worship we're praying that the angry citizens among us will soon come to their senses. Fellow Americans, you're being used. Years from now this episode is not going to be one of America's proudest moments. Those who stand up for tolerance and cohabitation, especially when it's unpopular, are the heroes, the defenders of liberty. Those who exploit public fears should be ashamed, and many later will be. The dead in military cemeteries may have crosses, crescents, or stars of David over their names, but they all served their country with equal devotion and courage. Let's not endanger further the soldiers and sailors who are still serving.

[The online version of this post includes a photograph from *The New Yorker* of the mother of Kareem Rashad Sultan Khan, who was awarded the Bronze Star and Purple Heart in Operation Iraqi Freedom, mourning at his grave in Arlington National Cemetery (Sept. 29, 2008).] Gen. Colin Powell hinted that he wept when he saw this photograph in *The New Yorker*. The sight of this photograph, amid the anti-Islamic vitriol that was erupting at McCain-Palin rallies in September 2008, was one of the factors that influenced the former secretary of state to come out and publicly endorse Barack Obama on *Meet the Press* (Oct. 19, 2008). Secretary Powell said to Tom Brokaw:

> I'm also troubled by . . . what members of the party say. And it is permitted to be said such things as, "Well, you know that Mr. Obama is a Muslim." Well, the correct answer is, he is not a Muslim, he's a Christian. He's always been a Christian. But the really right answer is, what if he is? Is there something wrong with being a Muslim in this country? The answer's no, that's not America. Is there something wrong with some seven-year-old Muslim-American kid believing that he or she could be president? Yet, I have heard senior members of my own party drop the suggestion, "He's a Muslim and he might be associated [with] terrorists." This is not the way we should be doing it in America.
>
> I feel strongly about this particular point because of a picture I saw in a magazine. It was a photo essay about troops who are serving in Iraq and Afghanistan. And one picture at the tail end

of this photo essay was of a mother in Arlington Cemetery, and she had her head on the headstone of her son's grave. And as the picture focused in, you could see the writing on the headstone. And it gave his awards—Purple Heart, Bronze Star—showed that he died in Iraq, gave his date of birth, date of death. He was 20 years old. And then, at the very top of the headstone, it didn't have a Christian cross, it didn't have the Star of David, it had crescent and a star of the Islamic faith. And his name was Kareem Rashad Sultan Khan, and he was an American. He was born in New Jersey. He was 14 years old at the time of 9/11, and he waited until he can go serve his country, and he gave his life. Now, we have got to stop polarizing ourself in this way.

When Senator John F. Kennedy was running for president in 1960, he was dogged by questions about his Roman Catholic faith. Would he take orders from the Vatican? Would he serve Rome first, then America? He tried repeatedly to answer questions and put the matter to rest, but still concerns remained, intensified by direct mail campaigns sympathetic to Republican candidate Richard Nixon. One of the greatest speeches of JFK's political career was his address to the Greater Houston Ministerial Association on Sept. 12, 1960, where he addressed head-on what he called "the so-called religious issue."

> . . . For while this year it may be a Catholic against whom the finger of suspicion is pointed, in other years it has been, and may someday be again, a Jew, or a Quaker, or a Unitarian, or a Baptist. . . . Today I may be the victim—but tomorrow it may be you—until the whole fabric of our harmonious society is ripped at a time of great national peril.

A rare—indeed, unprecedented—personal note, in the first person singular

I have known a good number of friends who are Muslim or whose parents moved to the U.S. from Arabic-speaking lands—friends from Turkey, Iran,

Egypt, and Morocco (the barber Aziz from Casablanca), including some girl-friends in and around college. I used to live in Baton Rouge, where Louisiana State University normally has about a 10% population of international students. A fair number of these are petroleum engineering students from Iran and elsewhere in the Middle East. When I worked at a restaurant in the 1980s the waiters included Shahram who went by "Shawn," and gave me tapes of beautiful Persian music, and "Tony" who, when asked, told the customers he was from Italy . . . After work we would go to, appropriately, the International House of Pancakes near campus and meet up with some of their friends, and drink from the bottomless urns of IHOP coffee and smoke and talk about everything. They said there was no family in Tehran that had not lost someone to the Shah's dreaded SAVAK secret police.

The concerns expressed above about freedom of worship and safety and security are concerns not only in the abstract but for individuals I've known— kind, intelligent, humorous, often devout but not always noticeably religious. They love America as much as anyone else, and sometimes appreciate its freedoms more than the native-born Americans realize because they've seen the difference. "They" is not the right word, for "they" are "we."

Pajama Party

Those bloggers need to take off their pajamas, get dressed and realize that governing a closely divided country is complicated and difficult.

Anonymous Obama adviser to NBC's John Harwood

OCT. 12, 2009—Wait: we have to get *dressed*? Drag! Our best pieces are done in our PJ's! We just sit here in our flannels, drinking coffee and making wise-cracks about the hard-working grown-ups who have real jobs. (Maybe we're still in our pajamas because—why bother dressing?—we can't find a job?)

Hey, you know what's difficult? Understanding how the Obama adminis-tration has let Wall Street get away with murder. You know what else is dif-ficult? Going on a third, fourth, and fifth tour of duty to Afghanistan when your marriage is falling apart and the bank is foreclosing on your house. You know what else is difficult? Understanding how an anonymous source in the White House thinks it's smart to whisper to John Harwood that the pro-gressives who supported Obama when most of the "dressed" people backed Hillary need to get serious. That's a real Sister Souljah moment—especially coming from an anonymous source. That'll put us in our place.

The best retort is from *Firedoglake*:

> That is just classic. After pandering to LGBT leaders last night
> the truth comes out. Dear gays: grow up and let us get about the
> serious business of governance. Signed, some dude who's too
> afraid to give his real name.

Who talks like this? Rahm Emanuel? David Axelrod? We're going to find out who this "adviser" is, and then we'll have a real pajama party. And that adviser may need a public option one of these days.

Winter of Our Discontent

DEC. 21, 2009—In the already-dark of the shortest day of the year, the first day of winter, rather than denying the obvious it feels appropriate to acknowledge a certain lowness of spirits, a mood that the holidays will warm temporarily but not dispel altogether. "Winter of our discontent" (besides opening Shakespeare's *Richard III*) was the title of a fund-raising e-mail *The Nation* sent out last week, and the phrase pretty well sums up the mood. This time last year, even though it felt like the U.S. and global economy was spinning down into an abyss, there was much hope in the air because of the outcome of the 2008 presidential election. (It felt almost too good to be true.) Now, the mood is not what one would call elation, or hopeful. "Yes we can" feels like a long time ago.

The Senate Democrats are moving along with their health reform bill, but it is hard to know what to think about it. A few conservative, corporate Democrats and a certain self-styled independent [Senator Joseph Lieberman of Connecticut] have been posing a greater danger to the ultimate passage than the whole united bloc of intransigent Republicans. So far, since Saturday, the Democrats have held together with the filibuster-proof 60 votes, and many of the outspoken progressive, liberal voices who were critical this time last week are holding their fire, realizing that if this fails, much more we hold dear could crash and burn besides.

A few weeks ago we explained at some length our discontent (grief and dread would be more accurate) about the president's decision to escalate U.S. troop (and, *ssshhh*, contractor) commitments to Afghanistan (and—*ssshhh*— to the undeclared war in Pakistan). Reading Steve Coll's magnificent magnum opus *Ghost Wars* gives us a more informed background on American involvement in that region (since the late 1970s) but no hope that the U.S. will withdraw from there in our lifetimes.

A further cause for dismay is reading Matt Taibbi's scathing account of Obama's Big Sellout in the Dec. 10 issue of *Rolling Stone*. Which sellout? The one to Wall Street, by loading his economic policy team and Treasury appointments with acolytes and protégés of Robert Rubin, with people more loyal to Goldman Sachs and Citigroup than to the "yes-we-can" community organizers and Main Street types who worked to get Obama elected. The article makes it quite plain why the U.S. government is in no position to make the big banks, which last year needed massive federal help to save them from utter ruin, now lend money again to the taxpayers whose money was used to rescue the financial institutions. The unemployment rate is, as the previous president used to say of the economy, "strong and getting stronger." Obama senses danger—his party is not likely to overperform in the midterm elections—but what is he really going to do? It was only two days after his West Point speech announcing 30,000 more troops to Afghanistan that he told a White House forum on unemployment that "our resources are limited." Now, why is that?

Take Off PJ's, Get Dressed, and Lay Off the Hallucinogens

As if all this weren't bad enough, now CNBC's John Harwood—wasn't he a reporter somewhere?—pipes in that "so much" of the liberal criticism of the health care reform bill has been "really idiotic." He opines that liberals who criticize the Senate bill for lacking universal coverage "ought to lay off the hallucinogenic drugs because we've had a vivid demonstration of the limits of political possibilities on this issue." Hey, is he quoting the same White House wit who said to him in October, "Those bloggers need to take off their pajamas, get dressed and realize that governing a closely divided country is complicated and difficult"? We strongly suspect Harwood's not that colorful a speaker; could he be parroting Rahm Emanuel? You betcha.

Even before this setback, things were not going our way. No public option, no Medicare buy-in (no serious White House push for either option), no winding down of the war in Afghanistan . . . In the midst of non-delivery of much of what progressives were hoping for (where's the new New Deal so many were writing about this time last year?), the right wing is hyperventilating with obstructionist foolishness and hysterical hyperbole as if Obama really were acting like Franklin Roosevelt. If only. (The Conservative Political Action Conference—CPAC—next February will be co-hosted by the John Birch Society. No kidding.) We say, if the right is going to excoriate you as a socialist, then go ahead and be one. Earn their enmity. Ramp it up. Be the real thing. But . . . that is not likely with the Goldman Sachs/Citigroup gang in place at Treasury. Also not likely with a president who has been overly conciliatory with a party locked against him. Though this is not his intention, in effect Obama has been cooperating with the forces of paralysis. But you never know: looking at a possible cataclysm in the midterm elections could bring about some more change we can believe in.

Sick and tired of being sick and tired? (It was worse before last November 4, wasn't it?) Though dismayed, we won't lie idle because the only thing worse than feeling defeated is giving up entirely, and that's not going to happen. It is only in resistance and efforts to make the world less bad than its power-possessors seem to insist on making it; it's only through persistence and repeated struggle that it's possible for true progressives to live with themselves. As the labor organizer Mary Harris "Mother" Jones (1837–1930) used to advise, "Sit down and read. Educate yourself for the coming conflicts." That sounds like good advice in this chilly winter of our discontent. It may get worse yet—after all, it's only the first day of winter. But we're not alone, and working keeps us warm.

Mad Tea Party with Chainsaws and Clowns

APRIL 8, 2011—Amid all the talk and worry of a Shutdown Showdown, is anyone else noticing that this crisis is happening as the United States is embarking on yet a third or fourth simultaneous, costly war? We and other prophets could see this thing coming even before last November's mid-term election when the Republicans were already warning that a Shutdown might be necessary to curb Washington's "out of control spending," though *of course* they hoped it wouldn't have to come to that. And if it did happen, it wouldn't be their fault. (Remember 1995?) A budget crisis complete with the grinding of chainsaws and the flashes of bloody meat cleavers was foreseeable last December when the Republicans were forcing an extension of the Bush (now Obama) Tax Cuts for Million- and Billionaires. Yes, the party demanding billions in spending cuts is the same that fought furiously for a high-end tax cut that will add $700 billion to the deficit over the next 10 years. The same one that sold us the $3 trillion Iraq war.

The Obama administration, which has gotten itself backed up against a wall yet again by "seeking common ground" and waiting again till the 4th quarter to speak up, warns that a government shutdown could furlough over 800,000 federal workers, interrupt military pay, and slow tax refunds.

We blame the Tea Party-infused Republicans for this mess, but we also hold the timid, mute Democrats responsible. (Democrats have already agreed to $33 billion in cuts, and still the Mad Tea Party demands more blood.) And

We the People are also responsible for this because we have not demanded forcefully enough that Congress and the White House stand up against this madness. Some of Us even voted for these extremists.

It's Not About the Budget Deficit

Conservatives cannot govern well for the same reason that vegetarians cannot prepare a world-class boeuf bourguignon: If you believe that what you are called upon to do is wrong, you are not likely to do it very well.—Alan Wolfe, "Why Conservatives Can't Govern" (*Washington Monthly*, July/August 2006)

Those driving the G.O.P. do not care about creating jobs or providing relief for the 24 million un- or underemployed—nor it seems do those trying to appease them. The ideologues are forcing this fight not so much to reduce the deficit as to end federal funding for Planned Parenthood or any abortion or family-planning services; to cut funding for NPR, health care reform, and the new consumer protection bureau; and to prevent regulation of greenhouse gases by the Environmental Protection Agency. (In 1995, too, G.O.P. insistence on unrelated policy objectives forced a shutdown.) Some of the basic, public-protecting functions of government are being gutted while the president seeks "common ground" (and reelection). Where are the forceful voices of the pro-government faction of the Democratic party? Why do they not boast of the many good accomplishments of the last two years? Why didn't they before the mid-term elections? (See "A Failure to Communicate—Not a Failure to Govern" and "Yes We Can Pass Good Legislation.") Do the networks still allow Democrats to appear before a camera? Are progressive Dems allowed inside the *Meet the Press* studio?

Who knows what will happen? No one knows how this plays out. It cannot end well, though, with an overly conciliatory, "post-partisan" president who wants to find common ground with extremist ideologues intent on shutting down the government. All we know is that it's time for Democrats and moderates and any sane, responsible Republicans still breathing (Dick Lugar is one) to stand up and begin, at last, to make the case for why government is good and necessary and must be not only preserved but reinforced with tax revenues from corporations and the very well-to-do—many of whom (like the Koch-funded "Americans for Prosperity" and "FreedomWorks") have fueled this fire. It is pathetic that the one nation on earth with the most stable, long-lasting democratic, representative government with a built-in balance of powers, so carefully constructed by wise and prudent men, is now apparently at the mercy of zealots driven by corporate money and 24-hour anti-government propaganda. Verily, the rich are killing us all.

They will over-reach, they will have to retreat some, but will the moderate general public ever rise up and say "Enough!"? We have little hope in our elected officials. The determined and courageous pro-labor citizens of Wisconsin and elsewhere in the Midwest give us some hope, but how bad does it have to get?

TAGS: Barack Obama, Democrats, Mad Tea Party, Party of Hell No, Silence of the Dems

http://www.leveesnotwar.org/mad-tea-party-with-chainsaws/

Arguing about How to Defuse
a Huge Ticking Bomb

*I certainly think you will see some short-term volatility. In the end,
the sun is going to come up tomorrow.*

Rep. Austin Scott of Georgia, president, House Republicans' freshman class

JULY 20, 2011—House Republicans laughed a former George H. W. Bush economist out of the room on Monday when he tried to warn them of the dire consequences of a U.S. debt default, according to John Stanton of *Roll Call*. Stanton says the number of let-it-crash denialists among House Republicans is actually increasing. They think the Aug. 2 deadline is artificial. The Honorable Louie Gohmert of Texas said in a radio interview that the Aug. 2 deadline is only for the convenience of the president so he can have a big Aug. 4 birthday celebration fund-raiser. Freshman Rep. Mo Brooks (R-Ala.) says there's nothing to worry about: "In fact, our credit rating should be improved by not raising the debt ceiling." The crazy just keeps on comin'. And the clock—or is it a time bomb?—is ticking. The rating agencies Moody's and Standard & Poor's may not wait till Aug. 2 to downgrade the United States of America's credit rating. Then what?

Burn-it-Down Nihilism Spreads Among
Tea-Infused House Republicans

Congress raised the debt ceiling 7 times under George W. Bush, 18 times under Ronald Reagan. But that was then. There is serious concern in the Republican leadership (in the Senate, for example) that House leaders John Boehner and Eric Cantor cannot control the fire-eating Tea Party members, who distrust them and Senate minority leader Mitch McConnell as RINOs

(Republicans in Name Only). The radicals have principles; they don't give a damn about reelection. Many of them scorn the Senate's "Gang of Six" plan as a betrayal because it involves revenues and does not cut spending deeply enough.

Self-styled Tea Parties of populist anger at overtaxation and nonrepresentation began to sprout at first spontaneously in 2009 (though maybe their rise should be dated to Sarah Palin's "goin' rogue" rallies of late 2008). As the G.O.P. and right-wing self-interest groups including Fox News began to feed the nascent movement with the steroids of corporate money and tactics training to direct their anger against the Obama administration's health care reform initiative—and then against everything else Democrats were up to—political observers on the right and left voiced misgivings that in dispensing the stimulants, the Koch brothers, FreedomWorks, Americans for Prosperity, and other Dr. Frankensteins were creating a monster that they would not be able to control. (Remember the GOP House members standing on the Capitol building porches waving "Don't Tread on Me" flags and egging on the Tea Party protesters down below shouting "kill the bill!" as the House was debating the health care bill in March 2010?)

Republicans "won't be satisfied until the family is out on the street."

The New Yorker's George Packer begins a Talk of the Town piece (July 25 issue) about the debt-ceiling fight titled "Empty Wallets" with a heart-grieving anecdote of a jobless Florida man whose daughter has bone cancer. Danny Hartzell is packing up the family to move in with a friend in Georgia with whom he has reconnected on Facebook, hoping for a fresh start. After being terminated from his $8.50 an hour job at Target—business is slow—his last biweekly paycheck after taxes is $140. Hartzell is hit by one ax-blow of bad luck after another, mostly in the form of Republican-legislated cuts of unemployment benefits or access to health care (votes cast by men and women who have health insurance).

Turning to the debt-ceiling impasse between Congress and President Obama, Packer compares the struggle as "like members of an ordnance-disposal unit arguing about how to defuse a huge ticking bomb."

Obama, securely in character, called on all sides to rise above
petty politics, acknowledged the practical realities of divided
government, and proposed a grand compromise that would
lower the deficit by four trillion dollars. According to the *Times'*
Nate Silver, Obama's offer, in its roughly four-to-one balance
between spending cuts and revenue increases, falls to the right of
the average American voter's preference; in fact, it may outflank
the views of the average Republican. . . .

The Republicans are also securely in character. They've
rejected everything that the President has proposed, because
Obama's deal includes tax increases and the closing of loopholes
for hedge-fund managers and corporate jets and companies that
move offshore. Ninety-seven per cent of House Republicans have
taken something called the "No Tax Pledge." . . . Representative
Paul Ryan's ten-year budget plan, which remains his party's
blueprint for the future, would impose a fifty-percent cut on
programs like food stamps and Supplemental Security Income,
which, as long as Danny Hartzell remains jobless, represent the
Hartzells' only income. By the last day of June, the Hartzells had
twenty-nine dollars to their name. The Republicans in Congress
won't be satisfied until the family is out on the street.

Packer notes that the sociologist Max Weber in an essay on politics as a
vocation distinguished between "the ethic of responsibility" and "the ethic
of ultimate ends"—between those who act on the basis of practical considerations and those motivated by a higher conviction, acting on principle
"regardless of consequences." They are opposites, but someone suited to a
career in politics forges some kind of union of the ethics of responsibility and
ultimate ends.

On its own, the ethic of responsibility can become a devotion to
technically correct procedure, while the ethic of ultimate ends
can become fanaticism. Weber's terms perfectly capture the
toxic dynamic between the President, who takes responsibility
as an end in itself, and the Republicans in Congress, who are

destructively consumed with their own dogma. Neither side
can be said to possess what Weber calls a "leader's personality."
Responsibility without conviction is weak, but it is sane.
Conviction without responsibility, in the current incarnation of
the Republican Party, is raving mad. . . . It was Lenin who first
said, "The worse, the better," a mantra adopted by elements of
the New Left in the nineteen-sixties. This nihilistic idea animates
a large number of Republican officeholders.

Packer concludes with the pessimistic observation that Barack Obama—whom we dimly remember as a man elected president on slogans of "hope" and "change" (our characterization, not Packer's)—"is now the leading champion of fiscal austerity, and his proposals contain very little in the way of job creation. . . . he no longer uses his office's most powerful tool, rhetorical suasion, to keep the country focussed on the continued need for government activism."

TAGS: Barack Obama, budget deficit, Mad Tea Party, Republican fiscal stewardship,
Republican Tea Party
http://www.leveesnotwar.org/arguing-about-how-to-defuse-a-huge-ticking-bomb/

The Credit Crisis and the Social Contract

OCT. 1, 2008—It's significant that the crisis threatening the U.S. and the global economy is a credit crisis, a collapse of confidence. The word "credit" derives from the Latin *credere*, to trust, believe. But how can financial institutions believe in each other when they've played Enron-like shell games to the point where no one knows what anything is worth anymore? How can anyone have confidence when regulations are legislated away and there is no adult supervision?

The dog-eat-dog feeding frenzy we've seen on Wall Street and Washington in recent years obviously does not provide a sound basis for a sustainable society and economy. It's inherently unstable: it's not good for business, and it's hell on people. We are all in this together, nationally and globally, and the way we see it, the only sustainable economy is one based on principles of the Golden Rule. Enough damage has been done and felt that this statement should be seen as a realistic, practical prescription for stability rather than as a sweet dream.

We call for managed capitalism and a restoration of the social contract, a repair of the social safety net and a more equitable distribution of wealth. To endure, to be fair, the economy and society must be based upon a two-way street of reciprocal obligation and fulfillment: Everyone must contribute, but no one should be left to sink or swim.

Part of the ancient idea of the social contract—the spirit of cooperation that made possible the evolution from a state of nature to civil society—is the deeply held notion, as deep as conscience, that if the ruler does not govern justly, then the people are not obligated to obey. Some say—and we agree—the people are justified in changing the government.

We see New Orleans after Katrina as the epitome of the social contract broken. As we've said before, the Lower Ninth Ward is the national predicament carried to an extreme. It is this vision that drives *Levees Not War*, and it is because we know Barack Obama and Joe Biden understand the need to restore fairness and hope to the American way of life that we are vigorous supporters of their campaign. And this is why we urge our readers to join us in contributing not only financially but with phone calls and door-to-door, get-out-the-vote efforts to change the government in Washington, and local government too.

For more about "managed capitalism" and for lucid, "razor sharp" explanations of how Wall Street and Washington got us into this mess, we highly recommend Robert Kuttner's excellent *The Squandering of America: How the Failure of Our Politics Undermines Our Prosperity* (2007).

TAGS: 2008 financial crisis, global economy, social contract
http://www.leveesnotwar.org/the-credit-crisis-and-the-social-contract/

The Destroyer

*I do solemnly swear that I will faithfully execute the office of
President of the United States, and will to the best of my ability
preserve, protect and defend the Constitution of the United States.*

DEC. 7, 2007—If a president recites this oath, is he legally bound to take care of the nation itself, or only to 'preserve, protect and defend the Constitution' of the United States (however White House legal counsel may interpret that clause)? Does he have some 'wiggle room' here? Does the oath pertain only to duly elected chief executives?

Although he has (twice) placed his hand on a Bible and spoken the words, George W. Bush has never been serious about protecting the United States—not on Aug. 6, 2001, when he was shown a Presidential Daily Briefing titled 'Bin Laden Determined to Strike in U.S.,' and not on September 11, when the nation's defenses were suspiciously slack. He disregarded his duty when for a year after 9/11 he opposed the establishment of a department of homeland security. And then there was Katrina.

The newly proposed cuts to cities and states' anti-terrorism programs—including DHS grants for police, rescue departments, firefighters, port security, and transit security—compound the budget cuts of 2006 when Bush slashed anti-terrorism funding for New York City and Washington by 40% and sprinkled a paltry $1.7 billion instead on such second- and third-rate targets as Charlotte, St. Louis, and Jacksonville. (No offense, but really . . .)

- In 2006 a DHS 'risk scorecard' claimed that New York, with the
  Statue of Liberty, the Empire State Building, and the Brooklyn Bridge,
  had 'zero' national monuments or icons. DHS's anti-terrorism grants
  that year for New York City were reduced from $207 million to

$124 million, and Washington's DHS budget fell from $77 million to about $46 million.

- In 2006 New Orleans's funds for security and disaster preparedness were slashed in half, from $9.3 million to $4.6 million, even as the stricken city was struggling to recover from Hurricane Katrina— a disaster compounded by Bush's earlier federal cuts to its flood protection system.

Bush Inc. has shown repeatedly that it views the possibility of terrorist attacks not as a threat to be countered effectively, without fanfare (as, say, the British do), but as a useful tool (like shock therapy) for frightening the American public into accepting policies and wars that are otherwise unjustifiable. (And recall the conveniently timed 'alerts' during the campaign year of 2004—what Keith Olbermann has termed 'the nexus of politics and terror.') In *The Shock Doctrine: The Rise of Disaster Capitalism*, Naomi Klein has demonstrated in abundant detail that the security-industrial complex can be highly profitable for friends of the Commander in Chief and his party such as Dick Cheney of Halliburton and Erik Prince of Blackwater.

Since January 2001, as we have witnessed the successive waves of disasters and domestic funding cuts while wars proliferate and military budgets escalate and chaos metastasizes, we have come to regard the president not only (ironically) as The Commander and The Decider, but, seriously, as The Destroyer. (Observe how, regardless of the new National Intelligence Estimate's findings on Iran's nuclear energy program, he stubbornly insists on portraying Iran as a grave threat, an enemy whom he will threaten but with whom he will not try to reason, negotiate, or seek to coexist. Instead, he warns ominously of World War III. [See "Horseman of the Apocalypse," posted Oct. 17, 2007.])

On the injustice of slavery, Thomas Jefferson once wrote, "I tremble for my country when I reflect that God is just, that His justice cannot sleep for ever" (*Notes on the State of Virginia, 1781–85*). Indeed, the stubborn consistency of this administration's reckless actions (and of its party faithful in Congress) only makes sense as the fulfillment of a curse upon this nation.

We citizens, meanwhile—we who count ourselves among the free and the brave—are duty- and honor-bound to resist The Destroyer and restore our nation to its rightful place as a "more perfect union" and a sanctuary of liberty and justice for all. To us, the only logical response to a world turned upside-down is to do as the Scottish novelist and artist Alasdair Gray once wrote: "Work as if you are in the early days of a better nation" (epigraph to *1982, Janine*; 1984).

TAGS: George W. Bush, Halliburton, oath of office, The Destroyer
http://www.leveesnotwar.org/the-destroyer/

Is the U.S. an Occupied Nation?

JUNE 16, 2007—Just supposing our national government were ever to be infiltrated, somehow occupied by invisible agents of a foreign power (without the public quite realizing it)—If this happened and then the public somehow became aware that the government had fallen into the hands of men loyal to an alien power, then would the people yank the usurpers out of office at once?

For what people—what free and rational people whose votes and taxes empower the government—would willingly entrust the powers of public spending, taxation, foreign relations, and war powers to officials loyal to a foreign power? . . . or to any authority acting without attention to or concern for the public well-being?

Would that government be called a representative democracy?

TAGS: democracy, government, national security, powers of public spending, representative democracy, taxation

http://www.leveesnotwar.org/is-the-us-an-occupied-nation/

Supreme Conservatives Drag U.S.
Ceaselessly into the (Jim Crow) Past

*Throwing out preclearance when it has worked and is continuing
to work to stop discriminatory changes is like throwing away your
umbrella in a rainstorm because you are not getting wet.*

Justice Ruth Bader Ginsburg, dissenting opinion, *Shelby County v. Holder*

JUNE 26, 2013—Yesterday, June 25, 2013, will go down in infamy as the day when a radically conservative majority of the Supreme Court ripped the guts out of the historic protections of the 1965 Voting Rights Act, "the crown jewel of the civil rights movement" that was so proudly signed by President Lyndon B. Johnson. Congressman John R. Lewis, who was beaten nearly to death by state troopers in the famous "Bloody Sunday" civil rights march in Selma, Alabama, in March 1965, declared the *Shelby County v. Holder* decision "a dagger in the heart" of the Voting Rights Act.

Re-Legalizing Electoral Racism;
Red State Republicans "Free at Last"

What the 5–4 decision, signed by Chief Justice John Roberts, does, nearly 50 years after its signing, is declare unconstitutional the single most important part of the Act (section 4), which identifies the states and counties that must submit to oversight (or preclearance) by the Justice Department before changing "any voting qualification or prerequisite to voting, or standard, practice, or procedure with respect to voting" in any "covered jurisdiction." In effect, the conservative majority struck down section 4 as a sneaky way of nullifying section 5, without actually ruling on the constitutionality of section 5. As *The New York Times*'s Adam Liptak explains:

> The majority held that the coverage formula in Section 4 of the
> Voting Rights Act, originally passed in 1965 and most recently
> updated by Congress in 1975, was unconstitutional. The section
> determined which states must receive clearance from the Justice
> Department or a federal court in Washington before they made
> minor changes to voting procedures, like moving a polling place,
> or major ones, like redrawing electoral districts. . . .
>
> The decision did not strike down Section 5 [which sets out
> the preclearance requirement], but without Section 4, the later
> section is without significance—unless Congress passes a new
> bill for determining which states would be covered.

These jurisdictions that were required to seek preclearance include the
very states—mostly in the Old Confederacy—that were the worst offenders
against minorities seeking the right to vote. Indeed, it is no accident that it was
Shelby County, Alabama—i.e., Birmingham—that brought the suit against
the U.S. Justice Department. In the 1960s it was the Justice Department, very
often backed up by the National Guard, that was on the front lines of protecting southern blacks against discrimination, vicious racism, and murder.

In "An Assault on the Voting Rights Act," *The New York Times* editorial
board declared the decision "damaging and intellectually dishonest," and that
was just in the first sentence. In a *Times* op-ed, Richard L. Hasen, author of
The Voting Wars: From Florida 2000 to the Next Election Meltdown, writes:

> The court pretends it is not striking down the act but merely
> sending the law back to Congress for tweaking; it imagines
> that Congress forced its hand; and it fantasizes that voting
> discrimination in the South is a thing of the past. None of this
> is true.
>
> In the *Shelby* decision, we see a somewhat more open version
> of a pattern that is characteristic of the Roberts court, in which
> the conservative justices tee up major constitutional issues for
> dramatic reversal. First the court wrecked campaign finance law
> in *Citizens United*. On Tuesday it took away a crown jewel of the
> civil rights movement. And as we saw in Monday's Fisher case,
> affirmative action is next in line . . .

John Roberts, who has long sought to weaken the Voting Rights Act, wrote in the majority opinion that because voter registration among black voters is higher than it was at the time the Voting Rights Act was passed, the protections afforded by the Act are no longer needed. (Click here for Justice Ruth Bader Ginsburg's scathing dissent, in which she wrote, "Hubris is a fit word for today's demolition of the VRA. . . . The court errs egregiously by overriding Congress's decision" to reauthorize the Act.) As though mere registration is the same thing as actually being able to vote, or your vote actually being counted. Ask the citizens of counties in Florida and Ohio in the contested elections of 2000 and 2004, or those who were forced to wait in interminable lines in 2008, 2012. *The New Yorker*'s Amy Davidson points out:

> Ginsburg quoted an F.B.I. investigation of Alabama legislators who referred to black voters as "Aborigines" and talked about how to keep them from the polls: "These conversations occurred not in the 1870's, or even in the 1960's, they took place in 2010." ("The Court Rejects the Voting Rights Act—and History," June 25, 2013)

The United States Senate approved an extension of the law in 2006 by a 98–0 vote, and the House by a 390–33 vote; 33 Republicans (all white men, except one white woman, from North Carolina) voted against it. Former President George W. Bush, who nominated Roberts as chief justice, said many fine words about the importance of the Voting Rights Act in a ceremony at the White House. If you watch the videotape he sounds sincere; perhaps he was. Had the Voting Right's Acts provisions been truly observed and enforced in the election of 2000, however—and had a similar 5–4 Supreme Court decision not ruled that Florida's recounting of votes be stopped—George W. Bush would not have been in the White House.

A Nation in Reverse

Coincidentally, we're sure, Confederate states such as North Carolina, Mississippi, Alabama, Texas, Georgia, and Florida (of course Florida!) immediately, on the same day as the Court's ruling, rolled out new legislation to restrict voting (less early voting, no Sunday voting, no voting on the same day you've registered). The AP's Bill Barrow reported, "Across the South, Republicans are working to take advantage of a new political landscape after a divided U.S. Supreme Court freed all or part of 15 states, many of them in the old Confederacy, from having to ask Washington's permission before changing election procedures in jurisdictions with histories of discrimination."

And Ed Kilgore writes at *Washington Monthly*'s Political Animal blog:

> . . . across the South, we've heard cheers from Republicans
> eager to return to a time when the feds didn't interfere with the
> sovereign ability of white southerners to decide who was worthy
> to vote. It's like watching a tape of the 1965 march across the
> Edmund Pettus Bridge in Selma in reverse.

One man's forward is another's backward. As some incremental, progressive legislative and judicial victories move liberties forward (healthcare reform and marriage equality are notable examples), other battles seemingly fought and won long ago are being reversed, dismantled. The United States is being torn asunder by well-funded and insatiable conservative forces that seek to drag the nation back to the days before the civil rights movement, before the women's liberation movement or Earth Day, before the New Deal, before Theodore Roosevelt's establishment of national parks, environmental protections, and food and drug regulations. Verily, sadly, after yesterday's odious ruling by the conservatives on the Court, William Greider's prophetic 2003 article "Rolling Back the 20th Century" is more true than ever.

God bless America. Please. In the words of the Old Testament prophet Amos, often quoted by the Rev. Martin Luther King Jr., one of the guiding-light heroes of this blog, "Let justice roll down like waters, and righteousness like an ever-flowing stream" (Amos 5:24).

Democrats in the 2010 Midterms:
A Failure to Communicate—Not a Failure to Govern

NOV. 3, 2010—A party that governs well but communicates poorly was set back by a party that obstructs well but is more interested in holding power than in governing.

What could have been a hideous wipeout following a grotesque campaign season was instead a series of setbacks, strong disappointments, and some reliefs and bright spots. Among the setbacks we sadly count the Illinois and Pennsylvania senate races where the Democratic candidates came very close. Among the strong disappointments were the losses of progressives like Russ Feingold, Alan Grayson, and Tom Perriello. *Ouch.* But we were relieved by the victories of senate majority leader Harry Reid, California senator Barbara Boxer, and among the bright spots are the gubernatorial victories of Andrew Cuomo in New York and Jerry Brown in California.

But the Democratic party is in serious trouble in the midsection of the country, with painful losses from Pennsylvania west to Wisconsin. Obama already is not strong in the South (which sometimes includes Florida), and that's not likely to change. (Also disappointing was Charlie Melancon's loss to David Vitter in Louisiana; Vitter ran against Obama, disregarding Melancon.) Obama and the Democratic party must get something in gear—something like employment, jobs programs, and a focused communications department—to regain support among the Rust Belt and Midwestern voters.

What the Hell Happened?

Of course Republicans are claiming a mandate, but that's ridiculous (and not at all supported by the CBS exit poll). We think the election results are more a matter of a sick economy (see below), Democrats' failure to clearly explain and promote their accomplishments, and massive GOP and conservative negative advertising + 24/7 Fox News propaganda (aka the Republican Noise Machine). While Republicans insist the election results are a "referendum on Obama's agenda" and "the voice of the American people," let's not forget that the GOP Tea Party candidates' ads and secret, shadow groups' attacks on Democrats were funded by millions of dollars from Karl Rove's Crossroads GPS and the U.S. Chamber of Commerce. Spending on congressional campaigns was expected to reach $4 billion. The GOP started campaigning around the inauguration; the Democrats, preoccupied with legislative accomplishments (see below), were late to the game. Further, remember that the so-called Tea Party, though it had grass-roots origins, has largely been co-opted and the Tea Party as it is now is not a people's movement in the traditional sense: it is corporate-sponsored, establishment-driven, not grass-roots but astroturf. Ask Dick Armey and the billionaire Koch brothers. So much for "the voice of the American people."

And "It's the Economy, Stupid." Comparisons with the 1994 midterms (after Clinton's first 18 months) are common, but the economy is far worse now. A closer comparison—which Republicans don't mention—would be 1982, after Reagan's first 18 months, when the unemployment rate was about 10 percent: Democrats gained 27 seats, cementing their majority. In 1994 unemployment was about 5.6 percent. It is now about 9.6 percent, with some 15 million people out of work, and that's only counting the people who have not given up in despair and not counting the under-employed (those working part-time instead of full-time). Reporter Robert Scheer says that for some 50 million Americans, either they've lost their homes through foreclosures or their home values are underwater: the amounts owed on their mortgages exceed the property's market value. (We recommend Sheer's new book, *The Great American Stickup: How Reagan Republicans and Clinton Democrats Enriched Wall Street While Mugging Main Street.*)

Need we add that the Republicans have done *nothing* to help create jobs, but instead have blocked extensions of unemployment insurance, voted against tax breaks for small businesses—often voting against their own ideas—and massively resisted the American Recovery and Reinvestment Act (the stimulus)? They wanted to intensify the economic pain and thwart the president in order to regain power. This will be their strategy for the next two years as well. Gird your loins.

Much Accomplished, Much More to Be Done

This blog has complained possibly too much about what the president and the Democrats have *not* done. Perhaps most frustrating, though, is that the Democrats in Congress and the White House *failed to communicate* to the nation the astonishingly productive legislative record that they have accomplished over the past 21 months. With bill after bill, the Donkey kicked ass, but you'd never know it from them.

On Monday, Nov. 1, *The Rachel Maddow Show* produced a 15-minute segment highlighting the many accomplishments of the 111th Congress. The list is impressive—"the most legislatively productive 21 months in decades"— and we only wish the DNC had boasted far and wide about these bills. With more effective messaging (and a more aggressive focus on job creation, of course), the Dems could have countered the GOP distortions and rallied stronger base support and thus invigorated voter turnout.

This Is What a Functioning Congress Looks Like

Take a look at these achievements (and spread the good word):

Lilly Ledbetter Fair Pay Act to help victims of pay discrimination—especially women—challenge unequal pay. Signed by President Obama Jan. 29, 2009.

Children's Health Insurance Program Reauthorization Act of 2009 expanded health insurance coverage to more than 4 million children and pregnant women. Signed into law Feb. 4, 2009.

Edward M. Kennedy Serve America Act (2009), giving about $6 billion over 5 years and increasing the number of full-time and part-time national service (AmeriCorps) volunteers from 75,000 to 250,000. Creates new programs focused on special areas like strengthening schools, improving health care for low-income communities, boosting energy efficiency and cleaning up parks, etc. Signed April 21, 2009.

Credit Card Accountability Responsibility and Disclosure Act (2009) sponsored by Rep. Carolyn Maloney (D-NY), described by *Money* magazine as the "best friend a credit card user ever had." Signed May 22, 2009.

College student loan reform, March 2010: as part of the health care reform legislation, a provision "that would cut funding to private student lenders and redirect billions of dollars in expected savings into grants to needy students" (*W. Post*).

Family Smoking Prevention and Tobacco Control Act gave FDA power to regulate tobacco. Signed by President Obama June 22, 2009.

Hate Crimes Prevention Act (aka Matthew Shepard and James Byrd Jr. Hate Crimes Prevention Act), made it a federal crime to commit assault based on victim's gender, sexual orientation, etc. Signed by President Obama Oct. 28, 2009.

Car Allowance Rebate System (aka "Cash for Clunkers"): Begun in June 2009, and by August the auto industry was reporting strong sales—only about a half year after GM and Chrysler were bailed out by Washington. Boosted sales of safer and more fuel-efficient cars, helping clear the air and stimulating the economy.

Veterans benefited from the Veterans Health Care Budget Reform and Transparency **Act** of 2009, the Consolidated Appropriations Act of 2010, and the Caregivers and Veterans Omnibus Health Services Act of 2010. The American Legion said "in our view the real successes [of the 111th Congress] were the passage of bills that affected nearly every veteran in America."

All this is even before the big-ticket items of the American Recovery and Reinvestment Act of 2009 (aka The **Stimulus**), the monumental (and incremental) Patient Protection and Affordable Care Act ("**Obamacare**"), and the **Dodd–Frank Wall Street Reform and Consumer Protection Act** (2010),

which included establishment of a Consumer Financial Protection Bureau, presently being (unofficially) headed by Harvard law professor and consumer advocate Elizabeth Warren.

And all of this was done with virtually no help from the Republicans in Congress. (Honorable Exception: Senator Orrin Hatch of Utah was one of the authors of the Edward M. Kennedy Serve America Act.)

Oh, and while all this was happening—you'd never know it to listen to the Noise Machine (or the Democratic Party)—Democrats actually reduced the deficit. The U.S. deficit shrank 9% in the fiscal year ending Sept. 30, 2010, the fastest one-year deficit reduction since 1984. The budget shortfall of $1.294 trillion was down $122 billion from the previous fiscal year. The deficit's ratio to economic output fell to 8.9 percent of the gross domestic product, down from an even 10 percent of GDP in fiscal 2009. What you also never hear from Republicans is how there was a budget surplus when George W. Bush took office in 2001 that had vanished before September 11.

This is a legislative record to be very proud of, and we are grateful to the House and Senate members who took difficult but principled votes in the public interest but who, for reasons large and small, complex and simple, did not win reelection. We regret that the DNC and the White House did not alert the nation about all the good policy work they were doing while the Republicans were busy hogging the microphones on cable TV.

Looking Forward to Pressing Onward

We anticipate gridlock, acrimony, more Republican Tea Party antics (cat fights and power struggles between Rand Paul and Mitch McConnell, for example, and between Sarah Palin and Christine O'Donnell).

Today in his press conference President Obama said, "Let's find those areas where we can agree."

Oh yeah? How's that going to work? Republicans have been repetitively transmitting "no compromise" messages for weeks now; longer, actually. In October Senate minority leader Mitch McConnell said, "The single most important thing we want to achieve is for President Obama to be a one-term president." And John Boehner, the likely speaker of the House, says of Obama's agenda, "We're going to do everything—and I mean everything we can do—to kill it, stop it, slow it down, whatever we can."

It is perverse and dismaying that in the two years since a near-catastrophic economic collapse they helped bring about, a Party of No has done nothing but stand in the way of efforts to repair damages they caused or enabled—wars, deficits, deregulation—and is rewarded by impatient, fearful, stressed-out voters whose anger that party has deliberately and cynically inflamed.

Dismaying but also energizing: we're not going to let them get away with the distortions, and we'll be pressing the White House and Harry Reid and other Democratic leaders to aggressively call out the GOP's lies and force the Republicans into votes that will show what they're really made of. We'll urge Reid and the president to assertively propose jobs and infrastructure and energy programs: let the GOP be seen in broad daylight saying no to jobs bills in the name of curbing the deficits they created.

This election was not a great rebuke of the Democratic party or of the president's agenda (again, see the CBS exit poll), but rather a predictable response to prolonged and widespread unemployment and economic anxiety. Further, as the president acknowledged, many voters may have misinterpreted the administration's emergency response to the economic crisis—support of TARP for Wall Street and the auto industry bailouts, for example—as a "big government over-reach" agenda, as if that was what Obama had wanted to do all along.

The president has delivered on a lot of campaign promises, but millions are still out of work. The Republicans will not deliver on jobs, either, unless they suddenly convert to New Deal–type employment programs. Of course they will not. They have no agenda but to extend tax cuts for the wealthiest and to serve the corporations who paid for their campaign ads, and to oppose Obama at all times. Just watch.

We also anticipate keeping our sleeves rolled up. We will try to help build support for President Obama's National Infrastructure Bank idea, which he mentioned again today in his press conference. When asked how he and the government could push forward with job creation measures that the GOP would oppose, the president replied that traditionally investments in infrastructure programs have bipartisan appeal, and he will press ahead on that initiative with congressional leaders. We like that idea very much. We'll have his back, and we'll be pushing Congress, too. (Connecticut Democratic congresswoman Rosa DeLauro is one of the principal parents of this idea. Obama has been talking it up since at least February 2008. See "Barack, You're Totally Our Infrastructure Hero" in Part II.)

More deep thoughts to come as we ponder and regroup . . .

Mr. Jindal, Tear Down This Ambition

FEB. 20, 2009—Who says brainy, high-I.Q. types can't be stunningly obtuse? Or cold-hearted?

We were already highly irritated with Louisiana governor Bobby Jindal, by some accounts an educated man, for supporting and signing the creationist, Orwellian-named Louisiana Academic Freedom Act, a law that officially weakens the teaching of evolution and now punishes New Orleans as a national science association sadly announces it would rather meet in Salt Lake City (!) than convene its 2,300 members in an anti-science state.

Now, Jindal says he'll reject $98 million from the recently passed economic stimulus bill that would go to extend unemployment insurance for up to 25,000 Louisianans. In today's G.O.P., a governor with presidential ambitions is a curse that we would not wish on any state.

Gov. Jindal is ready for his close-up, raising his national profile as one of several "principled conservative" Republican governors (with presidential ambitions) who say they'll refuse federal funding from the stimulus bill. He appears today on *Meet the Press* and on Tuesday night—the night of Mardi Gras, as it happens—he'll present the G.O.P.'s rebuttal to President Obama's address to the nation about the state of the economy. (See "GOP Calls on Exorcist to Break Obama Spell" at *People Get Ready*, and *The Daily Kingfish*'s account of Jindal's claim to powers of exorcism.)

Louisiana's unemployment benefits are already below the national average. As of 2006, the weekly maximum benefit was $258—the national average in 2006 was $277 per week—and the potential duration of benefits was 21 to 26 weeks (no more than half year). Louisiana's unemployment rate has risen to 5.9%, with about 122,000 jobless. Now help is on the way, right?

The stimulus bill (the American Recovery and Reinvestment Act) has three provisions for unemployed workers. One provides funds for states willing to allow a \$25-per-week increase in unemployment benefits. (Jindal will accept this.) The second provision extends the Emergency Unemployment Compensation (EUC) program that gives 20 weeks of federally funded benefits to the jobless who have already received all the state unemployment benefits they're entitled to. (Jindal says no.) A third provision widens the pool of unemployed eligible to receive benefits. (Jindal says no.)

As *The Times-Picayune*'s Jan Moller explains, "At issue are two pots of federal money that states can access only if they agree to change their laws to make it easier for unemployed workers to qualify for benefits.

> To access the first pot of money, worth \$32.8 million over 27 months, Louisiana would have to offer benefits to workers who have held jobs for as little as three months before becoming unemployed. Workers now have to hold a job for at least a year before they are eligible to collect unemployment. ("Jindal Rejects \$98 Million in Stimulus Spending," *Times-Picayune*, Feb. 20, 2009)

Jindal is not rejecting all of the stimulus money coming to Louisiana, but he is turning down \$98 million that he disingenuously claims would result in tax increases for businesses and would require that the state legislature amend a law to allow it to accept the money. "You're talking about temporary federal spending triggering a permanent change in state law," said Jindal. (Louisiana senator Mary Landrieu disputes this claim; the unemployment benefits are designed to be temporary.)

While a reasonable person might expect a state facing a \$2.1 billion deficit to welcome any financial assistance available, the Jindal administration seems to be looking for reasons to reject the money. (The G.O.P. is watching.)

This "fiscal discipline" posturing is beyond frustrating. Activists work hard at pushing the government to spend more on infrastructure and social programs to alleviate suffering and disrepair caused by official neglect. Now, when money is actually available, the governor of a poor, ravaged state thinks first of his own political ambitions. This makes us worry about the effect this "principled" refusal will have on efforts to secure additional federal funding in the future. (Your governor said you didn't need help—so why come to us now?)

Governor Jindal, if you are so concerned about taking care of business, you might consider that, in addition to relieving your unemployed citizens' financial distress, extending unemployment benefits will also put money in the pocket of people who can then spend money at these businesses. Do you put ideology and personal ambition above your people's need to eat and pay rent? Perhaps you cynically assume the public is too passive and disorganized to protest?

Governor Jindal, your Rhodes Scholar intelligence and grasp of policy could be a force for good, precisely when there are positive forces in Washington that could provide the help Louisiana so badly needs. Just when there's a pragmatic president who is genuinely trying to move beyond partisan gridlock—as he did in the Illinois legislature and the U.S. Senate—you oppose his efforts. Precisely when your party is out of ideas, with no clear purpose, you as a young and energetic governor could be a leader for renewal and revival and fiscal discipline—if you directed your energies toward solutions that involve helping your people by spending, developing education (including science), health care (including Charity Hospital), and so on. Please, don't let your ambitions be a curse to your state. The party you seek to lead has been no friend of Louisiana in recent years. You can change that. You can at least try.

We know you won't, but we want you to remember the choice you left behind, along with your hard-pressed people.

We'll see how you are rewarded, how you're remembered.

Maybe one day you'll be out of a job.

TAGS: 2009 stimulus, American Recovery and Reinvestment Act, blind ambition, Bobby Jindal, Louisiana Academic Freedom Act, Louisiana unemployment rate, http://www.leveesnotwar.org/mr-jindal-tear-down-this-ambition/

Jindal: From Rising Star to Black Hole

FEB. 25, 2009—While "disastrous" was among the more charitable descriptions of Bobby Jindal's performance Tuesday night, we would like to thank him for mounting so ineffectual a response to President Obama's address to a joint session of Congress. (The joke in the White House press room is that Jindal has gone from being a rising star to a black hole.) We take no pleasure in the derision but we're glad that he put up no serious resistance to the persuasiveness of Obama's progressive agenda. Jindal has done us the favor of leaving his party even more leaderless and dispirited. His faux-optimistic speech, titled "Americans Can Do Anything," was clearly written before the G.O.P. knew what Obama would say; they were expecting a gloomy assessment of the economy without an equal measure of confidence that the nation can rebuild and come back stronger than before.

Speaking of storms and rebuilding, Jindal's use of Hurricane Katrina as an example of why the federal government cannot be relied upon in a time of crisis is beyond false and hypocritical (as we recall, it was his Republican party that was in charge at the time)—it was also self-damning and . . . simply incredible. The fact that one (government-despising) administration compounded the catastrophe should teach us that we can never improve government's effectiveness? (Further, surely lowering tax revenues as Jindal prescribes will make it only weaker, as happened before Katrina: sorry, we don't have enough funds for both stronger storm protection and the wars we're waging.)

So, even though the governor seems to have concocted his little Harry Lee anecdote (well, he did introduce it by saying, "Let me tell you a story"), we want to thank him for failing to rebut Obama's ambitious and perfectly logical focus on energy, health care, and education simultaneously. The Republicans' golden boy, their rising star, performed so badly that even conservative, right-wing commentators panned him. Only Rush Limbaugh is standing by his man. We don't like seeing our governor ridiculed, but if it eases the passage of Obama's agenda, we'll take it.

On *Meet the Press* on Sunday, Jindal repeatedly claimed a "fundamental disagreement" with the stimulus bill, but declined to mention that he is accepting about 98% of the stimulus money allocated for Louisiana (excepting the $100 million in unemployment funding). By our calculations, he has only a 2% philosophical difference. But enough to strike a convincing pose for his base. (And is there a racial element to the money he is refusing? Just asking.)

We were pleased to hear him say this on *Meet the Press*:

> Our state, by the way, $9 to $10 billion comes off of our coast in terms of federal oil and gas royalties. If that was federal lands within our state, we'd get 50 percent. We get virtually none of that. You look at 30 percent of the nation's oil and gas in some form comes off of our coast. It's important for the country that America rebuilds those levees, that America helps those communities get back on their feet.

And Jindal repeatedly referred to the "federal levees." At first we were encouraged to hear this acknowledgment of the builder, and the implied responsibility—or was he only giving another example of how government can't do anything right?

He is still wrong, though, morally and as a matter of economic policy, to deny his jobless citizens nearly $100 million in unemployment insurance funds from the stimulus bill. It is unconscionable to turn down money that would help one's people—and to refuse to amend state law to expand eligibility to include part-time workers. Further, since 2001, tax cuts as economic stimulus have been proven to be less stimulative than provision of unemployment benefits, state fiscal relief, food stamps, and middle class tax cuts.

We continue to hope that Jindal himself will soon be out of a job—first as his party's rising star, and then as Louisiana's governor. But he's still young; perhaps he can convert, as he's done before.

TAGS: Barack Obama, black hole, blind ambition, Bobby Jindal, Meet the Press
https://www.leveesnotwar.org/jindal-from-rising-star-to-black-hole/

Levees Not War's endorsement of John Edwards for president in January 2008—it felt right at the time—brought the blog a surge of attention when New Orleans–based blogger Karen Dalton-Beninato wrote about the endorsement on The Huffington Post *under the amusing headline "NOLA Endorsement: Edwards Will 'Kick Repubs in the Balls'." (Actually what we said was, "Democrats need a tough candidate who won't hesitate to kick the Republicans in the balls"—but who's quibbling?)*

Please see also the "Department of Corrections" addendum, posted two years later when it was painfully clear that Edwards, sullied by a tawdry tabloid scandal he got himself into, was not quite the man he had seemed. Still, many of his policy ideas were good, grounded in the social contract, and that is why these pieces still deserve to be included.

What John Edwards Brought Us

FEB. 2, 2008—We are voting for Senator Barack Obama in the primaries—as many times as possible. The more we see of him, the more we like. But first, we want to take a parting glance at the contributions our First Favorite, John Edwards, made to the presidential campaign of 2008.

We pushed hard for Edwards, and it's hard to let go, but we're grateful to him for returning the Democratic party to its populist roots. Our strongest gratitude is for the attention he brought to New Orleans and for the bold ideas he proposed, which, to the public's benefit, Obama and Clinton have incorporated to some extent into their own campaigns.

- Let's start with New Orleans. Edwards showed where his heart is by announcing his candidacy from a front yard in the Ninth Ward. He was the first to propose a definite plan for New Orleans. Last August, on the second anniversary of Hurricane Katrina, he pitched six good ideas for helping the city and the Gulf Coast—proposals that could be easily applied to other American cities and disaster areas. What impresses us is Edwards's specificity: A politician tends not to think in such detail unless he really cares.

One proposal we particularly liked is "Brownie's Law," which would require that senior political appointees "have demonstrated qualifications in the field related to their job." Edwards also called for fully funding the Road Home program and for the appointment of both a Gulf Coast Inspector General and a Chief Recovery Officer "to channel presidential leadership, ensure accountability, cut red tape and deliver results for the people of the Gulf Coast" (please!).

We have seen no comparably detailed ideas from Hillary Clinton. Barack Obama has recommended (and we agree) that FEMA be made independent of the Department of Homeland Security, as it once was, and that its director be appointed to a six-year term and have the direct, cabinet-level access to the president that James Lee Witt had with President Clinton (1993–2001). Obama also recommended the closure of the Mississippi River–Gulf Outlet (MR-GO), a good idea that was already being proposed by its original builder, the Army Corps of Engineers.

- In January Edwards called for the removal of all U.S. troops from Iraq in 10 months. He said the U.S. should immediately withdraw 40,000 to 50,000 troops, and have nearly all forces out within ten months, leaving only a contingent of no more than 5,000 to protect the American embassy and possibly humanitarian workers. We have heard no such call from Obama or Clinton.

- On health care, as Paul Krugman has pointed out in convincing detail, it was John Edwards who did the seemingly impossible and mandated universal coverage through a practical, public-private hybrid solution that gives you the option of staying with your private insurer and letting you buy into a government-sponsored, Medicare-type plan. And he was bold enough to call repealing the Bush tax cuts on incomes of over $200,000 to help pay for it.

- Edwards also took the lead on the environment—in March 2007—with ideas for halting global warming, achieving energy independence, and strengthening the federal commitment to the Clean Air and Water Acts. The environmental website Grist.org called his proposals "far and away the strongest, most comprehensive climate and energy plan among the three front-runners. . . . On these issues, Edwards has done his homework, and he's not trimming his sails."

Well, that was then . . .

With two star candidates to compete against—plus a former president to boot—he had a hard time breaking through. TV cameras seemed only to have eyes for Obama and the Clintons, and reporters seemed to have the attention span only for two Democrats at a time. (Curiously, the multitude of Republican candidates did not seem to present a similar attention deficit.)

As Krugman observed, "the willingness of his rivals to emulate his policy proposals made it hard for him to differentiate himself as a candidate; meanwhile, those rivals had far larger financial resources and received vastly more media attention. Even the *Times*'s own public editor chided the paper for giving Mr. Edwards so little coverage." ("The Edwards Effect," Feb. 1, 2007).

Edwards's fighting populist message could not have been appealing to the mega-conglomerates that run the networks or to their corporate advertisers such as the drug companies and oil and war profiteers. But we thank him for reminding America of the idea of the social compact (who else was talking about the social contract?), for standing in the cold with striking workers, speaking for the poor and the working class, the workers of all levels who have been burned by downsizing or the loss of jobs to lower-wage workers overseas.

In announcing the end of his campaign in New Orleans on Jan. 30, Edwards said: "I don't know when our party began to turn away from the cause of working people, from the fathers who were working three jobs literally just to pay the rent, mothers sending their kids to bed wrapped up in their clothes and in coats because they couldn't afford to pay for heat." His one request to Obama and Clinton, when he called to advise them that he would be withdrawing, was that they commit to making the ending of poverty a central theme of their campaigns. Promises are cheap in politics, and it is up to these candidates' supporters to hold them to their pledge. It's our fellow citizens, ourselves, who will suffer if we do not.

Finally, we thank John Edwards for never forgetting New Orleans, and reminding the nation that there is a great city and a wide swath of America still devastated by a natural disaster + manmade disaster (failure of levees) as well as by unnatural, inhumane governmental disregard. We are grateful to Edwards for having the good sense of dramatic closure by bringing it back home to the Ninth Ward when he announced his withdrawal from the race, and we'll do our part by pressing the remaining candidates and other office-holders to fulfill the ideas proposed by Edwards for New Orleans and for the United States of America so that we can be One Nation once again.

Department of Corrections

About That John Edwards Endorsement

FEB. 18, 2010—Mardi Gras has come and gone, and Ash Wednesday too, and now it is Lent: *"Remember that you are dust, and to dust you shall return."* Speaking of dust and repentance . . .

Two years ago we endorsed John Edwards for president. That was before we realized how far superior Barack Obama was (is), and before we read Heilemann and Halperin's *Game Change* from beginning to end. Now, our endorsement got a bit of attention through *The Huffington Post* (because we said "Democrats need a tough candidate who won't hesitate to kick the Republicans in the balls"), but apparently the endorsement caused no irreversible damage. Still, we would like to issue a correction, an admission of error of character judgment.

We were not alone, and there were very good policy reasons why we thought John Edwards was the superior choice: his progressive ideas for health care reform (bolder than Obama's or Hillary's) and ending the Iraq War, for aggressive action to address climate change, and his focus on the poor, his advocacy of the social compact and his populist, anti-corporate combativeness. But oh, what we did not know about his personal life! How reckless, selfish, and delusional he was, after his tawdry affair with what's-her-name (beginning two years before the 2008 Iowa primary), to pursue the presidency and then to plead desperately with go-betweens for appointment as Obama's attorney general. As if. The damage he could have inflicted on the nation and the party if these matters had blown up, as they would have—it makes you shudder as you read. Former campaign staff spilled because he and Elizabeth Edwards used their aides shabbily, and worse.

So, though we stand by our reasons for liking his message—health care reform, assistance for the poor, rebuilding one America—we must acknowledge that John Edwards was not the champion we thought he was.

He ended his campaign, as he began it, in New Orleans. As he withdrew, he said:

> I don't know when our party began to turn away from the cause
> of working people, from the fathers who were working three jobs
> literally just to pay the rent, mothers sending their kids to bed
> wrapped up in their clothes and in coats because they couldn't
> afford to pay for heat.

Now, this is a little hard to take when you read in *Game Change* about the enormous house he built in Chapel Hill, "a two-building complex totaling 28,200 square feet, with an indoor basketball court, swimming pool, and squash court, two theatrical stages, and a room designated 'John's Lounge.'" (Still, Democrats campaigning in the 2010 midterms—and those already in office—would do well to remember these hard-pressed working people and the jobless.)

There was also the matter of his role as "senior adviser" for Fortress Investment Group "for which he reaped a minor fortune"—the same group that purchased mortgages on properties in the Katrina-damaged areas of New Orleans and the Gulf Coast with the intention of foreclosing on the mortgages through affiliates.

After the self-inflicted damage, Edwards needs redemption (don't we all), his reputation rehabilitated. If we may humbly suggest a way to regain some measure of self-respect and public trust: he could come back to New Orleans and roll up his sleeves again and do some more carpentry work as he did for the cameras in the Lower Ninth Ward when he announced his run for the presidency. He could start simply, modestly, without notifying news organizations, but by volunteering his physical labor, his intelligence, his genuine empathy for the downtrodden. He could advocate for a continuation somehow of Charity Hospital's free health care for the indigent and uninsured (with or without LSU and the VA and their plans for a bright shiny new medical corridor), and he could put his environmental concerns to work by pitching in with coastal restoration groups. Or he could assist in Ivor van Heerden's legal defense against LSU pro bono.

Come to think of it, there might be other fallen politicians in need of rehabilitation who could join him in these and other efforts. New Orleans could always use more help. It's a fairly tolerant and forgiving city, and wouldn't hold their misbehavior against them. Come on down.

TAGS: Barack Obama, Charity Hospital, Game Change, Hillary Clinton,
        Ivor van Heerden, John Edwards, social contract
http://www.leveesnotwar.org/department-of-corrections-about-that-john
-edwards-endorsement/
http://www.leveesnotwar.org/what-john-edwards-brought-us/

PART V

Activism, Tributes, Remembrances

Photograph by Nathan Benn/Corbis

On the tenth anniversary of September 11, 2001

We're Not Forgetting

SEPT. 11, 2011—Except for posting this brief comment, we are among the millions of New Yorkers who are doing anything but "commemorating" the 10th anniversary. We are not reading the magazines' special commemorative editions or watching the solemn and reverent broadcasts brought to you by our sponsors of the corporate media. We live in New York City—we don't need to be reminded. It's with us every day, in every heavily armed National Guardsman at Penn Station, every fire station you pass by, etc., just as you can still hear Hurricane Katrina howling through New Orleans, not only on the anniversary of Aug. 29, 2005.

Let Us Remember These Attacks
Could Have Been Blocked

While we remember the dead, and those who died bravely trying to save lives, while our sincere condolences go out to their families, the children who never knew their daddy who died that day—

While we are never forgetting let us also recall that for eight months in early 2001 Bush, Cheney, Rumsfeld, and national security adviser Condoleezza Rice blew off counter-terrorism adviser Richard A. Clarke's repeated requests for meetings to brief them on the threat of Al Qaeda; and that Bush was specifically warned in an Aug. 6, 2001, CIA briefing titled "Bin Laden Determined to Strike in US" but remained on vacation till Sept. 4 and never did call Clarke. And we will never forget watching the towers burning—we could see the smoke from an elevated subway track in Queens a few miles away—and then on a TV in our office in midtown Manhattan watching the towers burning, hearing about another plane striking the Pentagon, and looking out the window and wondering, "Where is the f—in' goddamn air force?!"

The first plane to hit the World Trade Center was American flight 11 out of Boston. It took off at 7:45 a.m. After 8:13 there was no more pilot contact with air traffic control. Around 8:20, two flight attendants called American's headquarters to report a hijacking. Under normal conditions that plane would have been stopped, shot down if necessary. But NORAD and the FAA claimed NORAD wasn't contacted until 8:40. Even then, the first fighter jets weren't scrambled until 8:52. American flight 11 hit the north tower at 8:48—*thirty-five minutes* after Boston lost contact. McGuire Air Force Base in New Jersey is only 70 miles from Manhattan—an F-15 at top speed could have been there in three minutes—but instead the order went to Otis AFB in Cape Cod. *Cape Cod?* It would have been strange enough for the system to fail for Flight 11, but the same thing happened with *all four* hijacked flights: FAA is tardy in telling NORAD, then NORAD is slow to order up fighter jets from unnecessarily distant bases, then the fighters don't arrive till after the damage is done. For Washington, the obvious base is Andrews, 10 miles away, but instead the jets were ordered from Langley AFB, 130 miles from Washington, *after* the Pentagon was hit. (The USAF was budgeted $85 billion for fiscal year 2001.)

While human beings, many of them with their clothes on fire, were jumping out of the burning towers and splattering like eggs on the concrete plaza a quarter mile down, the commander in chief was in Sarasota, Florida, sitting virtually paralyzed as a class of second-graders read a story about a pet goat. Four different accounts attest that he had been notified about the attacks in New York before he entered the classroom for the photo-op.

(Imagine the reaction if any of this happened with the current president, or any Democrat, in the White House.)

This is not the part they want us to remember today. Sorry. This *is* what we remember and always will, just as we'll never forget the entire city abandoned by that same administration (with the president this time on a five-week vacation), children and elderly and all ages in between suffocating and dehydrating in the Superdome and outside the Convention Center for days after Hurricane Katrina and on rooftops all around the sweltering city of New Orleans in late August and early September 2005.

And God shall wipe away all tears from their eyes; and there shall be no more death, neither sorrow, nor crying, neither shall there be any more pain: for the former things are passed away. —Revelation 21:4

et absterget Deus omnem lacrimam ab oculis eorum . . .

Il essuiera toute larme de leurs yeux . . .

TAGS: 9/11 exploitation, Condoleezza Rice, Dick Cheney, Donald Rumsfeld, George W. Bush administration, Hurricane Katrina, Richard A. Clarke
http://www.leveesnotwar.org/we're-not-forgetting/

On July 4, Yearning for a Progressive American Revolution

We hold these truths to be self-evident, that all men are created equal, that they are endowed by their Creator with certain unalienable rights, that among these are life, liberty and the pursuit of happiness. That to secure these rights, governments are instituted among men, deriving their just powers from the consent of the governed. . . .

from the Declaration of Independence, Philadelphia, July 4, 1776

JULY 4, 2013—The coinciding of the anniversary of the Declaration of Independence, that cornerstone and launching pad event of the American Revolution of which we Americans are justly proud, with another massive wave of revolutionary fervor in Egypt and the second ouster of that ancient country's head of state in two years, makes us wish for a more vigorous *liberal* revolutionary spirit here in the nation that likes to call itself "the world's oldest democracy." What we wish for is a revolutionary spirit—a constructive energy—among those who would spread and defend liberty for the common folk, for the downtrodden poor, the near-exhausted middle class.

Especially on this day of all days in the year there is a strong yearning to glory in the specialness of our nation, to love our country and wish it a happy birthday with a childlike simplicity and sincerity, to love it not only as it can be but as it is, now, today. Increasingly, however, this *amor patria* is a difficult feeling to sustain while also facing the facts of our nation's recent history.

This country is composed of states, but they are far from united. Two political parties hold power, but, though similar in their dependence on money, they are far apart in their governing philosophies. One seeks to govern, to administer programs for the general good, while the other seeks power, control.

When the most powerful, aggressive political energy is that of conservative reactionaries fired by a zeal to abolish longstanding functions of government, to abolish programs and departments, to roll back liberties hard-won by the common folk and minorities, to make life for the poor even harder, to scorn the less fortunate as undeserving even of the little that they have . . . then indeed it is hard to love the actuality, and one is driven to nostalgia for better times that once existed ("the greatest generation," etc.), and to hope and pray for better times to come. And who will lead us?

There is a revolutionary spirit at work in this country, but rather than pushing for greater freedoms for the average citizen it is a spirit of reactionary zeal, like that of the Jacobins such as Robespierre and his dreaded Committee on Public Safety that became known for a Reign of Terror after the French Revolution. The revolutionaries now at work in the U.S. do not wear overalls or rags but Brooks Brothers and Armani suits. They are not grassroots organizers but are funded by conservative billionaires, acting in the name of the average Joe. They do not recognize the legitimacy of the popularly elected executive; since his inauguration they have plotted massive resistance to his moderate, centrist agenda; and seek the repeal of his publicly supported, and needed, legislation.

The two Supreme Court decisions last week that received the most attention in the press, on June 25 and June 26, concerned the Voting Rights Act of 1965 and marriage equality, or "gay marriage" rights. One decision was disastrous for this nation's democracy, and the other was a positive step forward in the establishment of equal rights. Though we applaud the marriage equality decision, we wish it had not come so soon after the deplorable ruling against the Voting Rights Act, as its publicity and celebrations wiped the Voting Rights story off the screen—and the poor and disenfranchised are already ignored too much.

The week after these decisions, delivering more bad news for the average worker, the Obama administration announced a one-year delay—from 2014 to 2015—in the Affordable Care Act's mandate that larger employers provide coverage for employees or face a penalty. The Commerce Department felt business's pain—but what about the suffering and anxieties of over 45 million uninsured? The health care reform law, passed in 2010, was already overly gradual in its deployment of benefits for the public—a politically calculated "time-release capsule." Although the administration downplays the practical significance of this new delay, Republicans jumped with joy—See? The whole damned thing should be abolished!—and health reform advocates are disheartened by the Democrats' latest display of cowardice in advance of the 2014 midterm elections. (*The New York Times* quoted Sara Rosenbaum, a professor of health law and policy at George Washington University and an advocate of the law: "I am utterly astounded. . . . It boggles the mind. This step could significantly reduce the number of uninsured people who will gain coverage in 2014.")

And in mid June, the Obama administration, which had been admirably cautious about getting involved in the very complicated Syrian civil war, announced that the U.S. would begin arming certain groups of Syrian rebels. Officials claimed, without showing proof, the Bashar al-Assad regime has used chemical weapons against its own people. This was a public announcement of what had been secret U.S. policy for some time. There is always a war (or wars) beneath the visible war.

What does it take, foreign visitors often wonder, to get the Americans out into the streets? Perhaps one day we shall see . . . Till then, we have patriotic marching bands and awesome fireworks displays . . .

I hold it, that a little rebellion, now and then, is a good thing,
and as necessary in the political world as storms in the physical
Thomas Jefferson, letter (from Paris) to James Madison,
January 30, 1787

On Independence Day, with Help from a Founding Mother

In the new code of laws which I suppose it will be necessary for you to make I desire you would remember the ladies, and be more generous and favorable to them than your ancestors. Do not put such unlimited power into the hands of the husbands. Remember all men would be tyrants if they could.

Abigail Adams, letter to John Adams, then in Philadelphia, March 31, 1776

JULY 4, 2011—On holidays we like to take a break from our often critical attitude about "what fresh hell" is breaking forth and to say something affirmative about the meaning of the day and why it is celebrated.

Everyone knows that the Fourth of July, which we prefer to think of as Independence Day, celebrates the new United States of America's (declaration of) independence from Britain. This is true, and this is good.

But, today, after reading that the median pay for a CEO of the top 200 corporations in the U.S. is $10.9 million—*$10.9 million for a single individual*—up 23% since 2009 (how many jobs could that money create when the unemployment rate has exceeded 9% since May 2009, with at least 15 million lacking any job at all?) . . . and knowing that Congress in its wisdom recently extended the reduced (35%) rate of taxation for those millionaires (rather than let it return to 39%), a reduced taxation that continues for the 10th year to starve the national treasury of desperately needed revenues . . . and while as a related result "leaders" of a purportedly serious and fiscally responsible political party insist in budget deficit talks that revenue increases of any kind are "off the table" . . . Then we have to ask what *freedom* and what *liberty* do the ordinary people of this nation have anymore?

Are we the people free from corporate dominion? Are the press and the airwaves free? Are the 15+ million unemployed free to work and earn a living wage? Are the young graduates of our schools free to find jobs worthy of their skills and intelligence? Are workers free to negotiate with employers about their wages and working conditions? Are we citizens free to see a substantial portion of our tax dollars go to education (as in Pell Grants for college) and social safety net programs like health care assistance and Social Security? Are we free to say that the tax dollars we're compelled to pay will not go to the wars that a majority of the population wants to end? Are women free to determine their own reproductive choices without shame or criminal prosecution? Are their doctors free to advise them simply on the basis of medical science?

Truly it seems that a different form of servitude—or maybe there's another word for it—has taken hold of this country while a hypnotized, narcotized, War-on-Terror-ized populace is reminded constantly of "our freedoms." Would these be the same freedoms for which American soldiers who can't find a job anywhere else are sent to fight in tour after tour of duty in three simultaneous wars, then are brought home, if not in a box, to fend for themselves for jobs and health care?

Just askin'.

But on a more positive note, which we really do want to strike: We do sincerely tip our hats (we wear several) to salute those brave patriots of the Revolutionary War, and to the Founding Fathers who composed the Declaration of Independence and the Constitution of the United States— but also to the *Founding Mothers* we rarely hear about, such as Abigail Smith Adams (1744–1818), aka Mrs. John Adams.

Particularly in a year that has seen, "from sea to shining sea," systematic and relentless efforts by state and federal legislatures to strip away the rights of workers and voters, and rape-like assaults on women's reproductive freedoms—and when a couple of women are campaigning for the presidency even though they appear not to believe in the idea of governing, or of learning—some passages from the wise Mrs. Adams are worth pondering, and practicing, enacting.

Selections from Abigail Adams's Letters to John Adams

*Patriotism in the female sex is the most disinterested of all
virtues. Excluded from honors and from offices, we cannot attach
ourselves to the State or Government from having held a place of
eminence. . . . Deprived of a voice in legislation, obliged to submit
to those laws which are imposed upon us, is it not sufficient to
make us indifferent to the public welfare? Yet all history and every
age exhibit instances of patriotic virtue in the female sex; which
considering our situation equals the most heroic of yours.*
(June 17, 1782)

*In the new code of laws which I suppose it will be necessary for
you to make I desire you would remember the ladies, and be more
generous and favorable to them than your ancestors. Do not put
such unlimited power into the hands of the husbands. Remember
all men would be tyrants if they could.*—letter to John Adams,
then in Philadelphia (March 31, 1776)

*Whilst you are proclaiming peace and good will to men,
emancipating all nations, you insist upon retaining an absolute
power over wives. But you must remember that arbitrary power is
like most other things which are very hard, very liable to be broken
. . .* (May 7, 1776)

*If we mean to have heroes, statesmen and philosophers, we should
have learned women. . . . If much depends as is allowed upon the
early education of youth and the first principles which are instilled
take the deepest root, great benefit must arise from literary
accomplishments in women.* (Aug. 14, 1776)

*It is really mortifying, sir, when a woman possessed of a common
share of understanding considers the difference of education
between the male and female sex, even in those families where
education is attended to. . . .* (Feb. 15, 1778)

I regret the trifling narrow contracted education of the females of my own country. (June 30, 1778)

Learning is not attained by chance, it must be sought for with ardor and attended to with diligence.—to John Quincy Adams (May 8, 1780)

TAGS: 4th of July, Abigail Adams, Declaration of Independence, executive compensation, holidays, income disparity, Independence Day, Revolutionary War, Socialist Party of Louisiana, Tyranny Disguised as Fiscal Discipline, United States of Inequality

http://www.leveesnotwar.org/on-independence-day-with-help-from-a-founding-mother/

Occupying Wall Street with Nurses, Teachers, Transit Workers, and the Rest of America's Middle Class

"We are the 99% . . . You are the 99%."
"Banks got bailed out / We got sold out!"
"Whose street? Our street!"

OCT. 6, 2011—Yesterday into last night we gathered near New York's City Hall and marched with what looked and felt like at least 100,000 "marginal fringe elements" such as nurses' and teachers' unions, the New York City Transit Workers' union, the AFL-CIO, and innumerable others through Lower Manhattan to Zuccotti Park near Wall Street, the home base of Occupy Wall Street. We've been on numerous protest rallies in Manhattan and Washington and London with hundreds of thousands, and this felt as jam-packed as the anti–Iraq War marches in 2003, 2004, 2005.

But this—this feels like a revolution.

This Is Not the Fringe. This Is the Middle Class.

Yesterday's marchers in the tens of thousands were nurses, teachers, professors, bus drivers, subway track workers, secretaries, students, at least one World War II veteran on an aluminum walker (according to the sign around his neck), many children on foot and in strollers, and so on. This is the middle class. As the signs and chants say, "We are the 99%. You are the 99%."

Among the unions that announced their support and sent members to the march were National Nurses United, AFL-CIO (AFSCME), United Federation of Teachers, New York State United Teachers, Service Employees International Union, SEIU 1199, the Transport Workers Union, Transit Workers Union

Local 100, Working Families Party, Communications Workers of America, United Auto Workers, and Writers Guild East.

A Few Things to Know about Occupy Wall Street

- Whatever you see on TV or read in the newspaper is probably a distortion, a minimizing dismissal, a marginalizing caricature. If you want the view of a seasoned journalist who has spent a lot of time with the OWS activists, read Chris Hedges, Pulitzer Prize–winning former *New York Times* reporter, at *Truthdig*. In an interview on *Truthdig* he describes the Occupy Wall Street activists as "the best among us." Check YouTube for the video of Nobel Prize–winning economist Joseph Stiglitz and Jeff Madrick, author of *Age of Greed*, talking with the Occupants through the "people's microphone" (bullhorns are forbidden).

- The OWS organizers, a loose-knit, non-hierarchical network, are not fringey radicals, but mostly well-educated, social media–savvy young people, creative and resourceful, and organized. They have worked hard in school but there are no jobs. The system—both the economy down to its foundations and the government—is not working for anyone but 1%. It's over.

- The Occupation was inspired by both Tahrir Square, Cairo, and the Arab Spring, and by Adbusters.org. (See Tracey Samuelson, "Meet the Occupants," *New York* magazine, Oct. 2, 2011.)

- This Occupation is not limited to Wall Street in Lower Manhattan. Occupy Together lists meetups in 588 cities. L.A. Chicago. Philadelphia. Boston. Seattle. Albuquerque . . . Tomorrow, more. London, you're next.

- The activists are not "unfocused" or lacking in specific aims. They have some very specific demands, including raising the tax rates on upper incomes; calling on the federal government to protect homeowners from arbitrary foreclosures by banks; establishing a financial transactions tax; and closing the "carried interest" and "founders stock" loopholes that, in the words of *New York Times* columnist Nicholas Kristof, "allow our wealthiest citizens to pay very low tax rates by pretending that their labor compensation is a capital gain."

- Americans prefer Occupy Wall Streeters to Congress. *New York* magazine reports: "A new Rasmussen poll shows that 33 percent of Americans have a favorable view of the Wall Street protesters, compared with the 14 percent or so who said the same about the legislative branch. A whopping 79 percent also agreed with what Rasmussen characterized as the movement's main statement: 'The big banks got bailed but the middle class got left behind.' "

Do the Police Know We're on Their Side Too?

Before the march got going, we asked a crew-cut, man's man–looking fellow in a red Communications Workers of America T-shirt, what would he and his fellow union members say to the police who have shown their dislike the whole Occupy Wall Street thing (e.g., NYPD Deputy Inspector Anthony Bologna pepper-spraying women held within an orange plastic fence).

This union man said he and his union members would say, "We support you when you're negotiating for a new contract. We're there for you, and we expect you to be there for us. Just let us protest this unfairness and don't give us a hard time."

There were many people with press passes interviewing union members and taking down notes, and it seemed nearly everyone had a camera—at least an iPhone camera—taking pictures of each other's signs.

The atmosphere was festive, though still charged, passionate, determined. Some chanted against police brutality, against racist police. This was no Obama kumbaya feeling as in 2008. That was so long ago. In the signs and the comments between fellow marchers (you chat as you walk, or when the march stalls), the people are pretty much as disgusted with the Democrats as with the other party. One sign said OBAMA = BUSH.

We're Peaceful, But Screw with Us and We Multiply

The NYPD seemed unprepared for the massiveness of the turnout. Once we got to walking, after the speeches that very few could hear in Foley Square near City Hall, we were channeled into narrow, Dixie straw–like passages on sidewalks or on the margins of the streets while large spaces of the streets were occupied by the white shirts and the regular blue-uniformed cops. At one point along an east-west street between Centre Street and Broadway, we were held up, absolutely still, for five minutes or more. People started shouting, "The light says walk! The light says walk!" Others were chanting something indistinct but provocative against police. We were carrying a sign that read "We're Peaceful, But Screw with Us and We Multiply," and weren't too comfortable being penned in among anti-NYPD chanters. Nearby were yellow signs saying "NYPD Protects and Serves the Rich." Finally someone lifted the steel barricades and several dozen of us moved through across the street. Police yelled, "Stay on the sidewalk!" The cops didn't like that freedom of movement and came running to slam the gates shut to keep the cattle penned in.

The videos of police violence later in the evening were doubtless instances of the crowds spilling out of the designated perimeter, the chain of steel barricades penning in the multitudes. ("Whose street? Our street!") The talk among the crowds is that the police, the authorities want conflict, want confrontation—the media certainly do ("If it bleeds, it leads"). You can feel that they are on edge. They don't like us, even though we are there for them, for all of us. The authorities want to know who the leaders are so they can decapitate the Occupation, but it's dispersed, decentralized, like the Internets.

Around 7:30 we peeled off to take the subway back home. The marchers were still coming, about 8 to 10 abreast, down Broadway, pouring into Zuccotti Park at Liberty Place, holding up signs, chanting, beating drums. It was a beautiful sight. Someone said, "The French are here!" Across the street we saw a large white banner, "LIBERTÉ, EGALITÉ, FRATERNITÉ."

There is no telling where this is going, but we know it's growing, and it's spreading. There will be violent repression, and the movement will continue to grow. As they said in Madison, Wisconsin, "Screw with us and we multiply." The popular uprising will give some backing to the president's newfound populist push against the Republicans and put some courage in the spines of the Democrats to stand up against the rich, but in a way it's too late. In the signs, the chants, the conversations, in the passion and conviction of the people marching toward Wall Street yesterday, you could feel that the people have already moved beyond the politicians, perhaps even beyond the old American economy and society as we've known it.

https://www.leveesnotwar.org/occupying-wall-street-with-nurses-teachers-transit -workers-and-the-rest-of-america's-middle-class/

In Honor of Medgar Evers
and *Res Publica*

You can kill a man but you can't kill an idea.
Medgar Evers (1925–1963)

JUNE 12, 2013—Fifty years ago today, Medgar Wylie Evers was killed in his driveway in Jackson, Mississippi, after returning from an NAACP meeting at a nearby church. Evers, a graduate of Alcorn A&M whose application to the University of Mississippi law school was rejected on racial grounds, had served as the NAACP field secretary for the state of Mississippi since 1954. One of his tasks was an investigation of the 1955 murder of Emmett Till. He was one of the first members of Martin Luther King Jr.'s Southern Christian Leadership Conference (SCLC, est. 1957). The assassination of Medgar Evers was commemorated in Bob Dylan's song "Only a Pawn in Their Game" (1964) and more recently in season three of *Mad Men*. Evers, who had served in the U.S. Army in France in World War II and was honorably discharged as a sergeant, was buried in Arlington National Cemetery.

It was late on the night of June 11, and the killer was hiding behind a bush. Myrlie Evers found her husband on the front steps where he had managed to drag himself after being shot in the back. His car keys were still in his hands, and in his arms was a stack of T-shirts reading JIM CROW MUST GO. For thirty years the murder went unprosecuted (a trial in 1964 ended with a hung jury), until Byron De La Beckwith was convicted of murder in 1994. Throughout the 1994 trial De La Beckwith wore a Confederate flag on his lapel.

On the night her husband was assassinated, Mrs. Evers and her children were watching a televised address to the nation by President John F. Kennedy in response to recent civil rights events, including Alabama Governor George Wallace's refusal to allow two black students to register at the University of

Alabama. (The president announced, "I am . . . asking the Congress to enact legislation giving all Americans the right to be served in facilities which are open to the public—hotels, restaurants, theaters, retail stores, and similar establishments.")

Conservatives' Rejection of All Things "Public" as "White Flight"

In an excellent 10-minute overview of the Jim Crow (segregated, apartheid) South into which Medgar Evers was born, and of early civil rights protests such as the lunch counter sit-ins, Rachel Maddow last night [6/11/13] mentioned that, rather than cooperate with the legislation that ordered integration of schools and other public facilities, many white southerners opted to withdraw from desegregated public society. ("Segregation today, segregation tomorrow, segregation forever!" as George Wallace put it.) Rachel explained:

> The southern part of the United States was forced to abolish its
> segregation laws. But it was a bloody, bloody fight. Throughout
> the old Confederacy, white people were asked, first as a matter
> of conscience, and then finally they were ordered as a matter of
> justice, to integrate on racial lines. And when the white people
> who had control of the laws and the government and the schools
> and the businesses, when the fight to hold on to segregation
> laws was a lost fight, and they knew they had no choice but to
> integrate the society they lived in, in many cases, instead of
> going through with that and living through that kind of change,
> *a lot of them just decided to quit that society*, they gave up public
> pools and public schools and in some cases movie theaters. They
> gave up whole cities and moved away. They called it white flight.
> The census from 1960 records a Jackson, Mississippi, that was
> majority white, almost two to one. By 1990 Jackson's population
> had made the turn toward getting much smaller and it was
> much blacker. By 2010 Jackson, Mississippi, had become the
> second most African American city in the nation. White people
> in the previously legally segregated South, and really across the

nation, abandoned places rather than see them change. [LNW's emphasis]

White Flight

From Orleans Parish, for example, tens of thousands fled to Metairie and Kenner in nearby Jefferson Parish. All over the South, public pools were closed, schools lost white students and teachers, theaters were closed. The middle class and affluent tax base withered, so all facilities and programs needing public funding were at a loss. For a while, to some extent, federal money helped supplement what was dwindling from local coffers. We all know the story. (For more on white southerners' responses to the advances of civil rights, read Jason Sokol's excellent *There Goes My Everything: White Southerners in the Age of Civil Rights, 1945–1975*.)

Rachel Maddow's comment above constituted just one paragraph in a larger overview, but it helps us understand the rejection of the public sphere that conservatives have made into a matter of hard-core principle over the last fifty years, and with increasing intensity during Barack Obama's presidency. Win friends and influence people by appealing to voters' resentments. That is how they get away with slashing, filibustering, or otherwise denying—even during a time of high unemployment, widespread suffering, and (deliberately) strangled economic recovery—government expenditures that are meant to benefit *everybody*.

Recall the Republicans' stubborn opposition to the $800 billion American Recovery and Reinvestment Act (the stimulus bill) in early 2009, one-third of which was tax cuts intended to win GOP votes; or the permanent campaign against health care reform, aka "Obamacare"—officially, for those who may have forgotten, the Patient Protection and Affordable Care Act, which the industrious, Republican-led House of Representatives has voted some 39 times to abolish. And think of all the "principled" Republican rejections of federal money that would, could help cover Medicaid, or FEMA-funded tornado shelters in Oklahoma; of stimulus money for rail projects spurned by GOP governors in Louisiana and Florida (among other places), and potential funding that could pay for other public needs. (At least for public show: see "Republicans Secretly (Seriously) Like the Stimulus" and "Public Works in a

Time of Job-Killing Scrooges.") Austerity is not about the budget deficit; it's an excuse to slash social spending. Austerity, so often prescribed for the public, seems never to apply to the budgets of the Department of Defense or the National Security Agency.

In *The Shock Doctrine: The Rise of Disaster Capitalism*, Naomi Klein has written in alarming detail about how the corporate-friendly, privatizing energies of the Republican party (and of their kin among the Democrats) want to abolish all things public that could more profitably be handled by private firms. The for-profit motive is usually behind most anti-government rhetoric and legislation.

And yet at the same time there is often a significant and ugly racial, racist element to the conservative rejection of the public sphere. "Why should I have to pay for their public schools?" (Think of Mitt Romney and the 47 percent "who believe that they are victims.") Lawrence Wright, Pulitzer Prize–winning author of *The Looming Tower: Al Qaeda and the Road to 9/11*, writes in his excellent memoir *In the New World: Growing Up with America from the Sixties to the Eighties* (1978; just republished in paperback):

> We talked about freedom all the time in Texas, and on my side
> of [Dallas] we had plenty of it, but we seldom talked seriously
> about equality. . . . What came clear to me was that *freedom and
> equality were mutually exclusive*; one came at the expense of the
> other. [LNW's emphasis]

The Latin phrase *res publica* was the term used in ancient Rome for "public affairs," "the things of the people," or "the things we have in common." *Res publica* is the source of the word *republic*. Now, if our "public things" are struggling to survive an onslaught of defunding and stripping down, then do we still have a republic? In this time of burn-it-down nihilism among tea-infused House Republicans, let us remember Diderot's admonition, "From fanaticism to barbarism is only one step."

TAGS: 47 percent, civil rights, GOP=Confederacy, Medgar Evers, public good, public sector, social contract, white backlash, white flight
http://www.leveesnotwar.org/in-honor-of-medgar-evers-and-res-publica/

Tom Hayden and Todd Gitlin on the Port Huron Statement at 50

The following is a two-part series on the fiftieth anniversary of the Port Huron Statement, not as famous as the Pentagon Papers but one of the most influential documents of the 1960s. The Statement was drafted primarily by an idealistic Irish Catholic boy from Royal Oak, Michigan, named Thomas Emmet Hayden who, as editor of the University of Michigan Daily, *had already interviewed the Rev. Martin Luther King Jr. and Edward "Dr. Strangelove" Teller. He had spent his twenty-second birthday in jail in Albany, Georgia, arrested as a Freedom Rider with SNCC civil rights activists, and it was there that he started drafting notes toward what would become the Port Huron Statement.*

The first part of our coverage gives some background about the Port Huron Statement and the remarks of Columbia University professor Todd Gitlin about its importance as an "articulation . . . of a moral awakening." The second part, below, summarizes the remarks of Tom Hayden and other participants at the commemoration at New York University on April 12 and 13, 2012.

Special thanks to Todd Gitlin, a former president of Students for a Democratic Society and author of The Sixties: Years of Hope, Days of Rage, *for permission to quote from his remarks.*

Todd Gitlin on the Port Huron Statement

APRIL 14, 2012—As we were strolling through Washington Square Park Thursday evening we saw a light shining from the south, and, behold, the brightness was the Tamiment Library & Robert F. Wagner Labor Archives on the tenth floor of the NYU library at 70 Washington Square South.

We followed the light and found a gathering of luminaries to commemorate the fiftieth anniversary of the Port Huron Statement, featuring Tom Hayden, Todd Gitlin, Robb Burlage, and Martha Prescod Norman Noonan as speakers. In the audience sitting among the ordinary folks like us were history-making New Left activists and organizers you may not have heard of, such as Alan Haber, the first president of Students for a Democratic Society, and Charles McDew of the Student Nonviolent Coordinating Committee, but their work in the civil rights, free speech, anti-war, and anti-poverty movements changed—that is, made more humane and more democratic—the world we live in today. In many cases, they also risked their very lives.

Roadmap to the 1960s, Blueprint for a Generation

Briefly, the Port Huron Statement (1962) was a sort of mimeographed mission statement of SDS: a new generation's call for participatory democracy; an assertion of humane, liberal values; and a critique of the Cold War mentality and the military-industrial complex that were strangling civic action and imagination and diverting precious resources from social needs such as ending racism and poverty. It marked a break from the old left that was anxious to prove itself anti-communist after the ravages of McCarthyism.

Students for a Democratic Society, a student division of the League for Industrial Democracy, was founded at the University of Michigan in Ann Arbor in 1960. The Port Huron Statement, initially drafted by Tom Hayden—22 years old at the time—and elaborated through discussion among fellow SDS members, was adopted at the first SDS annual convention of about 60 members on June 11–15, 1962, at the AFL-CIO's camp in Port Huron, about 100 miles northeast of Ann Arbor, near Detroit.

The statement, intended to be a living document, guided a generation until, with racial and Vietnam War tensions escalating, around 1967 and 1968, younger activists found it not radical enough. Many of SDS's ideas, values, and methods, however, live on in the energy and activism of the Occupy movement, the Arab spring, and the Wisconsin public workers' struggle. We are confident that, like the Declaration of Independence, it will be commemorated on its one-hundredth anniversary, too, and well beyond, as long as there is a United States of America.

The Port Huron Statement was typed and mimeographed by some of the people, now in their sixties and seventies, who were in attendance Thursday night. The first mimeographed printing, in August 1962, was of 20,000 copies; the second, of 20,000 copies, was in December 1964. Copies sold for thirty-five cents each. It is now a paperback published by Thunder's Mouth Press (2005).

We begin our commemoration by sharing the eloquent remarks of Todd Gitlin, who was kind enough to give us a copy. A cultural historian and professor of journalism and sociology at Columbia University, Mr. Gitlin, the author of many books, including *The Whole World Is Watching* and *Letters to a Young Activist*, is perhaps best known for his bestselling *The Sixties: Years of Hope, Days of Rage*. His *Occupy Nation: The Roots, the Spirit, and the Promise of Occupy Wall Street* was published in 2012. He was president of SDS in 1964 and 1965 and helped organize the first national demonstration against the Vietnam War, in 1965. His remarks Thursday night (slightly abridged below) were energetic and charged with an intimate sense of the beauty and love and also frustration and tragedy that characterized the experience of the 1960s and afterward.

On the Port Huron Statement
By Todd Gitlin | April 12, 2012

The Port Huron Statement was the clearest, most vivid and
energetic articulation of an awakening: one of those great
uprisings that are the crucibles of America struggling (against
much violence and cruelty) to become itself—a commonwealth
of free association and mutual aid.

The New Left wanted to make, out of the lonely crowd, the
beloved community—the kernel of a moral awakening that
would put intelligence to work in behalf of transcendent values
and overcome as much human ugliness as possible. . . .

The keen insight of the Port Huron Statement was that a life of
shared value mattered—and that it could be lived in common—
and that citizenship might matter and might, for some body of
people, be practical. The name that was affixed to that insight
was "participatory democracy."

It was, I think, intended more as a principle of social life
than as a way of holding meetings. It was not understood as an
alternative to strategy or to the collective work of intellect, but as
their fruition.

The genius of the Port Huron Statement, as it was structured, was placing its declaration of values up front. The movement would not be guided by interests but by values. It would not despise interests but it would insist that human life deserved to be less cruel and more lovely. The intimation that the world could be remade—starting right now and right here—this was the movement's idea—*all* of the movement, as Linda Gordon points out in her paper, not just the white guys.

The movement's idea *was not utopian*. Values were the starting point. They were not other-worldly. They were this-worldly. For some in the movement those values were spoken in an other-worldly spirit; for some not. It didn't matter. All the eyes were on the prize.

SDS insisted that the people had to consent to their government, but more than consent—they should *become* a people, held together by what was best and most decent in them.

There was a penetrating hope that breathed between the lines of this remarkable document. Within the lines, there were a lot of intellectual puzzles that the Port Huron Statement could not solve. No one has since. They may not be capable of solution. For example: What if most people do not want, at least not so much, to make the decisions at affect their lives? Shall we then disband the people and convene another one?

But the Port Huron Statement did not say: Follow us from Point A to Point Z. It said: Here we are, a bunch of people, "raised in at least modest comfort," who are going to make the effort to live lives we are not ashamed of, in order to live in a country we are not ashamed of. And that was a very great thing.

At the same time, we are all well aware of what we could not accomplish in the movements of that time. And that is why we ought to be refreshing the language of values, and reawakening the awakening, and acquainting and reacquainting ourselves with our better angels.

I mean not just ourselves, the core of a movement and its passions. I mean also the vast outer movement. Just as there was a conspicuous '60s, the one recorded in the photogenic confrontations and iconic images of courage and horror, there was also a subterranean '60s—less well known but just as important. The core American values of the New Left ignited many millions of people who did not necessarily subscribe to the movement's very doctrine and whim and style. Around kitchen tables and in their private nights they went beyond asking: What should the world be? They asked themselves, and asked each other: What should *I* do?

That subterranean movement, I suspect, is again or still, at work among us. So too is the aboveground movement, reawakening the awakening, reminding ourselves of our better angels.

What a crazy idea for a crazy country, which is no less a crazy country, though a differently crazy country, than it was half a century ago, in 1962. You can trace a line from then to now. It's not a straight line but a sinuous one, full of lurches, surprises, chasms, and leaps.

SDS National Council Meeting, September 1963. Tom Hayden stands at far left. SDS president Todd Gitlin is fifth from right (in dark jacket). Photograph courtesy of C. Clark Kissinger.

Today's Occupy movement, I think, holds open the promise of
a renewal, another great awakening, that moves us further along
the long and winding road toward a more respectful and less
cruel society, one which conserves the earth (and is therefore
in an honest sense "conservative") and takes seriously, again,
the inalienable rights of life, liberty, and the pursuit of happiness.

Tom Hayden, SDS and SNCC Alums: Happy 50th, Port Huron Statement!

*We are people of this generation, bred in at least modest comfort,
housed now in universities, looking uncomfortably to the world
we inherit. . . . First, the permeating and victimizing fact of
human degradation, symbolized by the Southern struggle against
racial bigotry. . . . Second, the enclosing fact of the Cold War,
symbolized by the presence of the Bomb. . . . The search for truly
democratic alternatives to the present, and a commitment to social
experimentation with them, is a worthy and fulfilling human
enterprise. . . .*

*If we appear to seek the unattainable, as it has been said, then
let it be known that we do so to avoid the unimaginable.*

Opening and closing sentences of the Port Huron Statement (1962)

APRIL 21, 2012—While "the dude," the amiable stoner played by Jeff Bridges
in the Coen brothers' 1998 film *The Big Lebowski*, claims authorship of the
Port Huron Statement, it is Tom Hayden's recollection that he was in a jail cell
in Albany, Georgia, after a Freedom Ride in 1961 when he composed the initial notes of what turned out to be the historic "living document" whose 50th
anniversary was commemorated April 12–13 at NYU's Tamiment Library
and Global Center for Spiritual Life. At the time of the Port Huron gathering

in June 1962, Hayden was the editor of the University of Michigan's student newspaper, and had already published the powerful "A Letter to the New (Young) Left" in *The Activist* (Oberlin College, Winter 1961). As he wrote in his memoir *Rebel: A Personal History of the 1960s*, "the primary question was changing the values of society, not just modifying government structures. . . . moral realignment had to precede political realignment, a view that became central to the manifesto . . ."

The 50th anniversary event was organized, and Hayden was introduced, by Robert "Robbie" Cohen, professor of history and social studies at NYU and author of *Freedom's Orator: Mario Savio and the Radical Legacy of the 1960s* (Oxford, 2009). The following remarks by Hayden are a blending of what he said on Thursday night and Friday morning; direct quotations are used only in a few instances; otherwise, we try to convey as accurately as possible the essence of what he said.

"This may be our last time together"

Tom Hayden began by saying our presence here is a sign of group love. "This is a blessed group." This will be (or may be) the last time we get together to talk about this. (Most of the members of the Students for a Democratic Society who attended the 1962 Port Huron gathering were about 20 at the time. Twenty-year-olds, by the way, could be drafted but could not vote; the national voting age was not lowered to 18 until 1971.)

Hayden spoke about courage, "a renewable resource" that everyone possesses. Often you do something not so much because you decide to be brave but because you can't leave your friends alone, or you can't stand what the police or the draft board or other authorities are doing; it strikes you as unjust and you have to put yourself in front of it to make it stop, to protect your friends.

Hayden spoke of Charles "Chuck" McDew III, who was sitting in the audience, a former chairman of the Student Nonviolent Coordinating Committee (SNCC), as "bravery in action. I owe my life, much of my career to Chuck." (More about McDew below.)

SNCC wanted as many white college students as possible to come and help in their civil rights movement in part because white college kids getting beaten up would attract news media attention, whereas black protesters getting killed could be (and often was) ignored.

In McComb, Mississippi, SNCC and friends from the North (perhaps after being arrested) were being interrogated by the White Citizens' Council. We were given the choice to leave the state or go to the dreaded Parchman state penitentiary. We were ashamed later at our choice to leave the state. We went back to Washington and in a meeting at the Justice Department we were told by a deputy attorney general under Attorney General Robert F. Kennedy that SNCC needed to get out of Mississippi. They should leave; they'll be killed if they stay. Hayden said in effect the man was saying that the United States Constitution does not extend to the state of Mississippi. The U.S. exports democracy abroad but does not protect it at home. The Kennedy Justice Department was not going to run the political risk, stick its neck out to enforce the Constitution and protect the student activists.

Hayden said our intention in going down to the Deep South was to go to the calcified hard core of the racist unequal society in America and break it open. We thought that if we confronted this racism and entrenched, enforced poverty at its core, if we could break open the nucleus there, we could help break its grip in the North, too, and everywhere else, to make the northern clergy, society, educational institutions and businesses answer, Which side are you on?

"The Dead Sea Scrolls of the Left"

We were trying to pull together a coalition movement of poor, middle class, white, black, labor, etc. It was hard to do, maybe impossible, and we failed, but it was the right thing to try to do. We failed in part because we did not know all of what we were up against. For one thing, we lacked the support of older people on the left, the Old Left, because we never could satisfy them that we were anti-communist enough. We certainly were not pro-Soviet Union, but for us, being anti-communist was not a priority. Racism and poverty in America were priorities; moral values and democracy were more important. We felt we were constantly on trial not only with conservative antagonists but even with older progressives; it was absurd and futile, like Kafka's *The Trial*.

Another obstacle that we could never quite see was the invisible collusion of labor and other supposedly democratic organizations with the U.S. government, namely the CIA. This may sound like a conspiracy theory, and maybe it is, but the federal government did not like our aim of de-escalating the cold war.

As Hayden wrote in *The Nation*:

> The unmovable obstacle to the coalition we hoped to build with organized labor was the secret pro–cold war element within liberalism, directly and indirectly tied to the CIA, which was fiercely opposed to our break from cold war thinking. On the one hand, the UAW's Reuther brothers helped fund and provide conference quarters at Port Huron; . . . On the other hand, the right-wing AFL-CIO foreign affairs department carried on the anti-communist crusade with its covert operations. . . . There was no way, in other words, that the New Left could have joined organized labor in 1964–65 around the Port Huron foreign policy vision, because the AFL-CIO was shackled to the CIA without our knowledge. ("Participatory Democracy: From Port Huron to Occupy Wall Street," *The Nation*, April 16, 2012)

We could not have anticipated the effects of the Vietnam war or all the assassinations. (Vietnam had not escalated into a full-blown war at the time of the Port Huron Statement.) I remember coming back on a bus from a Democratic party conference or event in February 1965, listening to Fannie Lou Hamer of the Mississippi Freedom Democratic Party, and learning of the assassination of Malcolm X. Some historian should analyze the effect of the assassinations on the New Left (in particular), how demoralizing and disorienting it was to lose these inspiring leaders one after another.

Our movement should be thought of not so much as an organization as an organism, an organism that is constantly adapting to a hostile environment. In this struggle to adapt we kept going back to first principles, the values expressed in the Port Huron Statement. We were learning by doing, by constantly keeping moving, adapting to changing circumstances. "I'm an organizer, but every organization I've ever been part of has fallen apart." (Laughter.)

We were influenced by Allen Ginsberg's "Howl" and Jack Kerouac's *On the Road*, *The Catcher in the Rye*, and the James Dean film *Rebel Without a Cause*. These were all about young people who felt out of place in the mainstream of

American life, who wanted a different kind of life. We grew up feeling maladjusted, wondered if we were crazy. These works told us we were not alone. As we met more people like us at the university, we realized we can't all be crazy and they can't lock all of us up. This period around 1960–62 was not "the sixties" as the decade came to be known. My first wife, Casey, who had been a member of an existential Christian group in Austin, said of those early years, "it was a holy time."

Concerning recent events, Hayden said that he did not predict Occupy Wall Street or anything like it, so he cannot or should not give advice or dispense wisdom about it. (He said this several times.) Although he finds Occupy Wall Street vital and important, he found the public workers' protests in Wisconsin more his idea of participatory democracy. In Wisconsin in early 2011, day after day, and weekend after weekend, 75,000 to 100,000 ordinary citizens—teachers, nurses, bus drivers, and other public employees—and their families went out in freezing temperatures to protest Gov. Scott Walker and the Republican state legislators' attempt to repeal public employees' rights to collective bargaining. The sign of a movement, said Hayden, is when people in the street are not members of an organization but are acting because they refuse to take any more of unacceptable conditions. One slogan he liked was "BEER, BRATS, CHEESE, UNIONS!" An organization did not make up that sign, he said; that comes from real, daily life. And when they're out there with thousands of others, they feel they are participating in history.

One of the organizers of the 2012 Wisconsin pro-union demonstrations was a former SDS member, Paul Booth, who had been at Port Huron in 1962. Just as he was back then, at Madison he was again acting as a field marshal, getting people making sure people had transportation and signs, etc. Although he was at Port Huron in 1962, he was later kicked out of SDS because he was not radical enough. (As the 1960s went on and leaders were assassinated and the Vietnam war and racial tensions escalated, some of the early, Port Huron–era SDS members were found by younger students to not be radical enough for what the times called for. For more about this, read Todd Gitlin's *The Sixties* and *The Whole World Is Watching*, and Kirkpatrick Sale's *SDS*.)

Hayden said that at some point around 1962 or 1963, some official in the Kennedy administration offered him a job with the Peace Corps, or in a Peace Corps–like agency, that would have taken him to South America. He was not sure if the administration was trying to arrange a meetup with Che Guevara (joke) or possibly just to get him out of the country for a few years. Hayden declined the offer.

At the five-day Port Huron meeting in June 1962, when the SDS members were working long hours discussing and revising the draft of the Statement (of which he had written the original draft), Hayden kept himself awake by sitting in a doorway with a toothbrush in his shirt pocket, and whenever someone stepped over him on the way to the bathroom, he would sit up a little and brush his teeth to keep himself awake a while longer.

Through a connection with one of our fellow SDS members' parents, we were able to get to the White House to give a copy of the Statement to Arthur M. Schlesinger Jr., the historian and special assistant to President Kennedy (1961–63). Did JFK read the part about de-escalating the cold war?

As an indicator of how influential, or dangerous, the Port Huron Statement has been perceived to be, the conservative jurist Robert H. Bork in his book *Slouching Towards Gomorrah: Modern Liberalism and American Decline*, describes the Statement as "disastrous," an "ominous document" and "a guide to today's cultural and political debacles."

"'Mickey, I've just seen the next Lenin,' Dick Flacks, the Jewish son of CP [Communist Party] members, exulted to his wife, a fellow child of Jewish Party members, after he first met Tom Hayden—who himself came from a thoroughly unradical Irish Catholic family," according to historian Michael Kazin in *American Dreamers: How the Left Changed a Nation* (p. 231). (This could explain the Peace Corps offer.)

A Talk with Tom Hayden and Other Participants

We got a chance to talk with Mr. Hayden for a few minutes after the panel discussion. Following are some notes on conversations with him and some of the other participants after the panel. ("Dead Sea Scrolls of the New Left," by the way, was Hayden's nickname for the Statement in an interview with *Democracy Now!* on Friday, April 13, the morning of his keynote address.)

After the initial waves of old friends and admirers and well-wishers, we got to talk with Mr. Hayden for a few minutes. We found him calm, kindly, tolerant, almost Zen-like, interested, still passionate but disciplined, focused. We talked some about the composition of the Statement, and told him about

Levees Not War, mainly a conjunction of infrastructure, anti-war, and environment. Ever think of those three things together? All the time, he said with a smile, in all seriousness. He said he'd been in New Orleans just the week before and enjoyed it.

Chuck McDew told us that when he was chairman of SNCC (1961–64), one of his organizers was arrested in Baton Rouge for addressing students at Southern University about registering to vote. McDew went to Baton Rouge with $10,000 in cash to pay the organizer's bail. McDew himself was arrested on spurious charges and spent many months in jail in Baton Rouge and more months at Angola state penitentiary. After that experience, he said, he wanted to leave the United States altogether.

One of the most remarkable comments of the night was spoken by **Robb Burlage**, who was editor of the student newspaper of the University of Texas at the time of the Port Huron meeting in June 1962. On Thursday night he said, We in the SDS (and the progressive movement generally in the 1960s) did not take enough responsibility, or prepare well enough, for "the craziness" that the '60s veered off into in the 1970s. There was so much to work on and there was only so much that could be accomplished in that brief period in history when the conditions were ripe, but looking back on it over the years it's clear that *we did not do enough to prepare for our accomplishments to last*, to cultivate relationships with younger waves of students and activists.

Burlage told us that when he was the editor of the University of Texas newspaper, his father got threatening, hate phone calls demanding that his son stop writing pro-integration, pro–civil rights editorials. His father shielded him from these messages at the time, and only told him later.

On the point of Burlage's lament about the New Left's failures, historian Michael Kazin addresses the shortcoming in his book *American Dreamers: How the Left Changed a Nation* (2012):

> Contemptuous of liberals, they failed to build durable interclass,
> interracial coalitions that might have sustained the new age
> of reform led by John Kennedy and Lyndon Johnson and
> prevented or delayed the rise of the New Right. Disenchanted
> with old formulas for remaking American society, *they gave
> little thought to devising new ones*. In the late 1960s and early

1970s, frustration at the lack of an alternative led an aggressive minority in the movement to take up one variety of Leninist dogma or another, while other activists sought to refashion a liberalism cleansed of Cold War hypocrisies. Neither project was successful. Soon, for the first time in over 150 years, *no American radical movement survived that was worthy of the name.* [LNW's emphasis]

And yet, Kazin goes on to say, "the New Left articulated a critique of everyday life which was in time taken up by millions. . . . [By the 1980s] Tens of millions of Americans, perhaps even a majority, had come to reject racial and sexual discrimination, to question the need for and morality of military intervention abroad, and to worry that industrial growth might be imperiling the future of life on earth. Neither the power nor the influence of the radicals who had helped promote these changes were what they had desired. But their message had certainly been received." (*American Dreamers*, pp. 212–13)

TAGS: Chuck McDew, Democracy Now!, Michael Kazin, NYU, Port Huron Statement, Robb Burlage, SDS, SNCC, Students for a Democratic Society, Todd Gitlin, Tom Hayden, Wisconsin

http://www.leveesnotwar.org/tom-hayden-sds-and-sncc-alums-happy-50th-port-huron-statement/

Jim Bohlen, a Greenpeace Founder, Dies

JULY 9, 2010—A quick note of appreciation for the life of James Calvin Bohlen (at left in photo), a cofounder of the environmental and peace action group Greenpeace, who died Monday in British Columbia. He was 84.

Navy Veteran, Peace Activist, Born on 4th of July

Bohlen was a member of a splinter group of Canadian Sierra Club members called the Don't Make a Wave Committee who opposed American testing of nuclear weapons at Amchitka Island in the Aleutian Islands (where he had served in the Navy in World War II as a radio operator). The Don't Make a Wave Committee later evolved into Greenpeace. The U.S. had been testing in the Aleutians, at a point midway between Alaska and the USSR, since 1965. Among the opponents' concerns was that the nuclear shock waves, so soon after the horrific Great Alaska Earthquake of 1964, would not only terrorize the already traumatized populace and release radioactive poisons but possibly also trigger new earthquakes (the test site was near a fault line) and tsunamis. In 1969, ten thousand protesters blocked a major U.S.–Canada border crossing, holding signs that read "Don't Make a Wave. It's Your Fault if Our Fault Goes."

Bohlen had complained to his wife, Marie, that the committee was taking too long to make up its mind about how to stop the tests; she said offhandedly why not sail a boat to the test site? When a reporter from *The Vancouver Sun* happened to phone to check on the committee's deliberations, Bohlen (perhaps to his own surprise) announced, "We hope to sail a boat to Amchitka to confront the bomb." When the remark appeared in the paper the following day, the die was cast.

The Don't Make a Wave Committee rented a halibut fishing boat, named it "Greenpeace I," and in September 1971 sailed toward the Aleutians, but was intercepted by the U.S. Coast Guard. The public outcry had an effect, however—boosted by a fund-raising concert starring James Taylor, Joni Mitchell, and Phil Ochs—and the U.S. stopped testing in 1971.

Regarding the concerns about radioactivity, an alarming "30 Years After" report in *In These Times* noted that "Highly radioactive elements and gasses, such as tritium, americium-241 and plutonium, poured out of the collapsed test shafts, leached into the groundwater and worked their way into ponds, creeks and the Bering Sea."

James Calvin Bohlen was born in the Bronx, and after World War II he earned an engineering degree and worked as an aerospace engineer. He moved his family to Vancouver in 1967 so that his stepson would not be subject to a U.S. military draft during the Vietnam War.

He was a director of Greenpeace (now in 40 countries worldwide, with 3 million members) until his retirement in 1993. His memoir, *Making Waves: The Origins and Future of Greenpeace*, was published in 2000.

May his memory be honored by similar (and repeated, persistent) acts of courage and conscience.

TAGS: Amchitka, Countdown to Zero, Don't Make a Wave Committee, environmental action, Greenpeace, James Bohlen, No Nukes, nuclear testing, Sierra Club

http://www.leveesnotwar.org/jim-bohlen-a-greenpeace-founder-dies/

"And Death Shall Have No Dominion"

A Tribute to President John F. Kennedy

*If we cannot end now our differences, at least we can help make
the world safe for diversity. For, in the final analysis, our most
basic common link is that we all inhabit this small planet.
We all breathe the same air. We all cherish our children's future.
And we are all mortal.*

John F. Kennedy, June 10, 1963

And death shall have no dominion

Dylan Thomas

NOV. 22, 2013—Rarely has a November passed by that this blog has not paused to pay respects to the memory of President John F. Kennedy. We keep an "eternal flame" of our own lighted not only because of a feeling of personal connection to him—from an Irish Catholic family kinship, and having been taken as a toddler to a 1960 campaign stop at an airport in the South, and being just old enough to watch the funeral coverage on a black-and-white TV—though these would be reasons enough. We repeatedly bring President Kennedy to our readers, or vice versa, because of what he stood for, what he accomplished, and what he symbolizes.

What Does "John F. Kennedy" Mean?

It may be that, despite the limitations of what he was able to accomplish during his too-brief presidency, because of the ideals he represents, because of the hope and activism he still inspires, President Kennedy is more influential postmortem than during his lifetime. And it's possible that the murky, still nebulous circumstances of his death (by whom, really, and why?) add to the mystique of the Dead King, the Slain Prince, and all that might have been possible, and might still be possible, if we summon his spirit. He dwells now on the mythological level, in the realm of ideas and legend. (This may explain the success of Jacqueline Kennedy's posthumous establishing of a "Camelot" myth. At least in the public mind, there was no Camelot connection with the Kennedy White House before Nov. 22, 1963: Mrs. Kennedy's myth-making began with an interview with Theodore H. White, author of *The Making of the President 1960*, a week after the assassination.)

Now, on the fiftieth anniversary of the assassination in Dallas (November 22, 1963, was also a Friday), many other voices are commenting on the accomplishments and significance of President Kennedy's "Thousand Days" in office—what he did and tried and what he failed to do. We only wish to honor his long-standing commitment to peace; his refusal to be bullied by the military chiefs or the CIA during the Cuban Missile Crisis of 1962 (especially after he was burned by the CIA's brilliant idea for an invasion of Cuba at the Bay of Pigs in 1961); his reluctance to escalate U.S. involvement in Vietnam and his intention to withdraw troops; his establishment of the Peace Corps, etc.

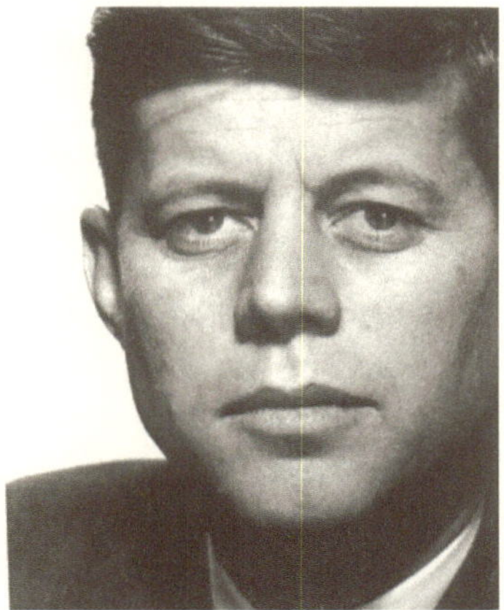

Photograph © Philippe Halsman Archive, 2015

He supported, though cautiously at first, civil rights and desegregation of public facilities, especially in the South. He had a plan for expansion of medical coverage for the poor and elderly that became what we know as Medicaid and Medicare, and he supported strengthening voting rights. Much of his desired or proposed legislation was left to his able successor, President Lyndon B. Johnson, to push through Congress—thus the Civil Rights Act of 1964, the Voting Rights Act of 1965, the establishment of Medicare and Medicaid in 1965 through expansion of Social Security.

Because of the historical circumstances of his time, the national priorities, and his own proclivities, Kennedy was more focused on foreign affairs than on domestic policy. But he also called the nation to put a man on the moon by the end of the decade (this too had national security components), and his vision was realized by the successful mission of *Apollo 11* in 1969.

And, of course, on this fiftieth anniversary, many pundits and historians are busy pouring concrete over the hardened conventional wisdom about the lone gunman, the "case closed," the truths "proved" by the Warren Commission Report, etc. This is not the occasion to expound our views on the assassination, but we have read enough books and articles, seen enough documentaries, and attended enough panel discussions to be thoroughly convinced that the president was shot at by multiple shooters, and we doubt that Lee Harvey Oswald was one of them. (As for the plausibility of a "conspiracy theory," remember that the attacks of 9/11, too, resulted from a conspiracy.) The most convincing explanation we have found of why Kennedy was killed is in the sober and methodical *JFK and the Unspeakable* by James W. Douglass.

> *John Kennedy's story is our story, although a titanic effort has been made to keep it from us. That story, like the struggle it embodies, is as current today as it was in 1963. The theology of redemptive violence still reigns. The Cold War has been followed by its twin, the War on Terror. We are engaged in another apocalyptic struggle against an enemy seen as absolute evil. . . . an enemy portrayed as irredeemably evil. Yet the redemptive means John Kennedy turned to, in a similar struggle, was dialogue with the enemy. When the enemy is seen as human, everything changes.*
>
> James W. Douglass, *JFK and the Unspeakable*

TAGS: Camelot, JFK, JFK and the Unspeakable, John F. Kennedy
http://www.leveesnotwar.org/a-tribute-to-president-john-f-kennedy/

PART VI

In and About New Orleans

What Is New Orleans?
Resilient, a Moveable Feast, and Growing, Slowly

OCT. 25, 2009—The moderator and panelists presented some very thoughtful and deeply felt responses to the question "What Is New Orleans" at Loyola's Nunemaker Auditorium Wednesday night. In his introduction, the moderator, New Orleans novelist John Biguenet, reminded the audience that in 2006 Republicans in Congress voted down a resolution that would have declared congressional commitment to rebuilding the Gulf Coast. (Biguenet blogged for *The New York Times* in 2005 and 2006 about the city's recovery—check out his strong, clear-voiced pieces—and he is profiled in the Fall 2009 *Louisiana Cultural Vistas*.)

Richard Campanella

In order of interest, first would be Tulane geographer and demographics whiz Richard Campanella (who actually spoke last), author of the fascinating *Bienville's Dilemma: A Historical Geography of New Orleans*. (Buy it. Read it. Then buy copies for your friends who are interested in the city's history and future.) Campanella—originally from Brooklyn, it turns out—is a sort of geography + demographics geek who makes statistics interesting and brisk-paced so your eyes don't glaze over. To wit: the city's population, about 450,000 before Katrina, dropped to nearly zero in Sept. '05, and is about 340,000 now. The population had risen to 200K on the first anniversary (2006), 300K on the second, and 320K by the third anniversary. From the second anniversary to the present, the population has risen by only 40,000 souls.

After presenting statistics on population and ethnic density in various parts of town, Campanella affirmed that New Orleans is enjoying a "brain gain" of talented people who want to be here to help rebuild (and possibly prosper). The city is now more mobile, more international, and (for tragic reasons) is more in the national consciousness than it has been in a long time. Among the consequences of the storm + flood have been greater citizen participation and decentralization of urban planning, public education, and health care (in part because the institutions are not delivering). There have also been some improved efficiencies through consolidation of the levee districts and boards and the tax assessors, among other official functions. He praised the city's (that is, the citizens') resiliency, their ability to recover from adversity through adaptation, reinvention, innovation.

Susan Saulny

Susan Saulny is a New Orleans native whose family roots go way back. She was a reporter for *The Times-Picayune* and *The Washington Post* before writing for *The New York Times*. Ms. Saulny spoke feelingly but with admirable composure of the family members—including elderly aunts and uncles—who have died after being displaced by Katrina. Some, though they were in their seventies and eighties, were determined to return and rebuild. Some were overwhelmed by the magnitude of the task, or may simply have died of heartbreak. But, on a more hopeful note, she said she likes the slogan (on stickers made by Dirty Coast) "Be a New Orleanian. Wherever you are." And she recalled Hemingway's tribute to the city of Paris that gives the title to his literary memoir: "If you are lucky enough to have lived in Paris as a young man, then wherever you go for the rest of your life, it stays with you, for Paris is a moveable feast." The same, she said, is true of her native city.

We highly recommend her powerful, sensitive report for *The New York Times*, "New Orleans Hurt by Acute Rental Shortage" (Dec. 3, 2007), on the homeless New Orleanians living under the Claiborne Avenue overpass and in tents near City Hall in late 2007 when the (all-white) New Orleans City Council was nearing a unanimous vote to allow the federal government to raze 4,500 public housing units *before* replacement housing had been built. A video accompanies Saulny's article. (Demolitions continue to this day, most recently at the Lafitte public housing site along Orleans Avenue.) See our posts from that sad time, December 2007, "Homeless for the Holidays" and "Who Would Jesus Evict?"

Lawrence N. Powell

Tulane history professor Lawrence N. Powell emphasized that much of American history, particularly concerning civil rights, and its culture (esp. music and cuisine) cannot be properly told without examining New Orleans's role and contributions, the good and the bad. In speaking of New Orleans as an "accidental city," Powell posited the notion—perhaps to be explained further in his history of the city forthcoming eventually from Harvard University Press (*The Accidental City: Improvising New Orleans*)—that John Law of "Mississippi Bubble" fame had originally recommended situating the new city of La Nouvelle-Orléans upriver where Bayou Manchac then led from the Mississippi to Lake Maurepas and thence to Lake Pontchartrain and on to the Gulf of Mexico. Law's plan, says Powell, was thwarted by Bienville's "seigneurial ambitions"—not to mention the bursting of the speculative venture known as the Mississippi Bubble—and Bienville's insistence on placing the city at its present location. We will want to read Professor Powell's *Accidental City* to learn more about this.

"What Is New Orleans" was presented by Loyola University's Center for the Study of New Orleans.

TAGS: John Biguenet, Lawrence Powell, Loyola University–New Orleans, Richard Campanella, Susan Saulny

http://www.leveesnotwar.org/what-is-new-orleans-resilient-a-moveable-feast -and-growing-slowly/

In Memoriam: Greg Peters

"Suspect Device" Artist and Blogger, Father, Friend

My message is kind of an emperor's new clothes thing: I'm making fun of them, but I'm also trying to remind people that you have a choice. And if you don't get involved in it, then it's going to continue, and they'll continue to put on the circus show for you, amusing you by proposing laws about pants that show ass crack, or Darwin being racist, at the same time that they're screwing over your future.

Greg Peters (September 24, 1962–August 2, 2013)

AUG. 3, 2013—It is with sadness that we note the death yesterday of our friend Greg Peters, an award-winning cartoonist, artist, and writer, following heart surgery at Oschner Medical Center in New Orleans. A native of Marquette, Michigan, who was an all-but-dissertation-Ph.D. in English and creative writing at the University of Louisiana (Lafayette), Greg Peters was 50.

In his own words (from his profile at Lafayette Creative ['artsy, without the fartsy']):

> Greg Peters is a cartoonist, writer and graphic designer living in Louisiana. He is available for freelance work, as well as speaking engagements, personal appearances at bachelorette parties, raucous press club luncheons, and swanky, black-tie bourgeois pig feeds, where his unassailable personal magnetism and colorful vocabulary make him a sure object of intense, whispered conversation.

Although we did not know Greg as well as we would like to have known him—living in separate cities, and meeting only at the Rising Tide conferences whose posters he designed year after year—we always admired his intelligence, artistic talent, his satirical wit and no-bullshit honesty, and his very wide and loyal network of friends, in New Orleans and beyond, who will be mourning his passing. We will miss Greg in much the same way as Ashley Morris is missed: talented life-forces who passed too early, too young, from this physical realm, but whose spirits live on among us and continue to inspire our best, most honest work and our best living, as if life itself, and how you live it, matters. We are not OK, because they are gone. But we'll be OK, because they're still with us on the inside.

Putting Art to Work Against Official Incompetence and Mendacity

Peters's award-winning "Suspect Device" editorial cartoon series (named after the song by Stiff Little Fingers) was published in the *Times of Acadiana* and *Gambit*, and other graphic work was featured in the book *Attitude 2: The New Subversive Alternative Cartoonists* (2004). He designed posters for the Port of New Orleans, among other clients, and, from 2007 on, he designed posters for all but one of the Rising Tide conferences on the future of New Orleans. He also created the cover for *A Howling in the Wires: An Anthology of Writing from Postdiluvian New Orleans* (2010), which includes two of his blog posts from *Suspect Device*.

Kevin Allman has posted a fine tribute at *Gambit*, noting that Peters was "funny—and always furious and rude, juxtaposed with sophisticated writing. In a 2004 profile of Peters and his work, former *Gambit* music editor Scott Jordan noted, 'Peters' craft is fueled by his punk rock-influenced DIY personality and educational background in literary criticism, Marxism, post-structuralism, and Buddhism—all meeting the surreal arena of Louisiana politics.'"

Other tributes can be found at NOLA.com, the blogs *Toulouse Street, Library Chronicles, Liprap's Lament, Pog mo Thoin* (an especially eloquent and touching personal recollection from a friend who is not of the New Orleans blogosphere), and on Facebook, where Greg's companion, *Gambit* contributor Eileen Loh, posted the following:

I'm gutted to have to tell so many of Greg Peters' friends that the world has lost a brilliant mind, a gifted artist, a scathing wit, a maestro of sarcasm, an ardent defender of the disenfranchised and the discriminated and the broken, and one of the gentlest, kindest, funniest and most fearless people I've ever met. He never got to live one day of his life without the congenital heart condition that got him in the end, and in my almost bottomless sadness, I am happy he's finally free. Please keep his boys in your thoughts; they are inconsolable.

Greg Peters is survived by his two sons, Magnus and Wilder; his companion, Eileen Loh, and his former wife, Saundra Scarce of Lafayette.

Memorial Services Announced

Eileen Loh announces on Facebook:

> There will be two memorial services for Greg Peters: one in Lafayette and one in New Orleans. The former is set for next Saturday, Aug. 10, at Martin & Castille Funeral Home, 600 East Farrel Road, Lafayette (337-234-2311). Visitation starts at 1:00, and the service is from 2:00 to 4:00. • The family is hoping that some of the guests might choose to prepare a 4- or 5-minute eulogy or remembrance to read at the service, largely so that Magnus and Wilder can hear many facets of their dad's truly one-of-a-kind personality.
>
> The New Orleans memorial service is TBA and will be a far less classy affair, a punk Irish wake in a New Orleans dive bar, as the gods intended . . . probably toward the end of August, 23/24, so that as many of his kick-ass friends from all corners can come. I will keep you posted.

Let the last words, for now, be those of Charles Bukowski, as quoted in a signature in an e-mail from Greg in 2009:

We are here to unlearn the teachings of the church, state, and our educational system. We are here to drink beer. We are here to kill war. We are here to laugh at the odds and live our lives so well that Death will tremble to take us.

Update 8/10/13: Be sure to read Mark Moseley's thoughtful tribute to his friend and ours at *The Lens*, "Remembering the unforgettable: a salute to the late, very great Greg Peters." Highly recommended.

TAGS: Eileen Loh, Gambit, Greg Peters, NOLA bloggers, Rising Tide, Suspect Device
http://www.leveesnotwar.org/in-memoriam-greg-peters-suspect-device-artist
-and-blogger-father-friend/

The following excerpts from or about several of the annual Rising Tide conferences between 2007 and 2013 are only tiny slivers of the totality of the gatherings. Please note that the transcripts were live-blogged, keyed hastily on the fly and should be read as paraphrases, not as literal, verbatim transcripts of the speakers' remarks. I apologize in case of any errors. ("Making Blogging Sexy" was the title of a post about Rising Tide 2 [2007], after the panel discussion "Making Civics Sexy" led by Bart "Editor B." Everson.)

Rising Tide

Making Blogging (and Civics) Sexy in New Orleans

What Is Rising Tide?

The Rising Tide conferences, held since 2006 on or near the anniversary of Hurricane Katrina (August 29), bring together bloggers, activists, techies and other geeks, teachers, writers, artists, and experts in education, public safety, infrastructure, Louisiana politics, sports, the environment, Internet technology, parenting in New Orleans, and many other topics pertaining to the area's ongoing recovery from hurricanes, "federal floods," oil spills, and other challenges.

Featured speakers have included David Simon (co-creator of HBO's *Treme* and *The Wire*); actor and activist Harry Shearer; New Orleans geographer and historian Richard Campanella, author of *Bourbon Street* and *Bienville's Dilemma*; John M. Barry, author of *Rising Tide: The Great Mississippi Flood of 1927 and How It Changed America*; Treme-born writer Lolis Eric Elie, director of the documentary *Faubourg Treme: The Untold Story of Black New Orleans*; former Tulane professor of history Lawrence N. Powell, author of *The Accidental City: Improvising New Orleans*; *Mother Jones* human rights reporter Mac McClelland; and Christopher Cooper and Robert Block, authors of *Disaster: Hurricane Katrina and the Failure of Homeland Security*.

Live-Blogging from Rising Tide 8 (2013)

http://www.leveesnotwar.org/live-blogging-from-rising-tide-8-in-new-orleans/

Keynote Address: Lt. Gen. Russel L. Honoré
on Leadership and Environmental Justice

SEPT. 14, 2013—The keynote speaker at the 8th annual Rising Tide conference was Lt. Gen. Russel L. Honoré, the no-nonsense "Category 5 General" who took command of Joint Task Force Katrina that coordinated military relief efforts following the August 29, 2005, hurricane and resulting "federal flood" of the city of New Orleans.

Honoré, a Louisiana native (born in Lakeland in Pointe Coupee Parish) and graduate of Southern University in Baton Rouge, was designated commander of Joint Task Force Katrina by President George W. Bush two days after the storm. Amid official incompetence from local to federal levels, Honoré exhibited decisiveness and a gruff management style, but also restraint and a local's understanding of the people he had been sent to assist. He knew that the task force was on a relief mission, and barked at one soldier who had flashed his weapon at a New Orleanian in a threatening way, "We're on a rescue mission, damn it!"

He is the author of Leadership in the New Normal *(2012).*

If oil and gas are so good for Louisiana, why are we one of the poorest states in the union? Why don't we all get to go to private schools? Just speaking critically of oil and gas industry and its effect on our state will get you criticized. We want tourism and visitors, and oil and gas industries can be here, but they can't trash the place.

. . . I was on CNN and I said I'm not going to call this the "Gulf oil spill," this is the *BP* oil spill. The Gulf of Mexico didn't cause this. This was created by a company.

. . . How is it that the EPA is prevented from coming into a state to take action against a violation of the Clean Water Act unless the state government invites it in? If there's a violation of a drug smuggling law, the federal forces can take action. But it was written into the Clean Water Act that the EPA is limited from enforcing the law. Self-regulating is not an option. These companies messing up this state don't even have their headquarters here. We've got to figure out how we're going to use our voice to influence our legislators.

We have a serious water problem. The aquifers are depleting seriously because of the industries' use. Why aren't they using the Mississippi River? Because the aquifers, which should be reserved for the local people's drinking water, are easier for the companies to draw from. And what are we going to do with the orphan wells? These old oil wells have been abandoned. Streams of oil all over the place, just leaking. You can see them all over Plaquemines Parish, still lying there, knocked over by Hurricane Katrina, and the companies have been allowed by the Louisiana legislature to leave them abandoned. We have to make it visible.

This is your war. This is our time. This is a great cause. How are you going to get your nieces and nephews and neighbors involved? The way we're going in the state of Louisiana, this place will not be fit to live in. What we have going on off our coastline is like what they have going on in Nigeria. How many of you could make a list of ten people you could bring on the team for environmental justice, for social justice?

We have a hard task, but through the power of connectivity, we can succeed. In a democracy, you can turn the situation around.

Live-Blogging from Rising Tide 6 (2011)

http://www.leveesnotwar.org/live-blogging-from-rising-tide-6/

AUG. 27, 2011—Usually we worry that Rising Tide might be disrupted by a hurricane—after all, it's held each year on the anniversary of Katrina. Ironically, this year, while Hurricane Irene is lashing at the East Coast and New York City is evacuating some 250,000 people from low-lying areas, the weather in New Orleans is warm (okay, hot), clear, calm. At the conference some of us are scratching our heads and asking of the millions who live along the East Coast, susceptible as it is to hurricanes, Why do they live there? [Ed. Note: This post appeared the year before Superstorm Sandy of late October 2012.]

Featured Speaker: David Simon

David Simon, creator of HBO's celebrated TV show Treme, *set in post-Katrina New Orleans, and of HBO's* The Wire.

Began as a reporter in Baltimore, covering police beat in a mainly African-American neighborhood. As a young reporter it struck me how few reporters would not want to ask questions to which they did not already know the answer. But I would ask anyone anything. Tells the story of a former Pulitzer Prize–winning *Herald Tribune* reporter who asked so many questions that an Esso executive complained to the editor, why did you send this idiot to interview me? He didn't know anything; I had to explain everything to him.

. . . As I approached New Orleanians to make the show *Treme* with Eric Overmeyer, I decided to hire local people, and determined to be very deferential to the people in this city who had suffered through such a terrible trauma.

. . . Recounts contentious phone call with Mayor Landrieu when bulldozers were aimed at houses in lower Mid-City where LSU Medical Center wants to build new center. A local preservation society had asked Simon to write a letter to the mayor to urge a halt to demolition of homes on Derbigny Street to clear ground for the new medical center. Simon mailed letter to mayor's office but it got lost, buried, not responded to. Then, without telling Simon, Preservation Society gave the letter to mayor and alerted the press. Mayor phoned Simon and yelled at him. Don't you realize how committed I am to preservation? These homes could not have been saved, anyway. Then he asked Simon if he (and HBO) had money to offer—to make a deal not to bulldoze? After the call, with the cameras rolling, the mayor said Who *is* this person [David Simon]? He's not from here. He doesn't realize how committed I am to preservation, etc.

. . . Your leaders will lie to you and suggest that no outsiders can tell us what to do. It keeps New Orleans isolated and weaker than it could be. It is not true that outsiders have no standing or understanding or caring about your city. There are people who are from here who do not have the city's best interests in mind, but rather their own profit.

[See "ReNEW, ReOPEN Charity Hospital" below.]

Panel: Recapping the Well, on the 2010 BP spill

Panelists survey the aftermath of the Deepwater Horizon / BP oil disaster and the future of the Gulf Coast.

Dr. Len Bahr, former coastal science adviser to five Louisiana governors, now editor of *LaCoastPost.com*; **Bob Marshall,** Pulitzer Prize–winning *Times-Picayune* reporter covering environmental issues [now at *The Lens*]; David Hammer, *Times-Picayune* reporter who covered the Macondo well; **Anne Rolfes,** founding director of the Louisiana Bucket Brigade; Drake Toulouse, BP and Gulf Coast Claims Facility critic, blogs at *Disenfranchised Citizen.* Moderated by Alex Woodward, *Gambit Weekly* staff writer.

Bob Marshall:

Nothing this big had ever happened and no one knew what would happen if such a big catastrophe took place. There were 39 possible time bombs out in the Gulf that likewise could blow and leak catastrophically. The pursuit of profit by both the industry and the state for the oil & gas royalties puts us at terrible risk; they say, well, there's risk in everything, as when crossing the street. Yes, but not all with such profound consequences. The oil industry didn't "rape" Louisiana; it was consensual sex. If you blame oil industry, look in the mirror. If the BP spill did not change our dysfunctional relationship with the industry, nothing will. We keep re-electing politicians who are close-ly allied with or beholden to the oil industry.

This hurricane [Irene] heading up the Eastern Seaboard makes me wonder, Why do they live there? [Audience laughter and applause] Congress is dominated by conservatives who do not want any regulation of any industry, particularly the oil industry with its drilling 5,000 feet below the surface. Obama budgeted millions for coastal restoration and study, but conservatives nixed it. One Republican said, What is the Corps of Engineers doing with coastal restoration? They should be dredging. Finally, after much struggle, supporters (including some Republicans) were able to get a mere $1 million for coastal Louisiana, and *The Times-Picayune* ran an editorial titled "A Win for Louisiana." [laughter] One of the things that takes so long for coastal restoration or tidal surge mitigation is that you have so many property owners' permission to obtain. Eminent domain? Why doesn't the legislature give "quick take" (eminent domain) authority to the state agency for coastal restoration, because it is in the public's interest. The coastal authority in the governor's office said that that would be the worst thing the state could do, even though the oil companies, if they want to drive a canal or lay a line through your property, do have the authority (or are granted permission) to do just that.

I recently re-watched *Louisiana Story*. In the 1930s, there was no sense that the oil exploration was going to destroy the environment. By the 1970s it was clear. The oil industries who said "we didn't know" did know by the 1970s, and what have they done since? What have these super-rich companies done for the state? When they threaten to leave, where are they going to go, Kansas? These riches are on public land, but they are not being made to pay, and the state is poor; it doesn't have to be this way.

Anne Rolfes:

Astonishing record of industrial accidents in oil industry, but the industry has strong defenders in Congress and Louisiana legislature. The oil refinery workers say the accident rate is much worse than reported by the oil firms. Curious parallel between Sen. Mary Landrieu and the American Petroleum Institute's language about the oil industry. They feed her the script, talking points. Louisiana seafood industry and oil industry "coexist peacefully."

. . . The BP disaster has opened up a small window for discussion of questions that were not heard before, such as Bob Marshall's column asking whether Louisiana's relation to oil industry is an example of Stockholm Syndrome or spousal abuse. Would you have been able to get an opinion piece in the *T-P* before the BP blowout? . . . We have an opportunity to make the oil industry accountable. Richard Campanella pointed out that oil refineries are on the same land where the plantations once were. They used to say that slavery would never be brought down, but it was.

Len Bahr:

I came to Louisiana (LSU) in 1973 out of graduate school to study the effects of oil and gas exploration on the Louisiana coast. Quickly learned how powerful the industry is, and how reluctant scientists are to "get political." So many connections between the terrible Katrina experience and the BP Deepwater Horizon experience. Bob Bea of Berkeley who studied why the federally built levees failed in Katrina also knows about oil and gas deepwater drilling but was not asked to become involved in studying what happened with Deepwater Horizon blowout.

Katrina gave us Bobby Jindal: the fight over Katrina with a Republican administration damaged the previous governor, Kathleen Babineaux Blanco, and paved the way for Republican conservative Bobby Jindal. Will the BP spill help make way for a Republican president? The Republican denial of science (climate change, sea level rise, evolution) is very discouraging for hopes for restoration of Louisiana's industry-damaged coastline.

Rising Tide 5 with Mac McClelland (2010)

http://www.leveesnotwar.org/live-blogging-from-rising-tide-5-in-new-orleans/

AUG. 28, 2010—*Rising Tide 5, held at the Howlin' Wolf in the warehouse district, was easily one of the best RTs ever. Following is a July 22 advance write-up of the program:*

> The conference will feature panel discussions on HBO's hit
> show *Treme* (set in post-Katrina New Orleans) with *Treme* co-
> creator Eric Overmyer and N.O. journalist and documentarist
> Lolis Eric Elie . . . "Paradise Lost" on environmental issues,
> including *LaCoastPost*'s Len Bahr, a coastal science adviser to

five Louisiana governors, and environmental law expert Rob
Verchick . . . flood protection discussed by Tim Ruppert, an
N.O. engineer and blogger . . . a public safety panel whose
guests will include NOPD Superintendent Ronal Serpas . . .
and Louisiana politics, moderated by Peter Athas and featuring
Clancy DuBos of *Gambit* and other N.O. journalists. And more!

*The keynote speaker was (Ms.) Mac McClelland, an intrepid investigative and
human rights reporter who was writing about the social, personal consequences
of the BP oil spill that had erupted four months earlier (April 2010). She writes
a column for* Mother Jones *titled "The Rights Stuff: Mac McClelland's Human
Rights Notebook."*

Keynote speaker: Mac McClelland

Reporting in the national media in years since Katrina has not kept up with
the facts here in New Orleans. Outside of Louisiana everyone thinks "everything's fine" because they're not seeing images and accurate on-the-ground
reporting from the real world in New Orleans. The oil spill is reported to have
dispersed, to no longer be a problem. Everyone wants to hear that it's all fine
now, in part because the truth is so sad and depressing. . . .

Reporters have a public responsibility for reporting on safety of seafood,
testing for safety of dispersants in Gulf waters. The U.S. is not testing for
safety of water, dispersant levels in the water. No reporter wants to be the
one to print that the seafood is not safe. Mac had originally come to write
an article for *Mother Jones* on public defenders. Then the oil spill happened.
Not so surprising that BP wasn't being cooperative, but what is surprising is
that the Obama administration has been secretive and not so cooperative. In
many cases they did not have the information we were looking for, such as the
number of cleanup workers. Coast Guard says the numbers you're looking for
are BP's numbers. We can ask, but sometimes they don't get back to us. This
is the Coast Guard. Coast Guard was disseminating BP's numbers and not
fact-checking, not overseeing. It was easier to get information from secretive
Burma than it has been from BP or U.S. agencies.

Dedra Johnson of "The G Bitch Spot" Wins Rising Tide's 2011 Ashley Award

AUG. 31, 2011—Congratulations to Dedra Johnson of *The G-Bitch Spot*—a blog that doesn't just have a great name, but shines with clear, independent thinking and sharp, sassy writing—in which "a mad black woman rants about New Orleans, insomnia, teaching, education, and 'education,' various -isms and anything involving a bitch, a spot or the letter g."

The coveted Ashley Award, established in 2008 and named in honor of the legendary, larger-than-life Ashley Morris, is presented each year to a blogger who has made outstanding contributions to writing about post-Katrina New Orleans. Ashley Morris, Ph.D., who died in 2008, was one of the founders of the Rising Tide conference and still a guiding spirit. He was an inspiration for the character Creighton Bernette (played by John Goodman) in HBO's *Treme*. The award is given each year to someone who embodies Ashley's fierce, passionate defense of New Orleans, its people, and its culture.

Dedra Johnson taught creative writing at Dillard University and is the author of *Sandrine's Letter to Tomorrow* (2007), a coming-of-age novel set in 1970s New Orleans. *Sandrine's Letter*, a runner-up for the William Faulkner–William Wisdom Award in 2006, was praised by Robert Olen Butler as "an important novel by a true artist" and hailed by Frederick Barthelme as "a remarkable debut novel" that conveys "the intricacies of a vexed family life." Dedra received her MFA degree from the University of Florida, where she was a finalist for the Hurston/Wright Award for College Writers.

"Where You Said You Live At? or Margaritas as Coping Strategy," posted at *The G-Bitch Spot* on March 19, 2006, conveys the fatigue of living in a battered, depopulated city that nearly drowned in floodwaters a half year earlier and is slowly being strangled by bureaucratic red tape and incompetence. The post also appeared in *A Howling in the Wires: An Anthology of Writing from*

Postdiluvian New Orleans, edited by Sam Jasper and Mark Folse (Gallatin & Toulouse Press, 2010).

Where You Said You Live At? or Margaritas as Coping Strategy

http://gbitchspot.com/gbitchspot/?p=41

Why no N.O. news, commentary, rants, pleas? Because it rankles enough to live it, much less reiterate it for the consumption of others. Each front page of the Times-Pic is demoralizing, infuriating—early pundits bashing New Orleanian stupidity in not getting flood insurance when a large percentage HAD flood insurance; every senator and representative bitching and moaning over the Gulf Coast being OK (and needing no more money) since they see clips of the French Quarter up and running on national news then being agog at their first superficial glance of Lakeview (where WHITE people and PROFESSIONAL people lived, not welfare queens and drug dealing pimps specializing in crack whores of all hues) and then the Ninth Ward, not even taking a look at the chaos of half-repaired and completely ignored traffic lights, piles of debris, refrigerators and 3+ weeks' worth of garbage and a coming election that is plagued by chaos, in-fighting, racial contempt and deep-seated conflict, federal neglect and unprocessed hurt and anger; and the bullshitting cockamamie half-assed amateurish job being done by all decision-makers and -influencers on the local, state and federal level; and then there's the particular chaos and neglect and fraud and graft that is FEMA.

I'm shattered and nothing happened to my house.

No one is being decisive or honest. Much of the money directed our way in the early days has been wasted. Entergy and LSUHC saw the post-Katrina atmosphere as one in which they could get concessions and privileges no one would give them

before—LSUHC closed Charity and University, "furloughed"
most of the employees (all while LSU hospital staff were retained
and many helped with housing), and claimed the Charity
hospital building was unusable and the federal government
needed to build a brand new hospital for them; and contractors
ran loose and wild with money, squishing the huge amounts
they got through more and more subcontractors and therefore
smaller funnels until those who actually did the work got paid
shit. It offends all my sensibilities, fuels all my social resentments
(one, that Entergy, a private for-profit company, owns a utility
at all; none of this would've happened if we still had NOPSI
[New Orleans Public Service, Inc.] b/c there would've been no
incentive/profit in delaying repairs or service or paperwork
gimmicks). Shaw made a shitload of money, too [the Shaw
Group, a Fortune 500 construction and engineering firm based
in Baton Rouge]. Meanwhile, no one knows what to do while
FEMA drags its barely-competent feet on new flood maps and
SBA loan requirements and amounts change at random and
Burger King pays better than most of the non-construction
jobs in town. I feel like my chest is weighed down, and also feel
forsaken. Again.

http://www.leveesnotwar.org/dedra-johnson-of-the-g-bitch-spot-wins-rising
-tide's-ashley-award/

Viva New Orleans—for Art's Sake!

AUG. 29, 2007—One of the happy (re)discoveries at the Rising Tide 2 conference of Katrina bloggers this past weekend was the New Orleanians' sheer vitality, creativity, and ingenuity—their will to survive, to renew, to make the city better than it was before. We came away reinvigorated, reassured that in at least one American city democracy and citizen activism are alive and well. (If you keep busy, it doesn't hurt quite as bad—and anyway, struggling for your very survival has a way of concentrating the mind.) In part because some public officials are lame and passive, and others are working but overwhelmed and underfunded, gutsy determined citizens are taking into their own hands the work of rebuilding, forming civic associations, alerting fellow citizens about opportunities and dangers (potential funding, criminal activity on the streets or in City Hall), etc.

And this vitality—this will to live, and to live better—made us realize that of all the reasons given for why New Orleans should be helped in its recovery, one that we've never heard mentioned (though it should be obvious) is the sheer creativity of the people in this city: the writers, musicians, artists, filmmakers, ceramicists and glass-blowers, gallery proprietors, booksellers, and all the ordinary citizens who so naturally invent whimsical Mardi Gras costumes and masks and floats and occasions for parties, and so on. New Orleans not only breeds talented musicians and writers, etc., from its own rich soil and dirty river water and humid air, but it also attracts creative types who thrive in the city's relatively tolerant society and inexpensive economy and lively calendars of festivals, readings, concerts, parades, gallery openings, jazz funerals, lectures, etc. (This hints at why New Orleans has been called not just a city but a civilization.)

So, in addition to all the other familiar reasons why the Crescent City warrants help in rebuilding—such as its seafood, the port, oil and gas, tourism, cuisine, and the rich musical heritage—America needs a healthy and happy New Orleans for the sake of its own cultural vitality, too. Now, we don't expect this argument to make a deep impression on everyone, but for those who understand, for those who need art and joie de vivre like most people need a good meal, just think about what could be lost if New Orleans is neglected. Think of what has already been lost.

http://www.leveesnotwar.org/viva-new-orleans—for-art's-sake/

ReNEW | ReOPEN Charity Hospital

NOV. 27, 2008—Our friend Schroeder at *People Get Ready* rightly points out that in a city beset by so many problems at once, New Orleans residents have to choose their battles. *Levees Not War* focuses on infrastructure and coastal restoration, but we also urge our readers—in the Sunken City and beyond—to help save Charity Hospital, a towering embodiment of the social contract built with obsessive attention to detail by Huey Long in the 1930s, from an expensive, unnecessary, and largely destructive plan by the LSU Medical School and the Veterans Administration that would raze it and about 250 structures in the surrounding neighborhood (all on the National Historic Trust for Historic Preservation's list of America's Most Endangered Places).

This aptly named, long-standing institution is an indicator of how a society treats its less fortunate members—a sign of how civilized and merciful a society is. This hospital (nearly as old as the city itself) and the struggle to save it may represent a last vestige of the social contract between the people and the powerful. If we can save Big Charity, New Orleans will be a better place to live, and the victory will embolden us for further efforts.

Charity, on Tulane Avenue, an architecturally beautiful art deco landmark, is a teaching hospital for the LSU medical school and is owned by LSU. Until Hurricane Katrina damaged its bottom floors, it was the central trauma unit for hundreds of miles around. (Visitors to Our Fair City, Charity was where you could get stitched up if you got drunk and injured during Mardi Gras.) The hospital has been closed since Katrina in 2005, and the state has shown no interest in reopening it. Now what we seem to have instead—as *The New York Times* recently reported—is interest in plans by developers to raze Charity and about 250 buildings in the immediate vicinity and to construct new buildings that will house the Veterans Administration and LSU Medical School facilities—even though these worthy institutions could be served by already existing structures. In an economic recession, the most rational option is to restore an already sturdy and spacious hospital whose hurricane damage was relatively slight.

The LSU/VA plan for Charity is "disaster capitalism" pure and simple, and is in keeping with the city's (HANO's) and the U.S. Department of Housing and Urban Development's refusal to restore the architecturally sound public housing units in New Orleans, but instead to spend unnecessarily high amounts on new constructions that lower-income residents cannot afford. (See "Homeless for the Holidays: Who Would Jesus Evict?" [LNW 12/23/07].)

Charity Hospital is a New Orleans institution that dates back to 1736 (the city was founded in 1718). Since its inception, it has been an institution for the care of the indigent—its original name was *L'Hôpital des Pauvres de la Charité*. Before the present art deco monolith was built under the direction of Huey P. Long in the 1930s, the hospital was located in the Faubourg St. Mary in the Central Business District. Jesus said, "the poor you will always have with you" (Matt. 26:11), and this is particularly true in New Orleans, a city that is rich in so many ways (mainly nonmaterial). Many of us have been helped by doctors and nurses at Charity at a time when we couldn't afford health insurance and didn't have the money to pay for treatment. We'll always be thankful that there was Charity to turn to, and that is why we feel a personal obligation to make sure it survives to help others in need.

Those who would profit from the unnecessary LSU/VA development plan are not people who have ever needed Charity—they don't know what they would be taking away from the less fortunate among us.

For the activists and 'political caregivers' among our readers who wish to help the city, we urge you to press hard on LSU to renovate and reopen Charity, and to contribute to the Foundation for Historical Louisiana to support its efforts to promote the restoration and reopening of this essential institution.

http://www.leveesnotwar.org/renew-reopen-charity-hospital/

Mardi Gras (Selections)

Do They Know It's Mardi Gras?

http://www.leveesnotwar.org/do-they-know-its-mardi-gras/

FEB. 21, 2012—Outside of New Orleans and southern Louisiana and Mobile, Alabama, Mardi Gras generally comes as news—if it comes at all—to people in the rest of the United States when they see footage on network and cable news. Oh, it must be Mardi Gras again. Look at all those crazy-dressed people milling around on Bourbon Street. Now back to work, or looking for a job.

There are emigrés from New Orleans and southern Louisiana all over the U.S. and around the world who feel Carnival coming for weeks before the big day arrives, and we know it's not a one-day affair (how could it be?). We look around at life going on in January, February, and sometimes March, and wonder how our fellow citizens cannot know that Carnival is coming, that it has already started, it's here. And especially on Fat Tuesday itself—which is today—seeing life go on as Just Another Day, earning just another dollar, we're reminded of the 1984 Band Aid song "Do They Know It's Christmas?" (recorded to raise awareness and aid for the 1983–85 famine in Ethiopia). It is not entirely a fair comparison, but there's a resemblance, and the question does come up.

Happy Mardi Gras 2011

http://www.leveesnotwar.org/happy-mardi-gras-2011/

MARCH 7, 2011—When the cares of this world grow too heavy, we all need a break from the ordinary, and that is why we have Carnival. And this festive season, which begins at Epiphany and whose climax is Mardi Gras (this year Tuesday, March 8), is a big part of the reason why this blog cares so much about the health and well-being of New Orleans: the city, its people, and its culture. It's the City That Care Forgot, but also a place that has lately seen too much to worry about (thanks most recently to a company called BP).

But we won't dwell on the cares just now—that's what Carnival is for. It's also for making fun of hardships and folly, flipping 'em around jujitsu-like with a sense of humor, satire, absurdity. Sometimes it's the only way to deal. Let it go for a while. Lighten up. The ancient Greeks and Romans, with their bacchanalias and Lupercalia (Carnival's deep-historical origins), understood that if you don't cut loose from time to time with a little madness here and there, you get hit with the big madness, the kind that doesn't go away. Therefore . . .

To all our friends in and around Louisiana, to all who "Be a New Orleanian, Wherever You Are"—we wish a lively and frolicsome Mardi Gras, a celebration of life, humor, imagination, and letting the good times roll, everybody all together.

Krewe du Vieux's "All Fired Up," Baby!

http://www.leveesnotwar.org/krewe-du-vieux's-"all-fired-up"-baby/

Postively Flamin'

FEB. 3, 2010—Of all New Orleans's wonderful (and some rather sedate) Carnival krewes, Krewe du Vieux is the sassiest, fiestiest, and wittiest, and it pains us to miss even one parade. Led by the great Dr. John as King, this year's parade's theme was "All Fired Up" (there was a fire last summer in the krewe's Den of Muses, quenched by the NOFD).

The krewe's full name is Krewe du Vieux Carré, and its subkrewes include Krewe de C.R.A.P.S., Krewe of Space Age Love, Krewe du Mishigas, Seeds of Decline, Mystic Krewe of Spermes . . . you get the picture. (Go to the URL below to see some pix from our friend Maitri Erwin's Flickr photostream.) The theme of Maitri's subkrewe, C.R.A.P.S., was "Walk on Burning Sphincters."

Oh, and did we mention the Saints are in the Super Bowl? Who Dat? Who Dat? Feelin' "Glory Bound," y'all.

New Orleans's Super Weekend

http://www.leveesnotwar.org/new-orleans's-super-weekend/

FEB. 8, 2010—We prayed for a one-two punch of good news, and the Saints and the voters delivered (helped no doubt by the prayers of the nuns and priests in Saints owner Tom Benson's posse). It is a delicious feeling of rejuvenation only four short years after the storm left us feeling devastated, unsure of the future. Now the nation and the world too are rejoicing for New Orleans and the Saints—everybody loves an underdog—and that too is a sweet thing. Not to downplay the significance of the Super Bowl triumph, but the first victory, Mitch Landrieu's in the mayoral race on Saturday (66% of the vote), may turn out to be the most enduring consequence of this Super Weekend. We shall see. (Karen Dalton Beninato tweeted, "The New Orleans mayoral election is now on Superbowl Eve while we dodge 8 parades to vote. Only in New Orleans.") We wish the new mayor and the amazing team and all their fans the best of luck—we're with you. We know the city will have a Carnival season like no other, more turbocharged with joie de vivre than perhaps any Mardi Gras there's ever been. (Fat Tuesday is Feb. 16: What a delirious week this will be.)

Mardi Gras, Lombardi Gras

http://www.leveesnotwar.org/mardi-gras-lombardi-gras/

FEB. 13, 2010—This is a Carnival where you don't have to say "Happy Mardi Gras" (tho' we do, anyway)—it simply is a happy Mardi Gras, and everyone's been in a crazy happy zone for weeks. People are changing their middle names to WhoDat. Maybe it's 'cause "Breesus Saves," and the rest of the Saints do, too. And "Hey Shockey Way." And then too there's a palpable relief that a popular new mayor has been elected to bring in energy and action where lethargy, passivity, absentia in officio, and lame excuses have held sway for lo these many years.

Viva Burlesque!

SEPT. 12, 2009—Will you pardon us while we take a break from being all-serious all the time?

This weekend, Sept. 11–13, The City That Care Forgot hosts the first annual New Orleans Burlesque Festival, which we hope will be the first of many to come. Featuring Foxy Flambeaux, Praline Dupree, and, yes, Dominic Moncada ("Bustout Burlesque's eye-candy for the ladies").

In the Festival's own words (we couldn't say it better):

The New Orleans Burlesque Festival (Sept. 11–13, 2009) is the first burlesque festival devoted to classic and traditional burlesque. The festival will pair glamorous and talented striptease dancers with live traditional jazz music, the way it was done in nightclubs during the glory days of burlesque. We'll assemble some of the best eye-popping burlesque dancers in the world to perform over three nights in sultry New Orleans. Comic emcees, singers, and variety acts flesh out the shows to provide the most entertaining and classiest risqué showcases you'll ever see. Fun and educational daytime activities for performers and enthusiasts of burlesque are spread over the three days. Celebrate this classic form of adult entertainment that made Bourbon Street famous worldwide!

Yet another reason why New Orleans must be protected by any and all means!

Ready for Burlesque Fest, New Orleans?

Time for the 5th Annual New Orleans Burlesque Festival, Sept. 19–21

SEPT. 19, 2013—*Of course* New Orleans is ready for another burlesque festival. A good warm-up for Halloween, perhaps. Or just a good warm-up for its own sake. If you're ready—or *might* be ready, as we totally are—for Coco Lectric, Dinah Might, Honey Touche and the Touchettes, Cora Vette with Dames D'lish, Ray Gunn, Jett Adore as Zorro (yes, dudes too), Miss PetitCoquette, Trixie Little & Evil Hate Monkey, and the Cheesecake Burlesque Revue, then the Burlesque Festival has the shows for you.

Opening night features the Strut at Harrah's: "Award-winning male burlesque stars deliver pure prime beef, emphasizing the masculine side of the tease with their sizzling surprise reveals, and tongue-in-cheek exploits! Starring world-renowned super troupe The Stage Door Johnnies!" You'll want to come for the Siren of the South ("Athena, the Goddess of the Bodice"), Mondo Burlesque ("A variety of burlesque entertainers perform acts that have driven audiences wild at clubs and theaters around the word. Sexy, funny, naughty, and très amusant!") and Bad Girls of Burlesque ("Luscious and lascivious ladies of burlesque entertain you in this rowdy, standing-room-only show . . . a celebration of the wicked, the wayward, and the wanton").

Cold shower time. We're all worked up just writing about it . . .

TAGS: Burlesque, burlesquery, feather boas, fun 'n' games, Sodom and Gomorrah
http://www.leveesnotwar.org/ready-for-burlesque-fest-new-orleans/

PART VII

Interviews

A FILM BY HARRY SHEARER
THE BIG UNEASY
BEFORE THERE WAS OIL, THERE WAS WATER.
"THE BIG UNEASY" SPECIAL APPEARANCE JOHN GOODMAN
WITH BRAD PITT JENNIFER COOLIDGE WENDELL PIERCE WILL LYMAN
MUSIC DAVID TORKANOWSKY EDITED BY ARLENE NELSON
TOM HOCHE NARRATED HARRY SHEARER
PRODUCED KAREN MURPHY CHRISTINE O'MALLEY WRITTEN DIRECTED HARRY SHEARER
Orleans

When Harry Met a Cover-Up

Shearer Talks about "The Big Uneasy"

OCT. 14, 2010—We sat down recently with Harry Shearer—that is, we sat down and e-mailed him some questions, and he sat down and wrote some thoughtful replies—to talk about his new film *The Big Uneasy*, which tells the real story of why New Orleans flooded in Hurricane Katrina.

You may not have seen *The Big Uneasy* yet because it hasn't found a distributor. Harry is working on that. Thus far it has been shown in New Orleans at the Prytania Theater uptown (it premiered before the Rising Tide conference in late August near the fifth anniversary of Hurricane Katrina), and it has run briefly in New York City and Los Angeles. We saw it at Manhattan's IFC Center (twice) and want to do all we can to spread the word about this excellent project—particularly to people with connections to film distributors with a social and political conscience.

[*Editor's Note (2015):* The Big Uneasy *is available on DVD.*]

Leave It to a Jester to Tell the Truth

Harry Shearer is famous as a versatile humorist, writer, and "voice artist" for *The Simpsons* and as Derek Smalls, the bearded, Ringo-like bass player in *This Is Spinal Tap*, so at first it may not seem that a movie about the flooding of New Orleans would be his natural subject matter. How funny can it be to explain the catastrophic engineering failure that led to the flooding of 80 percent of the city and about a thousand deaths? Although *The Big Uneasy* won't have audiences rolling in the aisles, this compelling and richly sourced new documentary does clarify the facts about the disaster-within-a-disaster. Misconceptions are corrected. Cover-ups are uncovered. Truths are told. Acts of professional courage are held up to the light.

Shearer's comic talent is for real, but his seriousness is authentic, too, as anyone knows who has read his *Huffington Post* blog pieces over the past several years or listened to his weekly radio program *Le Show* (KCRW, Los Angeles). He explains in the opening reel that he is a part-time New Orleanian. Through his work with Levees.org (no relation) and his blogging and other efforts—he was also the keynote speaker at Rising Tide IV in 2009—he has helped keep the spotlight on his adopted city's predicament with a commitment and persistence that should earn him some kind of Honorary Full-Time Citizenship award. You'll understand why when you see *The Big Uneasy*.

In a recent post on *HuffPo*, Shearer acknowledged that it's ironic that "a damn comedy actor" should be taking up the untold story:

> . . . the story that the flooding was a man-made catastrophe that
> developed over four and a half decades under administrations
> of both parties, and the story from a whistleblower inside
> the Corps of Engineers that the "new, improved" system for
> protecting New Orleans may right now be fatally flawed. . . .
> given that lapse among the professional journalists, it was up to
> a damn comedy actor to piece together the material that's been
> sitting there, on the public record, all this time . . .

A review in *New York* magazine by David Edelstein said it well:

> By the end of *The Big Uneasy*, I came to appreciate [Shearer's]
> self-effacement. He's not a filmmaker or an investigative
> journalist. He's not really in his element here. He just, finally,
> couldn't stand by and hear "natural disaster" one more time
> without picking up a camera and, like his protagonists, doing his
> civic duty for the city he loves so deeply.

Get This: The Flooding Was *Not* a Natural Disaster

The Big Uneasy is a feature film–length documentary about how and why New Orleans was flooded during Hurricane Katrina. It happened not because Katrina was so overwhelming: although it had been a Category 5 storm in the Gulf, Katrina was only about a Category 1.5 hurricane when it blew past (not straight through) New Orleans, sparing the city the brunt of the storm. The city flooded because of engineering failures in the federally built levees and walls of outflow canals that gave way under pressure even before the storm's winds did their worst. The film draws on engineers' reports, postmortem studies, and never-before-seen amateur video footage to show the flooding was not a natural but a man-made disaster. It was not inevitable. Contrary to predictable official claims that the storm was simply overwhelming and the levees were never designed to hold a storm of such magnitude, the flooding resulted from inferior engineering—a point that Ivor van Heerden of the LSU Hurricane Center began speaking out about very soon after the storm passed.

First-Rate Expert Testimony

To illuminate the fact that Katrina's worst damage to New Orleans came from the storm surge that blew apart the federally built drainage canal walls and levees, Shearer assembles a formidable cast of experts. In addition to Ivor van Heerden, former deputy director of the LSU Hurricane Center, we hear from Robert Bea of the U.C. Berkeley Department of Civil and Environmental Engineering; John Barry, historian and author of *Rising Tide*; coastal science legend Sherwood "Woody" Gagliano; and other authorities, including several representatives of the U.S. Army Corps of Engineers and attorneys and federal judge Stanwood R. Duval Jr. Additional expert testimony comes in the form of quotations from the very focused and eloquent 40-page letter from Dr. Raymond Seed, a Berkeley engineering professor and head of the Independent Levee Investigation Team that studied and documented the crime scene in the weeks and months after the storm. Also helping clarify matters are Tulane's Richard Campanella; *Time* magazine writer Michael Grunwald; Carlton Dufrechou, former director of the Lake Pontchartrain Basin Foundation; and Garret Graves of the Louisiana Governor's Office of Coastal Activities. It's amazing how much high-level expertise Shearer is able to fit comfortably into this 90-minute film.

Among the structural failures the film explores are the too-shallow pilings reinforcing the walls of the 17th Street, London Avenue, and Orleans Avenue outflow canals (built on soft, shifty soils) and the ill-fated Mississippi River–Gulf Outlet shipping channel known as MR-GO, all built by the U.S. Army Corps of Engineers and/or contractors without outside oversight. John

Barry says that one Corps contractor, Pitman, even brought a lawsuit objecting that the Corps' specifications were faulty and would lead to disaster, but he lost his court case and was directed to follow orders. One speaker characterizes MR-GO (built between 1958 and 1968 and obsolete before it was even completed) as "the cut that led to a thousand deaths." (Further details can be found in our interviews with Ivor van Heerden and with Mark Schleifstein, environmental reporter for *The Times-Picayune*, as well as in these authors' books, *The Storm* and *Path of Destruction*, respectively.)

Van Heerden, Bea, and others who conducted postmortem field tests (Team Louisiana and the Independent Levee Investigation Team, supported by the National Science Foundation) show that the flood control structures collapsed well before waves overtopped the walls. (In fact there was no overtopping.) Also hugely destructive was MR-GO's role as a "storm surge delivery system" to conduct massive volumes of seawater from the Gulf directly into the city. This "funnel effect" was exactly what Corps engineers had warned about in a 1988 study (and other experts before that). The 1988 study, however, was disregarded until it was disclosed in a recent lawsuit that found the Corps' poor maintenance of the shipping channel responsible for some of the worst flooding of St. Bernard Parish and the Lower Ninth Ward during and after Hurricane Katrina.

There were about two dozen ruptures in the federally built drainage canal walls and levees in the metro New Orleans area, including the infamous breaches in the 17th Street, London, and Orleans Avenue outflow canals, which let water into the city, in addition to breaches along the shore of Lake Pontchartrain. (The Mississippi River levee, a different type of construction from the outflow canals and shipping channels, did not breach, thank God.)

It is the regretful assessment of Berkeley engineering professor Raymond Seed (quoted, not filmed) that congressional and Corps cost-cutting has eviscerated much of the Corps' former engineering expertise. The cuts have reduced the USACE to a department of project managers who outsource much of the actual engineering work to outside, private firms. (Bob Bea was himself a Corps engineer in New Orleans at the time of Hurricane Betsy [1965], as was his father before him: Bea can tell from personal experience what has been lost.) This is not to say that there is no engineering expertise still on staff. But, like many other federal agencies, such as FEMA, the Corps has suffered from the privatizing drive (especially strong in the Rumsfeld years), diversions of talent and dollars to the wars overseas, and penny-pinching by Congress that must approve projects and funding. The Corps has not been able to compete for the level of talent that private engineering firms can afford.

The three members of the Corps of Engineers who are either authorized or willing to speak on the record are for the most part lame, defensive, or, as a lawyer might say, nonresponsive. (Some of the names don't inspire confidence, either: the current commander of the Corps' Hurricane Protection Office is named Robert Sinkler, and his New Orleans District office is located on Leake Avenue.) Karen Durham-Aguilera of Task Force Hope, wearing sunglasses at all times, refuses to speak about anything in the past, but says, incredibly, "I don't know what you mean by 'the funnel effect.'"

One Corps official who speaks quite candidly is Los Angeles–based civil mechanical engineer Maria Garzino. This whistle-blower still has her job, though in a diminished capacity. She was responsible for overseeing the quality of pumps being built by a Florida-based manufacturer to drive water out of the New Orleans outflow canals from the canals' mouth at Lake Pontchartrain. In a frightening likeness of the missile defense system tests that fail every time, the new pumps crashed or self-destructed in test after test. After each failure the Corps allowed the manufacturer to lower the performance standards. Still they failed. Originally the pumps were supposed to be good for 50 years; now the Corps, after spending some $700 to 800 million on their construction and installation, says the massive rig of pumps is an "interim" system, good for two or three years. Garzino doubts they'll function effectively even through one big storm. After she blew the whistle on the manufacturer's and the pumps' performance—doing her job, reporting the failures to her superiors in the Corps—she was demoted and then investigated by the U.S. Office of Special Counsel (which is supposed to protect whistle-blowers).

Help the Wetlands Help Save Us

In addition to the failings of the flood protection structures, Shearer introduces us to coastal and wetlands experts and activists—including Carlton Dufrechou, John Barry, Woody Gagliano, and musician Tab Benoit—who explain the importance of the Louisiana wetlands and the dangers posed by coastal erosion. Dufrechou (once a project manager for the Corps) explains that New Orleans was once well inland but is now essentially a coastal city. Coastal Louisiana is at greater risk from hurricane storm surge than when New Orleans was settled because the state has lost some 2,000 square miles since the late 1920s (mostly from oil and other industrial intrusion). The fragile wetlands act as a storm surge buffer—roughly every 3 miles or so reduces storm surge by a foot—but the protection is shrinking. Garret Graves of the Governor's Office of Coastal Activities says the state is now losing about 25 to 40 square miles every year. There are solutions to coastal erosion—none of them simple or cheap—but Tulane's Richard Campanella warns that New Orleans only has about 10 or 20 years, "no more than a generation," to solve the land loss and subsidence problem.

Fresh Thinking, Novel Approaches

Speaking of subsidence and solutions, one of the most interesting parts of *The Big Uneasy*—worthy of a whole new film—involves the "Dutch Dialogues" ideas of New Orleans architect David Waggoner. He has studied how the Dutch manage to live at and below sea level. One thing New Orleans should stop doing is pumping out all the water because soil without moisture contracts and sinks. More water = more safety. Counterintuitive as it may sound, New Orleans should instead allow more water into the city in the form of a veinlike network of small canals and bayous like Bayou St. John, to keep the soil "fat" and damp. Moisturized soil reduces the subsidence, or sinking, that puts the city at further risk of flooding (or of deeper floods). These ideas are practical, practicable—the kind of fresh thinking that the city needs to survive.

A related idea comes from Mississippi River historian John Barry, who says the wetlands can adapt to rising sea levels as long as they are getting enough new layers of sediment from freshwater diversions. We had never heard this before; this is good news. The two biggest river diversion projects currently under way, with help from the Army Corps of Engineers, EPA, and the U.S. Fish and Wildlife Service, are the Caernarvon and Davis Pond diversions of water from the Mississippi River at strategic openings to allow river water to spread across the wetlands and replenish the soil. Such projects could really do some good if they got sufficient federal funding, but there is not much time left.

But Wait—There's More

Much more. We haven't even talked about the Corps' stonewalling and obstruction of Team Louisiana or the National Science Foundation team's attempts to discover the cause of the structural collapses. There's also the conflict of interest in the American Society of Civil Engineers' getting $2 million from the Corps for a purportedly impartial "external review" of the Corps' IPET assessment of what went wrong. We haven't discussed the struggle between the Corps and Congress and others about which option to pursue for pumping water out of the city (the least expensive is not necessarily the worst option in this case). Nor have we mentioned LSU's firing of Ivor van Heerden and everyone else who worked on Team Louisiana, or van Heerden's lawsuit against the university for wrongful termination.

The Big Uneasy is impressively comprehensive in covering questions of what happened, the investigations, the parties involved, the answers arrived at (and attempts to block findings), what became of those who led the investigations, and what did not happen to those responsible for the engineering failures that led to the flooding. The film is well-paced, beautifully filmed in crisp, vivid HD. It's astonishing how much breadth and detail Shearer manages to compress into this 90-minute film, and yet it doesn't feel crowded. Out of all the very knowledgeable authorities interviewed, none go on too long, yet none appear to be cut short, either; they leave you wanting more. That's good editing.

The film concludes with colorful footage and snapshots of Carnival parades, Mardi Gras Indians, steaming bowls of gumbo and other mouth-watering culinary images of letting the good times roll. Quick glimpses of the rich culture that is endangered but doesn't have to be lost. The last words in the film, spoken by Carlton Dufrechou, concern the unity that we're going to need to save Louisiana. It is a place and culture worth saving, he says, and he's betting we're going to come together and do the right thing. But there's a plaintive, nearly grieving tone in his voice that suggests he worries the wetlands and the city may not be saved after all.

If the right choices and efforts are not made, it will be because not enough people saw and took to heart the truths and spirit so comprehensively and lovingly brought together in this fine work by Harry Shearer, to whom the city of New Orleans and the state of Louisiana owe a great debt. It is our hope that *The Big Uneasy* will find a courageous and imaginative distributor and that the truths and deceptions it shows will be seen far and wide, and acted upon, and soon.

Here, now, is an exchange between Levees Not War *and Harry Shearer on the making and content of* The Big Uneasy. *One question we forgot to ask him was how he got the eminent professor Bob Bea of Berkeley to talk with relish about how he likes to taste dirt, to test the quality of soil by sensing the granules on his tongue. We'll follow up on that question next time 'round.*

You've said that in President Obama's 3-hour "drive-through" appearance in New Orleans in October 2009, he used the phrase "natural disaster," and that that is what prompted you to make this film. Have you noticed any positive response? Is anyone learning that *Katrina itself did not flood the city*, but that *the levees' failure is what flooded the city*?
Harry Shearer: Very few, very slowly. People sometimes make reference to the levee failure in passing, as if it's a natural result of a storm like Katrina. But there still seems to be quite low awareness of the conclusion of the two independent investigations that, absent a badly-designed and -built "protection system," the worst Katrina would have inflicted on New Orleans would have been "wet ankles."

Had you thought of making a film on this subject before the president's remarks triggered you?
SHEARER: No, I don't recall giving serious thought to it, though I may have mentioned at Rising Tide IV in 2009 that wresting back control of the narrative of the city's near-destruction might have required somebody to do such a film. But I'd really not thought of myself as that somebody until I heard the President say something that he patently should have known was not true.

The time between the initial idea and the premiere was impressively short: about 10 months. Were you pushing to have it released in time for the 5th anniversary? Did it get a fair amount of attention, or was it overshadowed by other commemorative specials?

SHEARER: Yes, I was pushing from day one to have a big "event-type" release on the 5th anniversary, to benefit from the momentary re-focus of the media on the flood at that time. I regret to say it didn't get nearly the amount of attention I'd intended, for various reasons.

Did you already know quite a few of the interview subjects? Were there any experts or interview subjects you wanted to interview but who were not able or willing to participate?

SHEARER: I knew Ivor, Bob Bea, Maria and John Barry. They'd all been on my radio program. Ivor and John I'd gotten to know personally, Bob and Maria I'd just spoken to "down the line," so we first met when I arrived to film them. There were plenty of people we wanted in the film, many that we interviewed, who didn't make it into the final product. That's partly the result of shooting several people telling roughly the same story, and making choices as to how many different story-tellers we wanted. Ray Seed, Bob's partner in the ILIT [Independent Levee Investigation Team] investigation out of U.C. Berkeley, was the one person I really wanted to interview, but who, for reasons of his own, chose not to participate. I did get a lovely letter from him, though, after he'd seen the film.

Are there any subjects from this film that you wish you had had time to explore in more depth? Any thought about follow-ups? (One we would love to see would be on New Orleans architect David Waggoner and his Dutch Dialogues, especially combined with what John Barry said about the wetlands being able to adapt to rising sea levels as long as they receive new layers of sediment.)

SHEARER: I regret that none of the interviewees mentioned the role the oil industry played in hastening the wetlands destruction, but they didn't.

Your opening mention of "except for occasional oil spills" and another brief reference to the BP oil spill seemed sufficient. Did you consider including more of a mention, or would that have been off-topic?

SHEARER: No, I was very single-minded in what I wanted to focus on with this film. I felt I had 90 minutes (actually, 94) to undo five years of media misinformation, and I didn't think I could waste any more time on anything off-topic. Besides, I heard through the grapevine that Spike [Lee] was veering towards the spill for his film [*If God Is Willing and da Creek Don't Rise*], so I knew that subject was going to be covered.

What's with NPR? National Petrified Radio, as you write. (Afraid of being dismantled even under a Democratic administration?) NPR would not cover *The Big Uneasy* at all? (Is this the same kind of fear-of-retribution that got Ivor van Heerden fired from LSU?)

SHEARER: Can't tell you what's with them. They shunted me to "Talk of the Nation," a not widely heard midday chat show, and then used that as an excuse (citing their "dibs rule") for no coverage on the flagship newsmagazines. I can't guess at their motives, only at the circle of hell reserved for them.

Any attention from members of Congress or Obama White House or federal agencies such as FEMA? Are they about as petrified of the subject as NPR? If there's "a question of fear," why do you think that is? Fear of what?

SHEARER: FEMA's not really a subject of this film; we deal with the cause of the disaster, not the response. No reaction from Congress or the White House, as of yet.

Any response from the Corps, under the radar if not officially? (The film's treatment seems quite fair and evenhanded considering the Corps' culpability.)

SHEARER: I've seen some internal e-mails, all very upbeat and anodyne ("we'll just continue to do our good work"). This tells me we haven't hit a nerve yet with the level of public awareness.

http://www.leveesnotwar.org/when-harry-met-a-cover-up-shearer-talks-about-"the-big-uneasy"/

Ivor van Heerden

Author of *The Storm: What Went Wrong and Why During Hurricane Katrina: The Inside Story from One Louisiana Scientist*

JUNE 1, 2006—Ivor van Heerden of the LSU Hurricane Center is familiar to millions who watched the Katrina news reports as the straight-talking hurricane expert with a South African accent. In The Storm, *he has written a detailed, analytical, and compelling account of Hurricane Katrina and its terrible impact on Louisiana and the Gulf Coast. He shows what happened—and what didn't have to happen.*

What sets The Storm *apart from other Katrina books is that van Heerden, a professor of civil and environmental engineering, goes on to propose a workable and affordable plan for Category 5–strength storm protection, modeled on the Netherlands' successful system: a combination of reinforced levees, storm gates, and coastal restoration, including barrier islands.*

On the publication of The Storm, *we asked Dr. van Heerden to elaborate on some of his principal concerns about the aftermath of Hurricane Katrina, the Army Corps of Engineers' repair of the levees around New Orleans, and his hopes for political solutions to Louisiana's environmental predicament.*

[Editor's Note (2015): See page 45 for a piece about Louisiana State University's 2009 firing of Ivor van Heerden, who at the time of this interview was deputy director of the LSU Hurricane Center.]

Ivor van Heerden: I think what Hurricanes Rita and Katrina taught us and certainly we know from our computer modeling is that the whole of coastal Louisiana is super-susceptible to storm surges. In some ways New Orleans did dodge the bullet, because if Katrina had come west of the city and had slowed down just a little, she could have flooded the whole city. I mention in the book that Nature in some ways has given us a second chance, and this time we've got to get it right. The other thing is that the old system of doing business—however you look at it, whether it was building levees or whether it was restoring coastal wetlands—the old system didn't work, and unfortunately we don't see anything new right now. The Senate said we need a new version of FEMA, but nobody's saying we need a new version of the Army Corps of Engineers, which is to my mind what we do need.

[Ed. Note: Historically, the U.S. Army Corps of Engineers has had prima-ry responsibility for large public works of navigation and public safety on the nation's major waterways. In The Storm, *van Heerden recommends opening up the decision making to include scientists, engineers, and conservationists.]*

What can be done, or attempted, to loosen the Corps of Engineers' grip on all the projects in the United States?
VAN HEERDEN: Enough of a public outcry, and certainly if need be, perhaps a U.S. Senate investigation into the Corps. I know Senator Lieberman and another senator are proposing legislation that would rein in some of the activities of the Corps. The bottom line is, civil works projects like levees are long-term projects, but the Corps' management is extremely short-term. The colonels come and the colonels go. And if you think about Colonel Richard Wagenaar, the present chief of the New Orleans district, he's having to clean up somebody else's mess and before you know it he will be off and we will have another rookie running the New Orleans District.

Hadn't he just started a few weeks before Katrina hit?
VAN HEERDEN: Yes, and he's an absolute gentleman, but the bottom line is, as soon as he's picked up enough corporate knowledge to know what's going on, he's going to be gone. We've really got to come up with a civil works administration. What I've been proposing is a structure that is put under the Department of Commerce, because civil works are an important part of the economy. And you then have to set up a long-term management approach, then you can take a long-term look at projects, you can prioritize. And at the same time, the Corps survives on earmarks you've got to remove earmarks from the process completely. . . . By earmarks I mean various congressmen's

pet projects, such as that Alaskan Bridge to Nowhere. Oftimes a congressman gets his pet project funded by slipping it in at the last minute into some bit of legislation. Another word for it is pork. So you can't have an agency surviving on pork. You've got to have long-term goals and the civil works administration needs to develop a sustainable plan for the future . . .

One of the things we see here and certainly we've learned from the Dutch is that you've got to have external review of the designs of your system. And in many cases we need to be putting these large-scale projects out for design competitions, just as you would if you were building a skyscraper, and in that way we can get the best engineering and science. What happens right now is that with a number of the companies the Corps works with; the principals are former Corps employees. So a bad idea can be perpetuated for a long, long time.

When we talked back in February you expressed concern about possible cover-ups of both the reason for the levees' catastrophic failure, and then secondly, cover-ups or trying to mask the inadequate quality of the repairs being done. Has your view on that changed at all?

VAN HEERDEN: Yes, what we've seen on the repairs, and especially the areas that were concerning us, the Corps has heard us, they've heard the guys from Berkeley [Drs. Raymond Seed and Robert Bea investigating for the National Science Foundation], and they've come and as far as we can tell they've removed the sand and sandy silts, and used high-quality clays along most of the MR-GO. Along the Jefferson / St. Charles Parish boundary where they used the I-walls that sagged so badly, they're shoring it up with soils and with sheet piling. Overall the levee repairs are robust, that would be the best way to put it. In terms of what went wrong [in Katrina], I think between Team Louisiana and the Berkeley guys, we've shown exactly what went wrong, exposed the flaws in the design; the lack of accounting for the very weak soils; ignoring the latest science in sticking to a 1959 definition of a Standard Project (design) Hurricane . . .

Does the Corps appear to be willing to learn from its mistakes and to show a little flexibility or cooperation with the outside world?

VAN HEERDEN: What we've seen is that the planning's being done in a vacuum. We've been told by a senior governor's political appointee that Team Louisiana cannot participate in the planning.

Was that political appointee happy about this, or not? About Team Louisiana not being able to have input into the planning?

VAN HEERDEN: It sounded like he was making the decision. The unfortunate thing is that there is some politics, still that hasn't gone away, the reason being that we're still working with the old system. We've got to change it.

The other day I was talking with two staffers of Donald Powell's, you know, Bush's rebuilding czar. He could actually become the reconstruction czar. We could set up a Tennessee Valley Authority–like program, and we could tell the Corps we want this kind of thing constructed in this area, and so on. The Corps has the ability to let big contracts and manage big contracts. But get the design away from them, and also the management of the money, and put it under some kind of czar who's advised by a blue-ribbon panel of engineers and scientists. The same organization could have a National Levee Review Team who would go around and inspect levees throughout the country. Because what New Orleans has taught us, and as pointed out by the American Society of Civil Engineers, is that it's not only New Orleans's levees that we need to be concerned about. There are levees elsewhere, like around Sacramento.

Were Powell's deputies receptive?

VAN HEERDEN: They were listening carefully. I could see I was making my point. We've either got to do that, or better still with a longer-term view it's probably healthier to set up a civil works administration in the Department of Commerce. Take the best of the Corps, restaff it, make sure it's very well connected with academic engineering and natural science research programs the new administration has to have the absolute best data input. Set up review boards, set up design competitions, and come up with long-term strategies.

The problem with the New Orleans levees was that they were never a high priority for the Corps' New Orleans district. Their high priorities were navigation and dredging. And they never really seemed to have a long-term strategy of how they were going to get it done; the project kept slipping, the costs kept going up . . . And you get a new colonel every three years. It may take him a year and a half to even find out the ins and outs of the various district projects. The bottom line is, because he's new, he's learning from his own staff. By the time he may realize that he's not getting the right or best information from his staff his tenure is virtually over.

The solution is not the military. The military fights wars. It shouldn't be running civil works.

It sounds like, in some ways—even though the overall levee system, the three hundred and fifty miles' worth of levees were degraded by Katrina—it sounds like in some ways it's going to be better than it was before. Do you think so?

VAN HEERDEN: The situation is, to sink the city it takes only one wall monolith to fail. While the repairs are robust, there are many, many, many miles of levees that are in a compromised condition, and all the I-walls are suspect.

The bottom line is, we don't have any higher level of protection than we had before Katrina. If we get another Katrina we will see flooding in the city. That's all there is to it. We basically have Category 2 protection. Part of the reason for putting that big-picture plan in the book [chapter 11, "Now or Never"] was to get the debate going. If we don't head in that direction, if we get another Katrina or anything stronger, we might have to just switch the lights off and go. So it's absolutely critical that we start now and we come up with a consensual plan and we start building the necessary components, starting with the essential or the most critical works right away.

Priorities

VAN HEERDEN: To me the two things you've got to do right away are put a structure in the Rigolets Pass [between Lake Pontchartrain and the Gulf] and a structure in the funnel [where the Intracoastal Waterway and MR-GO canals converge; this has been built: see Editor's Note below]. The next thing would be the levees on the West Bank. You hire experts who can do the risk and probability analyses, and you use those to help you make the decisions, just the way the Dutch did. And also, once you understand the risks and probabilities, you have an understanding of how high you've got to make the levees, and so on.

If you think about the efforts that the Corps has put in in the last year that they've had all these different construction teams, they're constructing gates, they're doing this and that . . . They've rebuilt miles and miles of earthen levee. Well, just imagine if that sort of activity just continued for the next ten years, we'd have everything we wanted. None of this is impossible to do. We have all this levee activity going right now; just keep it going with the necessary components to come up with, in essence, Category 5 protection! And it has to include the wetlands. You can't achieve this without the wetlands.

What is your sense of the political will to do even half the things that need to be done? Are you somewhat encouraged?
VAN HEERDEN: If we can't even get the planning effort sorted out . . . If you're going to go and get the money from Congress, you've got to have one plan that the majority of people have bought into, it's got to be a scientific and engineeringly sensible plan. You've got to have the stakeholders along. And you don't achieve that by being politically selective about who participates in the planning and who doesn't.

What about the federal will to help?
VAN HEERDEN: I don't see it right now, but part of the reason is because the state hasn't come up with a plan.

So there is some truth to what the feds have said, that Louisiana hasn't proposed a plan?
VAN HEERDEN: I think when the state comes up with one sensible plan and goes to Congress and talks with one voice, then there's a chance in getting something funded, but we haven't succeeded on that part. When we tried to get funding from Congress through the CARA bill [Conservation and Reinvestment Act], just at the point where the vote was going to happen we had a consortium of businessmen say the first so many billions of dollars are going to go to creating a port down in southeast Louisiana, and the way this fits into CARA is that the port will be behind a big barrier island. And then we had the secretary of the Department of Natural Resources going around telling everybody you'll be able to use the money for sewerage and roads and so. So we're our own worst enemies. Instead of sticking to the plan we allow others to use this as an opportunity to push their agenda. The result was that even the environmental groups were advising Congress not to vote for the bill. [The 1998 Conservation and Reinvestment Act (CARA) was an oil and gas revenue-sharing bill that has stalled in the Senate. In 2000 the House of Representatives passed CARA by a vote of 315 to 102, and the Senate Energy

and Natural Resources Committee approved it by 13 to 7. Sixty-three senators signed a letter to the Senate majority and minority leaders urging that the bill be brought to a vote on the Senate floor, but, six years later, the bill has not been brought to the floor for a vote.]

Who in particular in the state government needs to be prodded to get such a plan developed?

VAN HEERDEN: The governor is in charge, and she, or he, whoever it is next time round, needs to take charge. The Louisiana Recovery Authority is doing a great job, but the Coastal Protection and Restoration Authority seems like it's become a political animal. You're not going to get anywhere if you just do the same old stuff. What's going to happen, they'll put a plan together and academia will shoot it down, and then environmental groups will shoot it down and citizens' groups will shoot it down, and we've gotten nowhere. . . .

So we need to press on the governor's office to focus on a definite plan that can be presented to the federal government to get behind, and we need to urge them to welcome the contributions of the LSU people, the local geologists and scientists, conservationists, and try to keep the politicians and lobbyists out of it.

You were saying in your book that if you get the right people together, in a week they could come up with a definite plan that would work.

VAN HEERDEN: The situation is you've got a bunch of people in the state planning efforts (many of them are Corps employees who still claim it was overtopping not breaching) who don't have the qualifications to be doing the comprehensive planning. And some people who do [have the qualifications] are being excluded from the process. And it's all about political control. So we aren't getting anywhere. I keep trying to warn people, we are as unsafe as we were before Katrina; nothing has changed.

[EDITOR'S NOTE (2006): The Mississippi River Gulf Outlet, commonly known as MR-GO, was built by the Army Corps of Engineers in the 1960s. MR-GO is not used as much by industrial shipping as its early boosters promised, and it is dangerous in hurricanes because it converges with the Intracoastal Waterway to form a funnel that directs storm surges from Lakes Borgne and Pontchartrain directly at the heart of the Orleans Parish bowl enclosed by levees. The sandy

MR-GO levees suffered massive breaches under Katrina, adding to the flood-waters that swamped St. Bernard Parish as well as the much-publicized Lower Ninth Ward.]

Is there any chance of closing MR-GO? People in Louisiana (other than businesses) want it shut down.
VAN HEERDEN: The state needs to make a decision and do it. It's been an argument for years and years and years, and it doesn't seem like it's going to be resolved any time soon. We've got to say, What's best for everybody? What's best for the greater good? The problem is that nobody's doing that. Nobody's asking what's best for the greater good. Everybody's saying I want my piece. I want to be taken care of. And that's not going to work. You've got to ultimately say what's best for the greater good of everybody? And then set up that system.

[EDITOR'S NOTE (2015): In 2007 the U.S. Army Corps of Engineers announced it would close MR-GO to all traffic. In 2008–9 a closure structure was built across the MR-GO at Bayou La Loutre, completed in July 2009. Closer to New Orleans, a strong $1 billion, 1.8-mile surge barrier was constructed to close the funnel at the convergence of the Intracoastal Waterway and MR-GO. This barrier, completed in 2011, was designed to prevent storm surges from entering the Industrial Canal and Intracoastal Waterway—and, hence, to reinforce the protection of New Orleans and vicinity from inundation.

After decades of salt water intrusion and loss of vegetation, the wetlands of cypress and swamp grass, etc., that were carved out to create the 76-mile-long Mississippi River–Gulf Outlet canal—authorized in 1956, completed in 1965—will probably never be restored.]

TAGS: Army Corps of Engineers, Ivor van Heerden, Katrina, LSU Hurricane Center, Mike Bryan, New Orleans, The Storm
http://www.leveesnotwar.org/ivor-van-heerden-author-of-the-storm/

Mark Schleifstein

Co-author of *Path of Destruction: The Devastation of New Orleans and the Coming Age of Superstorms*

NOV. 1, 2007—Pulitzer Prize–winning reporter Mark Schleifstein joined *The Times-Picayune* in 1984 as an environmental reporter after five years at *The Clarion-Ledger* of Jackson, Mississippi. Since 1996 he and his *Times-Picayune* colleague John McQuaid have written numerous major environmental series for the paper, most recently in January 2006. Schleifstein and McQuaid won the 1997 Pulitzer Prize for Public Service for their series "Oceans of Trouble: Are the World's Fisheries Doomed?"—a comprehensive eight-day series about the threats to the world's fish supply, including the effects of coastal wetlands erosion on fish in Louisiana and the Gulf of Mexico. In 1998 the *Picayune* published their series "Home Wreckers: How the Formosan Termite Is Devastating New Orleans," a finalist for the 1999 Pulitzer.

Perhaps their most famous project was "Washing Away," a prescient five-day series published in June 2002, three years before Hurricane Katrina, about the disappearance of the storm protection that southern Louisiana's wetlands once gave New Orleans, the likelihood of catastrophic flooding, and the frightening inadequacy of the city's storm protection infrastructure. (In his Katrina book *Breach of Faith*, fellow *Picayune* writer Jed Horne describes Schleifstein as "an Old Testament prophet possessed of a vision and the need to warn his people.") "Washing Away" won the American Society of Civil Engineers' 2003 Excellence in Media award.

For its reporting on Hurricane Katrina, *The Times-Picayune* in 2006 was again awarded Pulitzer Prizes, for Public Service and Breaking News Reporting, as well as a coveted George Polk Award. Schleifstein and McQuaid have won many other professional awards and wide acclaim for their environmental, political, and business reporting; the list might stretch longer than the text of the interview below.

Path of Destruction is one of the best Katrina books we've read—factual, well constructed, and humane. For anyone wishing to see the big picture, it is an excellent overview book that explains very clearly the science of hurricanes, the history of the river and the city and levees, and the background on disaster preparedness (or the lack thereof) on the local and national levels—including the effects of 9/11 and the federal government's subsequent concentration on terrorism that diminished funding for natural disaster preparedness—a fixation with disastrous consequences for FEMA and Corps of Engineers. The second half of *Path of Destruction* tells what happened during Katrina—the storm itself and the response, a disaster within a disaster. Interwoven with the narrative of the chaotic days that followed the storm are personal stories of about a dozen individuals in and around New Orleans—from Lakeview and the Lower Ninth Ward to St. Bernard Parish—as they make their way through the hellish aftermath. Schleifstein and McQuaid warn of a future of extreme weather that is a reaction to the warming atmosphere: Whether we are ready or not—and whatever we may believe about climate change—superstorms will be bearing down on human settlements all around the globe. This book shows what can happen when a city and a nation are unprepared for the worst, and shows human courage and compassion in the face of chaos both natural and man-made.

A Pulitzer Prize–Winning Team

Perhaps you could start by telling us about your Pulitzer Prize. You and John McQuaid together won the prize for Public Service in 1997?
SCHLEIFSTEIN: It was for "Oceans of Trouble," published in 1996, a series on fisheries and how they're affected by the loss of wetlands. I was doing the environmental beat in New Orleans and John was based up in Washington.

In 1995 we went to our sources—including scientists and politicians, etc.— and asked them what do you think fisheries are going to be like in 20 years?

And they all said, Oh, they'll be fine. We've figured out a management program to prevent over-fishing in the Gulf of Mexico. We don't think there will be a problem.

We said, "But if the wetlands in Louisiana continue to disappear at the rate they've been doing over the next twenty years, then what's the future of fisheries 20 years from now in the Gulf of Mexico?" They said, Oh, there won't be any.

Other than that, no problem.
SCHLEIFSTEIN: A little disconnect. They were replying to the question of managing over-fishing, but habitat is a completely different matter. If the habitat disappears, there's no place for the juvenile fish. We're actually seeing the effects of the loss of wetlands in the catch in the Gulf of Mexico. Since the majority of commercial fisheries that are caught in the Gulf of Mexico spend part of their juvenile life in the Louisiana wetlands, that would be a complete disaster.

So we went back to our editors and said, We think there might be a story here. John was covering the Washington angle, and I handled a lot of the habitat stuff. We looked at aquaculture and the way it was changing the industry of fishing, especially shrimping. The series went on for eight days—longer than the creation of the world. This was the first series where John and I worked together. We did another one a few years later on Formosan termites called "Home Wreckers" [1998].

You and John obviously have worked out a formula for a very fruitful collaboration. Great reporting, spadework . . .
SCHLEIFSTEIN: John has an ability of finding seemingly very odd but very important pieces of the story and explaining that importance and placing it in the context of the story. He's also very good, once we've got all our notes together, at assembling stuff out of everybody else's notes to make them into stories and make them ring.

The biggest plus I bring to things like this is the original ideas and some of the directions about the broader focus of the way things go. All three of the big series that we worked on together were originally my proposals. Largely because of our locations, I also had the ability of working the internal politics to be sure the series got off the ground.

Writing *Path of Destruction*

Tell us about how you conceived the book and planned its organization.

SCHLEIFSTEIN: We knew everybody would be doing a "tick-tock" of the storm, covering the Five Days of Katrina. We wanted to be different. We wanted to place the Five Days of Katrina in a context so that people could understand how that happened. When you look at the books that are out there, the tick-tock stories, you end up scratching your head and wondering why do people live in New Orleans? How come they didn't know about the levee system? What drove these things?

We wanted to answer those questions, so we went back to the beginning, looking at the geology of the area, explaining how southeastern Louisiana and the area where New Orleans was founded was actually formed, geologically, and what that meant for hurricanes. We used the reporting we did for the "Washing Away" series as our starting point—the history, getting into the science of storms, and things like that. It meant looking at how the city itself was formed. And the history of levees in the city, and the history of its expansion, and explaining that, so that people could understand why people could live below sea level, surrounded by levees. It meant explaining in as much detail as possible (but briefly) the history of hurricanes in the United States and the history of the way they're tracked, and the history of forecasting.

Most people would have been busy enough just putting their life back together, but you had time to write a book, too, at a pretty difficult time.

SCHLEIFSTEIN: How it all came about was, most of the staff had evacuated up to Baton Rouge, and we'd finally moved into our new temporary office park to produce the paper, and John calls me the week after the storm and says he's spoken with his literary agent. He says, "I've worked something up I think might work, and my agent thinks there might be a chance. I'll send it to you and—" And I said, "What, are you nuts?! My house is flooded I don't know how deep and I'm up in Baton Rouge bouncing from one living space to another, going from a room with 10 people in it to somebody's couch," etc. He said just do as much as you can. And so I make this really stupid decision: Sure, John, I've got nothing else to do.

So I'm continuing to do the regular day job 8 to 10 hours a day and in my "spare time" ended up working till about 2:30 or 3:30 every night, and getting up at 7:00 and starting it all over again.

We made ourselves assignments and John kept control over how it was going, what fit where—the way the book was put together, it was all John—and then when push came to shove we started tossing things back and forth to each other. . . . The book was published in August 2006, in time for the first anniversary of Hurricane Katrina.

What kind of reaction did the book receive? Did you feel it got a good reception, attention in the press, or from elected officials?
SCHLEIFSTEIN: It got some attention. It was one of about a dozen Katrina books that came out in August '06. It had a niche, and I think still does. We're still getting some action on it. John and I both made the rounds of radio talk shows for the second anniversary.

Including National Public Radio. That's very good.
SCHLEIFSTEIN: It was not a best-seller. I think Doug Brinkley's book [*The Great Deluge*] was that, because he has the name and the publisher behind him, and he had the critique of the mayor that everybody seemed to jump on that was a little different from ours. I think he's obviously the leader, and Jed Horne of our [*Times-Picayune*] staff, also, with *Breach of Faith*. Jed focuses largely on the human impacts and the effects of the storm on the African American community and the role of poverty and how it played out in the storm.

Did the publisher send the book to members of Congress, in addition to sending to the book reviews?
SCHLEIFSTEIN: Not that I'm aware of. I know that [former Louisiana governor] Mike Foster used to do that with books. He sent copies of Mike Tidwell's first book, *Bayou Farewell*, to everybody in Congress. And I think he did the same with *Holding Back the Sea* by Chris Hallowell.

Corps of Engineers Builds Levees to Withstand "100-Year Storms"

Let's talk infrastructure. We're told the flood control system is being restored to pre-Katrina levels. That's not quite what people were hoping for, or what the president seemed to be promising in his Jackson Square speech, but it seems to be all we're going to get, at least for now. What else is the Corps going to do?

SCHLEIFSTEIN: They're moving to raise the system to a level of hundred-year protection by 2011, and that is well under way. Huge amounts of contracts are in the process of being let or have already been let for the process of design and construction of the system. That will add a major amount of protection to the entire metro area.

One-hundred-year-level protection will exceed the strength before Katrina?
SCHLEIFSTEIN: Absolutely. One of the problems was that the Corps did not understand—really nobody did—what the risk was of flooding from a 100-year event in the city, and what that meant for the height of levees. And then you add in all the things the Corps did wrong, especially with the problems with the heights of individual pieces of the system of drainage canal walls and levees.

It wasn't that they measured wrong, it was that they kept using old measurements [see *Path of Destruction*, pp. 145–50], and had a policy of using the old measurements for old projects, and then using new measurements for new projects. They weren't updating the old projects or going to Congress or to the local sponsors and saying, "We have these real problems," until about three, four years before Katrina, when they did actually go to everybody and say, "These measurements are wrong and we need to do something about it, what do you want to do?"

But the answer never came. The Corps was waiting for a local sponsor to step up in each case as they were notified that their levees were too low, and say, "OK, Corps, we want you to go to Congress and tell them that we need to raise the levees to this level. We want greater protection."

What does this involve, bringing it up to 100-year-storm capacity?

SCHLEIFSTEIN: It involves a lot of things in a lot of different areas. If there's a keystone piece to this, it would be the V, that little triangle of wetlands that's in front of it [at the intersection of GIWW and MR-GO] called the "golden triangle" for some reason. I had never heard of that before Katrina, but that's what everyone calls it now.

The plan is to build a levee across the golden triangle, and a gate on the Gulf Intracoastal Waterway to the north, and then a gate or closure structure on the Mississippi River Gulf Outlet (MR-GO), which will give you a wall going all the way across from the St. Bernard levee to the Eastern New Orleans levee. That structure will be in some places like at the gates as high as 33 feet above sea level.

From there on down to the St. Bernard levee, that levee will be raised, depending on the location, 28 to 25 feet, maybe some places 23, and the same on the eastern New Orleans levee going east from that new structure. That's the key part [the golden triangle levee]. That's a huge increase in size of all of that area's protection. The idea there is that it will reduce the ability of storm surge to go over the top.

The goal of this is to reduce the chances of the amount of floodwater that occurs in the city once every 100 years from hurricane events. Events plural. They run these computer models that include 152 different kinds of hurricanes, ranging in intensity from a 50-year storm to a 5,000-year storm. (To do this they use a model called ADCIRC and several other models combined to put together this data.) They run all these hurricanes through the system and determine what the one-percent chance of flooding is, and that provides you with an idea of how high to raise the levees in each area.

The result of that is that you get this high levee. My shortcut for explaining this is: If you listen to the National Hurricane Center, they'll tell you that the return period for a Camille-like Category 5 hurricane, which is a very small but intense hurricane, is about 75 years, maybe 100. Camille [in 1969] hit the Mississippi Gulf Coast with a storm surge of 23 feet, approximately. And so if you run that storm at different pieces of the levee system, then to prevent it from overtopping the system, you have to raise the system to certain levels. And the difference between that storm and a Katrina is not very much. It could be a half-foot to a foot in terms of height.

What the Corps is hoping is that people buy into the idea that, at least for the start, until we can afford to do something better, if we raise it to a 100-year level, we will be protecting the area from a heck of a lot of flooding, and this will at least get the National Flood Insurance Program off our backs, and allow people to start getting insurance as we promised the National Flood Insurance Program that they would be able to get it.

How about the Inner Harbor Navigation Canal? Is it essential that it remain open? I ask because *The Times-Picayune*'s "Flash Flood" animation and the LSU Hurricane Center computer models show the storm surge rushing in through the funnel formed by the Intracoastal Waterway and MR-GO. In *The Storm*, Ivor van Heerden describes MR-GO as a "storm-surge delivery system."

SCHLEIFSTEIN: The Industrial Canal is a major industrial area, and nobody has any plans for closing it. And nobody has any plans of closing the Gulf Intracoastal Waterway (GIWW), either. That waterway will stay open. The Port of New Orleans, which has been dragged kicking and screaming to the closure of the MR-GO, has repeatedly, incorrectly said that you have to have the MR-GO open because if it's closed you can't get the space shuttles' external tank [from the Michoud Assembly Facility] out to the Gulf of Mexico and on to Cape Canaveral, and in the future you won't be able to transport the new rocket capsule that's going to be built at Michoud. The people who built the capsule and the external tank repeatedly have said, "You don't know what you're talking about. These are things that go on barges and their draft is enough that we can get them through the GIWW and into the Gulf without any problems at all." That is one of the reasons why the GIWW will not be closed.

From your point of view, is it okay that these waterways remain open?

SCHLEIFSTEIN: I think structures can be designed and levees can be designed so that it's not a problem that they stay open. I think it was stupid to build them in the first place, but that was seventy, eighty years ago. 1922 for the Inner Harbor Navigation Canal and the 1930s for the expansion of the Gulf Intracoastal Waterway. The GIWW has been there forever, but it was expanded significantly after the Industrial Canal was built. Doubled in size. It's not a problem. The other thing is, the 100-year plan calls for a gate at the northern end of the Industrial Canal at Seabrook [at Lake Pontchartrain near the Lakefront Airport] to stop storm surge from getting into the canal that way as well.

A Great Wall of Louisiana?

What do you think about the idea of a Great Wall of Louisiana as mentioned in the recent *Time* magazine cover story, across the Intracoastal Waterway, going out toward western Louisiana?

SCHLEIFSTEIN: That will never be built. I can tell you that right now. After Katrina and Rita there was this great clamor and a requirement by Congress that the Corps study Category 5 protection for the entire Louisiana coast. As part of that process, the Corps pulled out every single proposal that had ever been made about how to do that. One of those proposals was indeed all of these different levees that created this "Great Wall of Louisiana" idea that everybody has focused on. The state has made it clear that it's not interested in doing that, although the state has included it as an option in its plans. But at the moment they're just lines on the map.

Now, the Corps has what's called the Louisiana Coastal Protection and Restoration (LACPR) plan, which is this Category 5 study that Congress required of them. They basically are going to present Congress with a Chinese menu of projects to choose from, and it will include both coastal restoration projects and levee or hurricane protection projects, all in the name of hurricane protection. And then Congress will decide which ones they want to finance, and the state will decide which projects they want to finance and which ones they want to do.

What I think will eventually happen there is that you will see levees like the Morganza [Spillway]-to-the-Gulf project that is still awaiting official approval by Congress as part of the Water Resources Development Act (WRDA) that's now before Congress, but pieces of which are already under construction by the local sponsor. They basically are a U loop around the urban area, in this case Houma. You may see something like that around Lafayette, maybe some additional levee protection around Morgan City, and maybe around Lake Charles. But in terms of one long levee across the state, most people have dismissed that as both too expensive and unworkable, and also not able to get through the court system when the environmental organizations will challenge them.

The Corps Learns from Dutch Engineers

At the Rising Tide 2 conference in August I met Tim Ruppert, a very bright New Orleans–born Corps engineer. He says the Corps has been consulting with some Dutch engineers, getting ideas from them. I think they've traveled to the Netherlands to see their flood control works, and they've brought some of the Dutch over here. It's very encouraging that they're reaching out, because the Corps has not always welcomed outside expertise.
SCHLEIFSTEIN: They've been doing that continuously through this whole process, and indeed the IPET team, the Interagency Performance Evaluation Taskforce that did all the forensic work on why the levees failed, is a good example of that. You've got 150 researchers from all across the country, in and out of the Corps, and every other agency, and the Dutch were involved in that as well.

2008 Presidential Candidates' Visions for New Orleans

There's a presidential race going on, you may have heard. The only two plans I've seen are a *New York Times* article on Barack Obama's plan [published Aug. 26], and about that time John Edwards released a six-point plan for helping New Orleans. They both have to do with infrastructure and also police, nursing shortage, practical things like that. Are you aware of Hillary Clinton issuing any plan?
SCHLEIFSTEIN: I haven't seen either of those. I heard something about Obama's calling for the closure of MR-GO. That's nice. [laughs]

Well, one of the good points in Obama's plan is that he would make FEMA independent of the Department of Homeland Security. The FEMA director would have a six-year term and he'd have direct, cabinet-level access to the president the way he used to.
SCHLEIFSTEIN: That would be a major improvement, and it needs to be done. I expect that will be done by whoever gets into office. I really think there will be major changes in Homeland Security and FEMA, whoever becomes the next president.

Changes to Come at FEMA and Homeland Security

What kind of changes in Homeland Security and FEMA?
SCHLEIFSTEIN: There will be a huge amount of support—there already is—
for moving back toward a much more realistic all-hazards approach to emergency preparedness.

Instead of counter-terrorism-based?
SCHLEIFSTEIN: Nothing wrong with counter-terrorism emergency preparedness, just as long as you don't do things like happened here in New Orleans.
One of the problems with the way the federal government works is that when
they create a new program and provide it with lots of money to give out, then
local governments looking desperately for money go after those projects. New
Orleans was a perfect example of that prior to Katrina.

**When the 17th Street breach was discovered, there was a jurisdictional dis-
pute between the Corps of Engineers and the Levee Board about who was
responsible for fixing the hole. (It was like a variant on the state-and-federal,
Blanco-and-Bush dispute, like, who's in control here?) Have they settled on
a protocol so they'll know who's responsible for what next time?**
SCHLEIFSTEIN: It won't happen again. [Laughs] I can guarantee you that, at
least for the next five or six years, until people forget.

Basically there was no protocol available for how to deal with closing
breaches, and now there is a clear protocol. Added to all that was that on
the Corps of Engineers side you had a guy [district engineer Col. Richard P.
Wagenaar] who was not an engineer and was basically relying on his people
and he felt the Corps should be in control, while the locals thought they should
be in control, and it was a mess. The reality was it really didn't matter. With
the physical forces involved with the breach there was no way of plugging it
quickly. It delayed things for a while. But in the big scheme of things it wouldn't
have mattered that much, based on what they had available to work with. The
water was already coming in.

What will be the protocol next time? Who will be in charge? The Corps?
SCHLEIFSTEIN: Yes, at least for the short term, while things are under construction. The way things generally work is that when a levee is under

construction the Corps is in charge. At some point in the future the Corps will turn over that project to the local sponsor who will then be responsible for operation and maintenance. And at that point, things will get befuddled again, but hopefully not. Hopefully there will be a clear delineation of responsibility, and/or the local sponsor will have what's needed to deal with it and will do it.

Political Action

Who are some of the political allies, individuals who can help Louisiana push for flood control money? Who are the people we should focus on?
SCHLEIFSTEIN: [sighs] Unfortunately, number one with a bullet would be the next president, whoever that turns out to be. Whoever that is will be the one linchpin to additional support. Beyond that, the leadership of both parties is what's needed behind this. Both Landrieu and Vitter have worked extremely hard attempting to get that done, with varying success. And one of the unfortunate things is that things change with Congress, and I expect that the key players in this will be changing in the next few years. So that's going to be a real problem.

At the Rising Tide conference in August, one of the things that really impressed me was the citizen activism of the bloggers and organizers, and their imagination and determination. They're making public information websites, trying to start up a citizens' radio station, pressing on the city council members . . . They're taking matters into their own hands. There's a lot going on. It felt like democracy.
SCHLEIFSTEIN: The group I'm most familiar with is CHAT, the Citizens' Road Home Action Team, led by Melanie Ehrlich and Frank Silvestri. Melanie Ehrlich is a research scientist. She was never an activist, never involved in anything until she lost her house. All of the changes in the program have been a direct result of the continuous complaints of this group, and their pushes to get things straightened out. And they've been helping individuals by identifying the specific people they need to get in touch with, passing around the e-mail addresses of individual program officers, and that sort of thing. Extremely helpful.

How would you advise a citizens' advocacy group like *Levees Not War* to press the government to increase investment on infrastructure reinforcement, for coastal restoration, emergency preparedness and evacuations, and so on? Is there some way we can frame it in politicians' self-interest to take care of these essential needs?

SCHLEIFSTEIN: [laughs] I'd be much more direct than that. If there's anything that the Road Home program has taught me, it is that the squeakiest wheel is the most successful. I would recommend that any organization do what my wife has done over the last 18 months, and that is to find the name and e-mail address of every individual who is in a position of responsibility and bombard them on a daily basis with requests and demands until they are so pestered that they have no choice. That I'm convinced is the only way to get things done these days. And Congress is no different. The reality is that lobbyists in Washington have entrée because of campaign contributions and the ability of being there on a daily basis. And the only alternative for people who don't have the money or the ability of being in Congress every day that they have is to do just that: to find some way of tapping them on the shoulder on a regular basis and reminding them that we need a lot of money and we need some coherent direction down here.

TAGS: Army Corps of Engineers, FEMA, Hurricane Katrina, John McQuaid, Mark Schleifstein, Path of Destruction, Pulitzer Prize, The Times-Picayune
http://www.leveesnotwar.org/mark-schleifstein

Afterword

Around the time of Barack Obama's first inauguration, in January 2009, a friend asked if *Levees Not War* would continue, or be retitled, now that Obama was president. The question sounded naïve at the time, and sounds even more so now, when the United States is involved in more overseas conflicts than it can count or will officially acknowledge. What I answered then is, I think, still true: It's still the United States; the occupant of the White House doesn't—can't—change the national character or the nation's foreign policy that fundamentally. Given the American thirst for oil, the political and corporate resistance to renewable energy, the profitability of the war machine, and other chronic conditions, the need for anti-war advocacy is not likely to fade away anytime soon. But, despite many inevitable disappointments, the president we have now is a very good one whose temperament and instincts are to try for diplomatic solutions, international cooperation (such as the nuclear deal with Iran, reached after twenty months of negotiations—a truly global agreement, if it can be allowed to work). In his years as president, with good help from the State Department (and from some at Defense), he has shown a consistent talent for approaching tense situations with calm while not projecting weakness. I won't venture any predictions here except to say that if future presidents will follow the prudent example of Barack Obama—and if they will wind down our consumption of oil and remove U.S. forces from Islamic lands—the nation and the world will be a less dangerous place. The damaging effects of climate change, including global warming, may one day replace armed conflict as our primary national security threat—or will they only exacerbate each other?

So, between levees and war, who gets the money? And how have things changed over the past ten years?

Even among defense budget analysts it is difficult to agree on what should be counted in totaling defense appropriations, but the U.S. defense budget in 2005 was at least $462 billion; for 2006, $698.3 billion (probably including more agencies than the 2005 figure). Then, nearly ten years later, the 2014 budget as enacted (including Veterans Affairs, the Department of Energy nuclear program, and Overseas Contingency Operations, etc.) was $967.9 billion, and as requested for 2015, $1.009.5 trillion. These numbers come from the Straus Military Reform Project of the Center for Defense Information at the Project on Government Oversight (pogo.org).

How strong is the New Orleans area's flood protection system since Hurricane Katrina? Congress has allocated $14.5 billion to the U.S. Army Corps of Engineers to rebuild, reinforce, and install new protections. *Times-Picayune* reporter Mark Schleifstein describes it as "a $14.5-billion network of levees, floodwalls and pumps that nearly eliminates flooding for most so-called 100-year events and substantially reduces flooding from much larger hurricanes." The Corps is also spending about $1.2 billion to improve the city's drainage system, which accounts for the major work currently being done along Napoleon, Jefferson, and other avenues under which closed culverts convey excess water out of the city. The new system stood up well against Hurricane Isaac in August 2012; experts said that without the post-Katrina reinforcements, Isaac could have flooded the city as badly as the disastrous Hurricane Betsy of 1965. (See the interview with Mark Schleifstein in Part VII.)

There have been other important structural changes that should improve the area's safety from flooding. As noted in the interview with Ivor van Heerden, one of the main "delivery systems" of the inundation of New Orleans and vicinity was the convergence of the Intracoastal Waterway with the Mississippi River Gulf Outlet (MR-GO, known locally as Mister Go): The convergence forms a funnel that directs storm surges from Lakes Borgne and Pontchartrain directly at the heart of Orleans Parish, a low-lying bowl between the river and the lake, enclosed by levees. This danger was predicted before the U.S. Army Corps of Engineers built MR-GO in the 1950s and '60s. Following Katrina, a closure structure was built across MR-GO at Bayou La Loutre, completed in July 2009. Closer to New Orleans, a strong $1 billion, 1.8-mile surge barrier was constructed to close the funnel at the convergence of the Intracoastal Waterway and MR-GO. This barrier, completed in 2011, was designed to prevent storm surges from entering the Industrial Canal and Intracoastal Waterway—and, hence, to reinforce New Orleans and vicinity's defenses against flooding.

In September 2014 a federal judge found BP grossly negligent in the Deepwater Horizon disaster (it exploded on April 20, 2010, and was not finally capped until five months later). In July 2015, BP agreed to pay out $18.7 billion to settle the spill—$5.5 billion in penalties to the federal government, $7.1 billion to the five Gulf Coast states of Alabama, Florida, Louisiana, Mississippi, and Texas, and $6 billion to the states and local governments for economic damages. This brings the total amount BP will have paid out for the catastrophe to over $50 billion. The fines will be paid out over 18 years—not exactly gushing at the rate of the hundreds of thousands of gallons of crude oil that poured into the gulf each day—and will be used for environmental remediation and economic development. A *New York Times* editorial observed:

> Years of misguided flood control projects along the Mississippi
> River plus the slicing and dicing of coastal lands by the oil
> companies have cost Louisiana alone 2,300 square miles of
> wetlands over the last 80 years, with more erosion every day.
> This damage has robbed the state of natural protections against
> hurricanes and destroyed deepwater corals and coastal nurseries
> vital to the health of one of the world's richest fisheries. BP's
> money can help turn this around—but only if the officials in
> charge spend it wisely . . . ("BP Deal Will Lead to a Cleaner
> Gulf," July 8, 2015)

Two powerful books published in 2014 detail the staggering long-term costs of ignoring America's infrastructure and social safety net—which includes basic needs like public schools—and the inexorable reality of human-caused climate change (see Herbert, *Losing Our Way*, and Oreskes and Conway, *The Collapse of Western Civilization: A View from the Future*, in the bibliography). And even when (or if) the infrastructure and social care networks are mended, there remain the awesome challenges of curbing CO_2 emissions and trying to alleviate the severity of global climate change that is already under way whether we recognize it or not. The forecast is for more extreme weather—i.e., more intense and more frequent. The sea levels will continue rising—a big melt has already been set in motion—and coastal, low-lying communities will have to adjust, or retreat. But humankind is a mighty and resilient thing, especially when organized and pulling together as one. We just may manage to tough it out.

Acknowledgments

First, thanks, as always, to Janet, my co-conspirator and trusted adviser.

I am also very grateful to my talented and hardworking production team of Beverly Butterfield and Richard Sheppard, without whom this book would not have been possible.

Among New Orleans blogger friends (mentioned in the Introduction), I would like to thank and salute more than I can name, but foremost to me is my friend Mark Moseley of the blog *Your Right Hand Thief* ("Laughing off hard truths in New Orleans") and *The Lens*, as a role model of what a blogger should be, with humor, fairness, and sharp critical analysis, and a fine fellow besides. Mark is also one of the principal organizers, from its inception in 2006, of the annual Rising Tide conference on the future of New Orleans (see Part VI). I'm also grateful to Tim Ruppert of *Tim's Nameless Blog*; Maitri Erwin of *Maitri's VatulBlog*; Patrick Armstrong ("Cousin Pat from Georgia") of *Hurricane Radio*; Mark Folse of *Toulouse Street*; Bart "Editor B." Everson of *B.Rox*; George "Loki" Williams IV of *Social Gumbo* and *Humid City* . . . and many others I'm fond of and grateful to—you know who you are.

Levees Not War has benefited from the expertise of many experts I've consulted over the years, many of whom are named below. Any omissions are the fault of my memory but not of a lack of gratitude.

For their technical expertise and often for their friendship, I would like to thank Len Bahr of *LaCoastPost*, former director of the Louisiana Governor's Applied Coastal Science Program; John M. Barry, Tulane University; Richard Campanella, Tulane University; Joseph Cirincione, Ploughshares Fund; Christopher Cooper and Robert Block, authors of *Disaster: Hurricane Katrina and the Failure of Homeland Security* (2006); David B. Culpepper, Louisiana State Water Resources Commission; Mark S. Davis, Tulane

Institute on Water Resources Law and Policy, Tulane Law School, and former executive director of the Coalition to Restore Coastal Louisiana; Todd Gitlin, Columbia University; G. Paul Kemp, Coastal Ecology Institute, Louisiana State University; Clay Kirby, *noladishu.blogspot.com*; Lt. Joseph O. Labarriere, Harbor Police Department, Port of New Orleans; John A. Lopez, Lake Pontchartrain Basin Foundation; Neil M. Maher, New Jersey Institute of Technology; Sandy Rosenthal, *Levees.org*; Tim Ruppert of *Tim's Nameless Blog* and the U.S. Army Corps of Engineers; Mark Schleifstein, *The Times-Picayune*; Dana S. Scott, Carnegie Mellon University (emeritus); Ivor van Heerden, formerly of the LSU Hurricane Center; Joseph Wartman, Drexel University; and Aaron Viles, Gulf Restoration Network.

To close-reading friends and contributors through correspondence and givers of moral support, sincere thanks to David Spinner, Kevin Mulvenna, Ronald A. Lavine, Patrick Armstrong, Stephen R. Frankel, and the Rev. John R. Leech.

For design work on the Tenth Anniversary Edition I am also grateful to Kyle Kabel (interior) and again to Richard Sheppard (cover). For guidance on recent events and readings of the Preface, I wish to thank Mark Moseley, Tim Ruppert, Lisa Nicholas, and Janet Cameron.

Bibliography

Hurricane Katrina and the Environment

Barry, John M. *Rising Tide: The Great Mississippi Flood of 1927 and How It Changed America* (1998).

Baum, Dan. *Nine Lives: Mystery, Magic, Death, and Life in New Orleans* (2009).

Bergal, Jenni, et al. *City Adrift: New Orleans Before and After Katrina: A Center for Public Integrity Investigation* (2007).

Brinkley, Douglas. *The Great Deluge: Hurricane Katrina, New Orleans, and the Mississippi Gulf Coast* (2006).

Clark, Joshua. *Heart Like Water: Surviving Katrina and Life in Its Disaster Zone: A Memoir* (2007).

Coastal Protection and Restoration Authority, State of Louisiana. *2012 Coastal Master Plan* (coastal.la.gov).

Cooper, Christopher, and Robert Block. *Disaster: Hurricane Katrina and the Failure of Homeland Security* (2006).

Emanuel, Kerry. *Divine Wind: The History and Science of Hurricanes* (2005).

Fischetti, Mark. "Drowning New Orleans." *Scientific American*, October 2001.

Hallowell, Christopher. *Holding Back the Sea: The Struggle on the Gulf Coast to Save America* (2001).

Horne, Jed. *Breach of Faith: Hurricane Katrina and the Near Death of a Great American City* (2006).

Joyce, Cynthia. *Please Forward: How Blogging Reconnected New Orleans After Katrina* (2015).

Knapp, Bevil, and Mike Dunne. *America's Wetland: Louisiana's Vanishing Coast* (2005).

McPhee, John. "The Control of Nature: Atchafalaya." *The New Yorker*, February 23, 1987.

McQuaid, John, and Mark Schleifstein. *Path of Destruction: The Devastation of New Orleans and the Coming Age of Superstorms* (2006).

Rivlin, Gary. *Katrina: After the Flood* (2015).

Rose, Chris. *1 Dead in Attic: After Katrina* (2007).

Tidwell, Mike. *Bayou Farewell: The Rich Life and Tragic Death of Louisiana's Cajun Coast* (2003).

————. *The Ravaging Tide: Strange Weather, Future Katrinas, and the Coming Death of America's Coastal Cities* (2006).

Times-Picayune staff. *Katrina: The Ruin and Recovery of New Orleans* (2006).

Van Heerden, Ivor, and Mike Bryan. *The Storm: What Went Wrong and Why During Hurricane Katrina: The Inside Story from One Louisiana Scientist* (2006).

U.S. Geological Survey. "Wetland Subsidence, Fault Reactivation, and Hydrocarbon Production in the U.S. Gulf Coast Region" (2001). pubs.usgs.gov/fs/fs091-01/fs091-01.pdf

Documentaries About Hurricane Katrina

Lee, Spike, director. *When the Levees Broke: A Requiem in Four Acts* (2006).

————. *If God Is Willing and da Creek Don't Rise* (2011).

Lessin, Tia, and Carl Deal, directors. *Trouble the Water* (2008).

Climate Change

Federal Advisory Committee. *National Climate Assessment Report 2014.*

Gore, Al. *An Inconvenient Truth: The Planetary Emergency of Global Warming and What We Can Do About It* (2006).

Hansen, James. *Storms of My Grandchildren: The Truth About the Coming Climate Catastrophe and Our Last Chance to Save Humanity* (2010).

International Energy Agency. *World Energy Outlook 2011.*

Klein, Naomi. *The Shock Doctrine: The Rise of Disaster Capitalism* (2007).

————. *This Changes Everything: Capitalism vs. The Climate* (2014).

Kolbert, Elizabeth. *Field Notes from a Catastrophe: Man, Nature, and Climate Change* (2006).

————. *The Sixth Extinction: An Unnatural History* (2014).

McKibben, Bill. *The Global Warming Reader: A Century of Writing About Climate Change* (2011).

Oreskes, Naomi, and Erik M. Conway. *The Collapse of Western Civilization: A View from the Future* (2014).

And read these writers' excellent, fact-based environmental reporting: Elizabeth Kolbert at *The New Yorker* and Fiona Harvey and George Monbiot at *The Guardian.*

'I' Is for Infrastructure

American Society of Civil Engineers. *2013 Report Card for America's Infrastructure.* infrastructurereportcard.org.

Cohen, Stan. *The Tree Army: A Pictorial History of the Civilian Conservation Corps, 1933–1942* (1980).

BIBLIOGRAPHY

Flynn, Kathryn A., with Richard Polese. *The New Deal: A 75th Anniversary Celebration* (2008). Foreword by Anna Eleanor Roosevelt.

Kanter, Rosabeth Moss. *Move: Putting America's Infrastructure Back in the Lead* (2015).

Leighninger, Robert D., Jr. *Building Louisiana: The Legacy of the Public Works Administration* (2007).

LePatner, Barry B. *Too Big to Fall: America's Failing Infrastructure and the Way Forward* (2010).

Maher, Neil M. *Nature's New Deal: The Civilian Conservation Corps and the Roots of the American Environmental Movement* (2008).

Rohatyn, Felix. *Bold Endeavors: How Our Government Built America, and Why It Must Rebuild Now* (2009).

Taylor, Nick. *American-Made: The Enduring Legacy of the WPA: When FDR Put the Nation to Work* (2008).

War and Peace and War

Ahmed, Nafeez Mosaddeq. *The War on Freedom: How and Why America Was Attacked, September 11, 2001* (3rd ed., 2002).

Bacevich, Andrew J. *The New American Militarism: How Americans Are Seduced by War* (2005, 2013).

__________. *Washington Rules: America's Path to Permanent War* (2010).

Bin Laden, Osama. Declaration of War (Jihad) Against the United States (1996).

Burke, Jason. *Al-Qaeda: The True Story of Radical Islam* (2004).

__________. *On the Road to Kandahar: Travels Through Conflict in the Islamic World* (2007).

Clarke, Richard A. *Against All Enemies: Inside America's War on Terror* (2004).

Coll, Steve. *Ghost Wars: The Secret History of the CIA, Afghanistan, and Bin Laden, from the Soviet Invasion to September 10, 2001* (2004).

Dyer, Gwynne. *The Mess They Made: The Middle East After Iraq* (2007).

Filkins, Dexter. *The Forever War: Dispatches from the War on Terror* (2008).

Hoyle, Russ. *Going to War: How Misinformation, Disinformation, and Arrogance Led America into Iraq* (2008).

Johnson, Chalmers. *Blowback: The Costs and Consequences of American Empire* (2000, 2004).

Klare, Michael T. *Blood and Oil: The Dangers and Consequences of America's Growing Dependency on Imported Petroleum* (2004).

Maddow, Rachel. *Drift: The Unmooring of American Military Power* (2012).

Rashid, Ahmed. *Taliban: Militant Islam, Oil and Fundamentalism in Central Asia* (second ed., 2010).

Rich, Frank. *The Greatest Story Ever Sold: The Decline and Fall of Truth in Bush's America* (2006).

Scheuer, Michael. *Osama bin Laden* (2011).

————. *Imperial Hubris: Why the West Is Losing the War on Terror* (2004).

————. *Through Our Enemies' Eyes: Osama bin Laden, Radical Islam, and the Future of America* (revised edition, 2006).

Thompson, Paul, and Peter Lance. *The Terror Timeline: Year by Year, Day by Day, Minute by Minute: A Comprehensive Chronicle of the Road to 9/11—and America's Response* (2004).

Politics, Society, and the Social Contract

Cohen, Joshua, and Joel Rogers. *On Democracy: Toward a Transformation of American Society* (1983).

Conason, Joe. *It Can Happen Here: Authoritarian Peril in the Age of Bush* (2007).

Cowie, Jefferson R. *Stayin' Alive: The 1970s and the Last Days of the Working Class* (2010).

Edsall, Thomas Byrne. *The Age of Austerity: How Scarcity Will Remake American Politics* (2011).

Ehrenreich, Barbara. *Nickel and Dimed: On (Not) Getting By in America* (2001).

Greenhouse, Steven. *The Big Squeeze: Tough Times for the American Worker* (2008).

Greider, William. "Rolling Back the 20th Century." *The Nation*, April 24, 2003.

Hacker, Jacob S. *The Great Risk Shift: The New Economic Insecurity and the Decline of the American Dream*, revised and expanded edition (2006, 2008).

————. *Winner-Take-All Politics: How Washington Made the Rich Richer—and Turned Its Back on the Middle Class* (2010).

Harrington, Michael. *Socialism: Past and Future* (1972).

Head, Simon. *The New Ruthless Economy: Work and Power in the Digital Age* (2005).

Herbert, Bob. *Losing Our Way: An Intimate Portrait of a Troubled America* (2014).

Hitchens, Christopher. *Thomas Paine's* Rights of Man: *A Biography* (2006).

Johnston, David Cay. *Perfectly Legal: The Covert Campaign to Rig Our Tax System to Benefit the Super Rich—and Cheat Everybody Else* (2003).

Krugman, Paul. "The Tax-Cut Con." *New York Times Magazine*, September 14, 2003.

————. *The Conscience of a Liberal* (2007).

————. *End This Depression Now!* (2012).

————. *The Great Unraveling: Losing Our Way in the New Century* (2005).

Kuttner, Robert. *The Squandering of America: How the Failure of Our Politics Undermines Our Prosperity* (2007).

Madrick, Jeff. *Age of Greed: The Triumph of Finance and the Decline of America, 1970 to the Present* (2011).

————. *Seven Bad Ideas: How Mainstream Economists Have Damaged America and the World* (2014).

Nichols, John. *The "S" Word: A Short History of an American Tradition . . . Socialism* (2011).

Packer, George. *The Unwinding: An Inner History of the New America* (2013).

Paine, Thomas. *Rights of Man* (1791).

Reich, Robert B. *Aftershock: The Next Economy and America's Future* (2010).

————. *Beyond Outrage: What Has Gone Wrong with Our Economy and Our Democracy, and How to Fix It* (2012).

Scheer, Robert. *The Great American Stickup: How Reagan Republicans and Clinton Democrats Enriched Wall Street While Mugging Main Street* (2010).

Shipler, David K. *The Working Poor: Invisible in America* (2004).

Smith, Hedrick. *Who Stole the American Dream?* (2012).

Uchitelle, Louis. *The Disposable American: Layoffs and Their Consequences* (2006).

Wolfe, Alan. *The Future of Liberalism* (2009), especially the chapter "Why Conservatives Can't Govern."

Wolff, Richard. *Democracy at Work: A Cure for Capitalism* (2012).

Young, Alfred F., Gary B. Nash, and Ray Raphael, eds. *Revolutionary Founders: Rebels, Radicals, and Reformers in the Making of the Nation* (2011).

Social Contract

Gough, J. W. *The Social Contract: A Critical Study of Its Development* (1936, 1957).

Levin, Michael. "Social Contract." In *Dictionary of the History of Ideas*, edited by Philip P. Wiener (1974).

Locke, John. *Two Treatises of Government.* Edited by Peter Laslett (ca. 1688; 1960).

Social Contract: Essays by Locke, Hume, and Rousseau. With an introduction by Sir Ernest Barker (1947).

Activism, Tributes, Remembrances

The Port Huron Statement

Gitlin, Todd. *The Sixties: Years of Hope, Days of Rage* (1987).

Hayden, Tom. *The Port Huron Statement: The Visionary Call of the 1960s Revolution* (1962, 2005).

————. *Writings for a Democratic Society: The Tom Hayden Reader* (2008; includes excerpts from the Port Huron Statement).

————. "Participatory Democracy: From Port Huron to Occupy Wall Street," *The Nation*, April 16, 2012.

Hayden, Tom, and Dick Flacks. "The Port Huron Statement at 40." *The Nation*, August 5, 2002.

Kazin, Michael. *American Dreamers: How the Left Changed a Nation* (2011).

Sale, Kirkpatrick. *SDS: The Rise and Development of the Students for a Democratic Society* (1973).

Medgar Evers and Civil Rights

Branch, Taylor. *Parting the Waters: America in the King Years, 1954–63* (1988).

Evers-Williams, Myrlie, and Manning Marable, eds. *The Autobiography of Medgar Evers: A Hero's Life and Legacy Revealed Through His Writings, Letters, and Speeches* (2005).

Holsaert, Faith S., et al. *Hands on the Freedom Plow: Personal Accounts by Women in SNCC* (2010).

Morris, Willie. *The Ghosts of Medgar Evers: A Tale of Race, Murder, Mississippi, and Hollywood* (1998).

Nossiter, Adam. *Of Long Memory: Mississippi and the Murder of Medgar Evers* (1994).

Payne, Charles M. *I've Got the Light of Freedom: The Organizing Tradition and the Mississippi Freedom Struggle* (1995, 2007).

Vollers, Maryanne. *Ghosts of Mississippi: The Murder of Medgar Evers, the Trial of Byron de la Beckwith, and the Haunting of the New South* (1995).

John F. Kennedy

Dallek, Robert. *An Unfinished Life: John F. Kennedy, 1917–1963* (2003).

Dallek, Robert, and Terry Golway. *Let Every Nation Know: John F. Kennedy in His Own Words* (2006), book and CD.

Douglass, James W. *JFK and the Unspeakable: Why He Died and Why It Matters* (2008).

Garrison, Jim. *On the Trail of the Assassins: My Investigation and Prosecution of the Murder of President Kennedy* (1988).

Groden, Robert J. *The Killing of a President: The Complete Photographic Record of the JFK Assassination, the Conspiracy, and the Cover-Up* (1993).

Manchester, William. *The Death of a President: November 20–November 25, 1963* (1967).

Schlesinger, Arthur M., Jr. *A Thousand Days: John F. Kennedy in the White House* (1965).

Sorenson, Theodore C. *Kennedy* (1965).

The Men Who Killed Kennedy (DVD, 1988).

In and About New Orleans

Campanella, Richard. *Bienville's Dilemma: A Historical Geography of New Orleans* (2008).

Colten, Craig E. *An Unnatural Metropolis: Wresting New Orleans from Nature* (2005).

Jasper, Sam, and Mark Folse, eds. *A Howling in the Wires: An Anthology of Writing from Postdiluvian New Orleans* (2010).

Joyce, Cynthia, ed. *Please Forward: How Blogging Reconnected New Orleans After Katrina* (2015).
Piazza, Tom. *Why New Orleans Matters* (2005).
Powell, Lawrence N. *The Accidental City: Improvising New Orleans* (2013).

Interviews

McQuaid, John, and Mark Schleifstein. *Path of Destruction: The Devastation of New Orleans and the Coming Age of Superstorms* (2006).
Shearer, Harry. *The Big Uneasy* (2010). Available on DVD.
Van Heerden, Ivor, and Mike Bryan. *The Storm: What Went Wrong and Why During Hurricane Katrina: The Inside Story from One Louisiana Scientist* (2006).

Illustration Credits

Following are credits and thanks for assistance with illustrations and quotations of written material. (Regrettably, because of space limitations, some images for which permission was granted were not able to be used after all.)

For their kind assistance with permissions for images and quoted material, thanks to permissions managers Steve Bello and Jennifer Bello, Philippe Halsman Archive; Jeff Gates, Chamomile Tea Party; Blake Haney, DirtyCoast .com; Bob Meyers, Greenpeace; Alicia Samuel, Corbis Images; Tiffany Serna, Salon Media Group; Michael Shulman, Magnum Photos; Marianne Sugawara, Creators News Service.

Cover photo by NASA: Hurricane Isaac (August 29, 2012). Thanks to Bert Ulrich and Connie Moore of NASA.

Introduction

Photograph: collection of the author.

Part I: Hurricane Katrina and the Environment

Part opener illustration: Hurricane Katrina. Photo by NASA.

"BP Found Grossly Negligent in Deepwater Horizon Spill": photo by U.S. Coast Guard.

"Diagnosis of a Stressed-Out Planet: Penguins Are Melting": Antarctic warming trends image by NASA Earth Observatory, 2009.

Part II: 'I' Is for Infrastructure

Part opener illustration: Detail from Works Progress Administration poster. Allan Nase, artist, for WPA Federal Art Project, Pennsylvania (1936 or 1937).

"Infrastructure, Baby, Infrastructure!": Quotation from Joe Conason's "Rebuilding an American Legacy" by permission of Creators Syndicate, Inc.

"A Reply to 'Obama Our Infrastructure Hero': Letter from a New Orleans Engineer/Blogger": Used by permission of Tim Ruppert.

Part III: War and Peace and War

Part opener photograph: A soldier in the 503rd US Infantry rests after a day of heavy fighting. Restrepo outpost, Korengal Valley, Afghanistan, 2007. Photograph by Tim Hetherington/Magnum Photos. Used by permission.

"Eisenhower on the Opportunity Cost of the War Machine": "I Like Ike" image found online.

Part IV: Politics, Society, and the Social Contract

Part opener photograph: "Bushwick, Brooklyn, 2002," by Genevieve Hafner. Used by permission.

"Democrats in the 2010 Midterms": "Mothers of Democrats" image courtesy of Jeff Gates and the Chamomile Tea Party, chamomileteaparty .com. This work is licensed under a Creative Commons Attribution-NonCommercial-NoDerivs 3.0 United States License.

Part V: Activism, Tributes, Remembrances

Part opener photograph: Shadows of the World Trade Center cross lower Manhattan, February 18, 1988. Photograph by Nathan Benn/Corbis. Used by permission.

"Tom Hayden and Todd Gitlin on the Port Huron Statement at 50": Quotation from remarks on the Port Huron Statement by kind permission of Todd Gitlin.

__________. SDS National Council Meeting, September 1963. Photograph by C. Clark Kissinger. Reprinted by kind permission of C. Clark Kissinger.

"Jim Bohlen, a Greenpeace Founder": Photograph courtesy of Greenpeace.

"'And Death Shall Have No Dominion': A Tribute to President John F. Kennedy": Photograph by Philippe Halsman, 1952. Used by permission.

Part VI: In and About New Orleans

Part opener illustration: "Be a New Orleanian. Wherever You Are": Illustration by DirtyCoast.com. Used by permission.

"Rising Tide: Making Blogging (and Civics) Sexy in New Orleans": Poster for first annual Rising Tide conference, 2006. Used by permission. Illustration by Brad Jensen/IconVisuals.com.

"Dedra Johnson of 'The G Bitch Spot' Wins 2011 Ashley Award": Reprinting of "Where You Said You Live At? or Margaritas as Coping Strategy" by permission of Dedra Johnson.

"Viva Burlesque!": Poster for 2009 New Orleans Burlesque Festival, courtesy of Rick, New Orleans Burlesque Festival.

Part VII: Interviews

Part opener photograph: collection of the author.

Index

About the Author

Mark LaFlaur grew up in the South, mostly in Louisiana. He earned an MFA degree at Louisiana State University, where he worked on the literary magazine *Exquisite Corpse*. The author of *Elysian Fields*, a novel of New Orleans, he has also written for *The American Scholar*, *The New Criterion*, *Los Angeles Times Book Review*, and *The Village Voice*. He has worked in book publishing in New York, San Francisco, and in New Orleans, where he wrote *Elysian Fields*. After Hurricane Katrina in 2005 he  founded *Levees Not War*, a New York–based, New Orleans–dedicated blog focusing on infrastructure and the environment, which led to his second book, *What Fresh Hell? The Best of* Levees Not War: *Blogging on Post-Katrina New Orleans and America, 2005–2015*. He is a senior production editor for a major book publisher and lives with his wife, Janet, in New York City.